CONSCIOUSNESS AND BEING

CONSCIOUSNESS AND BEING

MARK EISENHARDT

CONTENTS

Introduction

It has been said that to be a philosopher means being interested in what everyone is interested in without knowing it. Given the significance to philosophy of the "mind-body" problem, or more generally the question of the relation between mind and matter or of consciousness and object, this statement may be more insightful than we might at first imagine. For as we will see, this problem is not merely an esoteric issue solely of interest to philosophers but is the underlying motivation of all human desire and all existence.

The purpose of this book is to explore this thesis and to understand the relation between what we know as mind and matter. Many books have been written from the perspective of neuroscience explaining how the brain and perceptual systems work and their association with the phenomena of consciousness. However, at best these accounts are only correlative. They tell us which parts and activities of the brain are associated with particular experiences but do not get at the real question of why or how these physical structures and events correspond to subjective experiences. For example, they do not explain why the firing of a particular light receptor in the eye results in the experience of "redness", or why vibrations of the tympanic membrane in the ear are perceived as sound.

On the other hand, there are also many spiritually oriented books that speak of a fundamental unity of all things, but they generally do not help us understand how this is possible. They might cite anecdotes about paranormal experiences that seem to support the idea of unseen connections between the mental and the material, or perhaps cite modern scientific findings such as quantum entanglement and the role of the observer as evidence of a connection between consciousness and physical phenomena. They may refer to feelings and states of a mystical unity of self and world but do not lead to a direct experience of this oneness or to a rational comprehension of how the inner and outer are connected. Ideas of union with the absolute and of non-dualism go back to ancient times in the mystical tradition, but its literature exhibits the same problem. There are allusions to non-dual unity with the absolute, but the states leading to this experience seem incapable of articulation in a way that allow us to directly grasp it for ourselves.

What is needed is not merely an account of the correlation between inner and outer as provided from the perspective of neuroscience, nor a description of subjective feeling states as offered from the viewpoint of spirit, but an understanding of how a relation between the two is possible. Relation requires a common ground on which a connection is possible. To join these two perspectives in relation is in effect to unify them. The primary objective of this book is to show how mind and matter are aspects of the same thing. A second goal is to understand the significance and meaning of this problem. The reconciliation of mind and matter is important to philosophy, but also underlies all desire and purpose in life and existence. The opposition of subject and object is the most fundamental problem of existence, and the desire to resolve it philosophically is the most general abstract form of the specific concrete desires of all that flows out of being. It is through the unfolding of the world and the development of mind that the nature of mind and matter is known, and their identity realized.

Chapter 1 lays out the basic problem of consciousness and its relation to the world of objects. We consider what is necessary for the possibility of consciousness and how the opposition between consciousness and object arises while also allowing us to recognize a relation between the two. We consider the various approaches taken towards this relation and consider how the history of thought has been an unresolved conflict over the primacy given to the subjective or objective. We look at the question of whom or what has consciousness, and then drive deeper into consciousness to its most basic form, arriving at an initial understanding the fundamental relation between subject and object.

Chapter 2 examines the proposition that reconciliation of the opposition between mind and matter is not merely a question of academic interest but is the fundamental issue driving the desire and activity of man and world. We start by looking at the question in the abstract to find a clearer understanding of its underlying meaning and argue that its end is ultimately the self-consciousness of being. We then examine various desires and activities of man and show how they are all aspects of and attempts at realizing this same basic desire. We work from the approach of psychologies that define hierarchies of human needs, e.g., the physiological, sex, love, self-actualization, etc., and consider how each can be seen an aspect of a drive of consciousness to know and realize itself in the world. We then consider this drive not only in man but also in the development of the universe and life that led to human consciousness.

Chapter 3 returns to the relation of consciousness and object, shifting from the investigation of pure consciousness in Chapter 1 to the world of human consciousness and explores how it relates to the specific vehicle of the human body. The aim is to understand how the appearance of the world comes about in relation to the specific structures and activities of the body, and to uncover what constitutes human experience of the world at the most fundamental level. Everyday experience largely consists of complex objects and concepts, but at bottom these are compounds of relatively few basic sensory and cognitive elements. Understanding these elements provides a means to better understand the relation of experience to the physiological, but they are also important for understanding conscious experience itself. Comprehending the basic categories, or parameters of consciousness, is the means to approaching the earliest emergence of consciousness of a world out from the wholeness of being. Chapter 3 focuses on the "objective" side of experience, i.e., that which accounts for and makes up the appearance of an external world of independent objects. Chapter 4 continues with inner "subjective" experience, addressing phenomena such as internal body sensations and feelings, emotion, thought, desire and the experiences of subjectivity and intersubjectivity.

Chapter 5 addresses what is known as the "hard problem" of consciousness, i.e., how can we explain subjective qualia. For example, we may have a reasonable understanding of the physiological structures and neural processes involved in color vision and how they correlate with the experience of the visible spectrum; however, it is not so easy to understand how this activity of flashing neurons is somehow experienced as redness or greenness. In this chapter, we explore the relation between these inner and outer perspectives.

Having examined the meaning of consciousness and broken down its objects to their component qualia, chapter 6 examines the means of overcoming the separation of the two, i.e., knowledge. This chapter addresses issues of epistemology in relation to our subject. We start with general issues such as the definition, meaning and limits of knowledge. Then we consider the development of knowledge to its ultimate form, in which consciousness bridges the separation from its objects and comes to consciousness of self in the object of knowledge.

Chapter 7 considers issues in the philosophy of science. The main purpose of the chapter is to address problems with reductive materialist approaches to consciousness. We look at what science actually does and what its usefulness says about human psychology. We question the adequacy of the natural science method as a means to gain understanding of the phenomena of consciousness and consider the possibility of alternatives that are both adequate to the subject matter and yet meet the criteria for science. We also look more closely at objects of science through a consideration of its measures.

Finally, chapter 8 returns to the elemental parameters of consciousness to see if we can find a deeper unity between them where the world collapses into the awareness of pure consciousness. We see how that which makes up the objects of consciousness is of the same nature as the structure of consciousness itself. We thus come full circle and see how it is possible for subject and object to be one and how consciousness realizes itself in self-conscious knowledge.

CHAPTER 1

Consciousness and Object

The most basic aspect of experience is the sense that there exists a world of objects and something that perceives these objects. The experience of this latter, the "having" or awareness of objects, is what we call consciousness. We identify with this perceiver for whom the world appears. There is a sense of an "I", a subject. I am this seer, this consciousness. I am a self, separated from the things of which I am aware. No judgment is intended as to the truth of this perception, but only a description of how the world appears to naïve, pre-philosophical, pre-scientific consciousness.

However, we are not completely separate from the objects of consciousness. There is one object that is unique: the body. Specifically, there is a particular body that we experience as "our" body, and we sense that it has an intimate connection to the "I". We experience this body as the place where the self resides. We identify with it. On the one hand, we experience our body like any object. We can see it; we can touch it, etc. On the other hand, the body seems to directly relate to consciousness. The contents of consciousness depend on what the body does or what is done to it. There are also experiences unique to interactions between world and body that do not arise with the consciousness of any other object. These are phenomena such as the sensations of the body, and feelings of pleasure and pain.

There is a notion of two distinct things: consciousness, and a body in which it seems to reside. This body directly affects what is present to consciousness, but what exactly is their relation? How is it possible that they interact? This is what we know as the "mind-body" problem. This, however, this is framing the question too narrowly. Our interest is in more than just the specific interactions and correlations of awareness with the body, but with the general relation between what appears as mind and matter, or even more abstractly between consciousness and object. This is an ancient problem for both Eastern and Western thought. A distinction has always been made between what are variously referred to as mind and matter, body and soul, or spirit and the material, etc. Modern accounts of the mind-body relation usually begin with the dualism of Rene Descartes. Cartesian dualism seems to philosophically represent the naive "folk" understanding of everyday lived consciousness, i.e., the sense of two distinct domains that somehow interact. The common notion is of a body opposed to a soul. However, this is more a description of the problem than a solution. If they are truly two separate realms, how do they interact? Descartes hypothesized the pineal gland as the point of connection between them but did not explain exactly how this worked. Modern dualisms provide alternative concepts of the relation but seem no more successful in explaining how these separate spheres interact. Monistic approaches have the opposite problem. Monism does away with the problem of explaining the interaction of independent domains but leaves the problem of how separate classes of experience arise within a singular mind or substance. Extreme materialism tries to avoid the problem by denying consciousness altogether, or least denying that certain categories of experience (e.g., the non-quantifiable) can be scientifically studied. However, this is only avoiding the problem. Conscious experience is self-evident. We may question the existential status of objects of experience or our understanding of them, but we cannot deny the experience itself, i.e., of an external object in opposition to something that has the experience. Perhaps many of our ordinary folk psychology conceptions of consciousness are flawed, but the underlying sense of a subject-object opposition is prior to any conceptualization of it.

The problem with materialism is not the recognition of a relation or even a dependence of specific contents of consciousness on the physical. We take for granted that the state of the body relates to and affects conscious experience. No one questions that we depend on our eyes and ears to see and hear. We have long understood the relation between injuries to specific parts of the brain and particular manifestations of mind. Modern methods such as fMRI have led to an explosion of research in the area, and we can now even observe the correlation of brain activity with reports of specifically conscious experience. However, as with everything else in science, correlation is not causation. There is a relationship between conscious experience and the body, and in some sense a dependence of the nature of the former on that of the latter, but a reduction of consciousness itself to brain activity or as something that somehow emerges from the material does not necessary follow. The problem with materialism is the primacy accorded to the "physical", i.e., the belief that what is really only a particular quality of experience has some greater or more fundamental reality, and that consciousness is an illusion or by-product that somehow arises out of this "true" physical reality. Yet consider the source of our knowledge of these material structures and processes. How can we claim a greater reality for something that is only known through and depends on the experience that the observer can bring to it? We only know the material as material through the consciousness of a particular set of experiences such as the qualities of the senses, the appearance of a particular series of views through which it manifests, the feeling of restriction or resistance to movement of the body when we touch or try to move an object, etc. There is nothing outside experience that provides assurance of a material hyper-reality.

All of which might lead to some form of idealism which makes consciousness the true reality. However, this raises the opposite problem of how matter precipitates out of mind. We face the problem either of how separate domains interact and affect each other, or of how a single "substance" develops into different forms. Any position that reduces the world to one side or the other just avoids the problem. Therefore, there seems to be more promise in theories that accord an equal reality to both sides. This is the class of views variously referred to as dual aspect theory, neutral monism or panpsychism. Although they have their differences and variations, in general they share the idea that mind and matter are in some way different aspects of the same thing. However, the real problem is to conceive exactly how mind and matter are the same and how they can interact with one another. In order to interact there must be some common ground on which relation is possible. If they have some underlying identity, we should be able to demonstrate how one becomes the other. If we start from matter, how do we get to consciousness? If we begin with consciousness, how does it become the material?

The opposition of mind and body is a central problem for the philosophy of mind but conceived more broadly has a significance that goes far beyond its place in a specialized branch of philosophy or for the problem of understanding of the relation between psychology and physiology. The issue pervades the history of philosophy in a larger sense as an endless debate over the dominance of the subjective or objective, with the rise and fall of schools of thought reflecting changes in the emphasis or supremacy accorded to each side. The history of thought shows an enduring conflict between these two poles, where for a time, subject or object temporarily becomes ascendant, but never achieves a decisive victory. A new version of one side gains ascendency only to eventually exhaust itself. Then a new approach from the other faction seems to provide promise only to play itself out in turn. Thus Plato's idealism is followed by Aristotle's empirical approach to the study of nature. Neo-Platonism greatly influences Christianity and dominates philosophy through the Middle Ages only to be challenged by the rise of science in the Enlightenment. Modern philosophy opens with the rationalism of Descartes and Spinoza to be followed by the empiricism of Locke and Hume. Kant tries to synthesize the two, but ultimately sets limits to knowledge with the unknowable thing-in-itself, thus leaving the problem unsolved. Hegel's idealism attempted to get beyond this issue, and his system to unify the subjective and objective in absolute spirit is perhaps the greatest attempt to resolve the subject/object dichotomy. Whether his arguments actually work is a separate question. Regardless, Hegelian idealism is soon turned on its head in Marxist materialism. This is followed by other developments of the objective position via positivism and analytic philosophy. On the subjective side, the twentieth century brought developments such as phenomenology and existentialism. And so on. The problem is that overemphasis of either opposing pole will eventually be found lacking. Each philosophy fails because of the inherent lack in its one-sidedness. A final solution can only exist on the razor's edge, at the point of transition between subject and object.

The issue seems to be more than just an intellectual debate over principles derived from reason, but also reflects a fundamental divide of human psychology in how we relate to the world. Jung psychologized the issue in his concepts of extroversion and introversion. Despite the popular understanding these terms have acquired as referring to gregarious versus reserved social behavior, Jung actually meant something more fundamental than that. For Jung, the primary split was an orientation and interest towards the objective in the case of the extrovert and towards the subjective for the introvert. More importantly, the intensity of the opposition and pervasiveness of attempts to reconcile the subjective and objective suggests that this divide reflects some basic human lack or desire, which, as suggested above, is a fundamental issue for life and existence itself.

WHAT IS CONSCIOUSNESS AND HOW IS IT POSSIBLE?

First, we should establish what is meant by "consciousness" here, as the term is commonly used in reference to a number of different phenomena. For example, there is a medical usage in which consciousness refers to a level of responsiveness to the world, ranging from comatose states, to sleep-like and drowsy conditions, to delirious or confused states, to normal, attentive waking consciousness. Then there are many spiritual and "self-realization" notions of consciousness. These ideas generally emphasize different states or levels of consciousness, describing its development. Whatever their value, these theories seem to be more descriptive of the kinds of objects available to consciousness or an orientation towards these objects rather than about consciousness itself. This distinction is an important one, for as we will consider below, many of the arguments regarding what consciousness is or what has consciousness arise from confusion between consciousness itself and the objects available to consciousness. Here the term consciousness refers to the basic sense of existence of something for a subject of awareness.

What does it mean to exist "for" something? When someone speaks of being conscious of something, we intuitively grasp his or her meaning, yet we are hard pressed to provide a precise definition. Look up consciousness in the dictionary and we find it described as the state of awareness. Look up awareness and we find words like "perception", "knowledge", and "realization". As we continue this process, it quickly becomes circular, as definitions of perceiving and knowing then refer back to the attaining awareness of some information or thing. The term "realization" might be the most useful clue to its meaning. Realization is the bringing into concrete existence of something. This is perhaps the simplest meaning of being consciousness of something. To be conscious of something is to affirm its existence. It is there.

However, not only is there something that exists, but there a sense of something for which it exists. This sense of a witness seems closer to the meaning of consciousness, but what accounts for it? Initially, we identify it with what we think of as the "self" and its associated body. An object of consciousness does not exist independently, but immediately refers back to the self and what the self brings to it. For example, recognition of an object requires an act of judgment, where its qualities are compared to set of qualities residing in the mind of the observer. In addition, any object is viewed from a particular perspective of the body, so the meaning of its presentation must be in some way interpreted with respect to the subject. What we perceive with the senses also comes with a wider set of associations regarding its significance to the feeling and desire of the self.

There is thus a kind of exchange between perceiver and perceived, but is this self of relation truly subjectivity itself? Much of what we think of as the self is actually object rather than subject and awareness itself. When we are "self-conscious", we are taking ourselves as an object of experience, perhaps a unique object, but an object nevertheless. Consider what this self-object consists of. There is a visual image of the body. There is a set of facts we attribute to this self. We are a certain age, come from a particular place; make a living in a given profession. We have particular credentials and affiliations. We have specific interests and beliefs. We have done certain things or had particular experiences and have memories of them. We have desires and feelings, things we like and dislike. Yet regardless of whether these attributes are unique to the subject, they are not subjectivity itself but another set of appearances to it. Even inner feelings and sensations that seem to belong intimately to the subject are experienced as something observed and apart from the observer itself. We say, "I feel X", not "I am X." I feel something but am not identical to it. "I" am viewing or judging the feeling. Where pleasure and pain are involved, sensations might be highly significant to or even have dominance over the subject but are still experienced as something present to consciousness rather than as consciousness itself.

How can we make sense of the notion of a subject of awareness and its relation to that of which it is aware? As noted above, simply positing a substance of mind as did Descartes does not really help. Mind itself is what needs explaining, and merely pushing it off to a separate domain does not add anything to understanding. Nor does Descartes provide any insights into the "how" of interaction with the material.

Yet modern accounts from the perspective of neuroscience do not do any better. Consider a simple act of visual consciousness, the seeing of an object such as an apple. A natural science explanation starts by saying that certain frequencies of light reflect off the apple and travel through the pupil and lens to project an image onto the retina. The light creating this image interacts with the rods, cones and ganglion cells of the retina and is converted to electrical signals that make their way down the optic nerve and eventually reach the visual cortex. For the time being we put aside the problem of how that which we know from an external perspective as electrical impulses and patterns of neuron firing comes to be experienced as an object with particular qualities such as redness and roundness. For now, we are concerned not with the question of the connection between externally observed brain activity and the specific qualities of internal experience, but rather with how there is any experience at all. At this point, all that has happened is that the body has changed its state in response to a particular differentiation in the "physical" world. The body has internalized a representation of the apple, or at least of what the apple can be for the body given its ability to respond differentially to whatever is "out there".

However, the question remains how this transfer of information leads to "seeing". How does consciousness "look upon" something? It is hard to understand how there can be a subject that somehow steps back from and yet engages the object. Some representation of the object gets imported into in the brain via the senses, but it seems to require some kind of viewer inside that sits back and perceives it. This is what Daniel Dennett referred to as the idea of the "Cartesian theater". Even if we claim it is all of a physical nature, the problem remains. We might speculate that consciousness emerges out of a particular complexity or organization of the brain. Perhaps there are higher-level structures that operate on and connect the sensory data. However, this only defers the problem, as it leads to the question of how this higher order structure "sees". We are left another version of the homunculus infinite regress problem. If we imagine some sort of viewer, whether of mental or material nature, within the brain that "sees" the internal representation, we must also ask how that viewer or structure sees, and we arrive at the conclusion that it would require a viewer of its own. In turn, would not the second order viewer also need another for it to see, and so on? Such higher order structures might explain the existence of more complex or abstract objects but get us no closer to awareness itself. A different way of conceiving consciousness is necessary.

We might start by considering what is necessary to make consciousness possible. First, there must be something of which it can be aware. Thus, the first prerequisite for consciousness is the existence of difference. As in the night in which all cows are black, where all is the same there is nothing of which to be conscious. Consciousness requires first a differentiation of existence. For the time being, we must defer the question of what this differentiation is and how it takes place. The point here is the need for difference. This, however, is only the first step. The existence of difference and plurality is necessary but insufficient for consciousness. Awareness requires the recognition of difference itself. Object A only exists in relation to object B. Thus, differentiation must be followed by integration, where separate entities exist together. In visual perception, for example, each light receptor on the retina and its mapping onto the visual cortex is in itself an only individual "pixel", separate and undifferentiated. However, each neuron is connected through the many multiple synaptic direct and indirect connections between them, creating a visual field where the individual parts are laid out in an array side by side where the state of one can affect another.

Yet it still is not clear how this results in conscious awareness. Imagine being immersed in a field of red light. Being wholly in redness there is no consciousness of redness. Now suppose the light changes to blue and we are now in a totality of blueness. The fact of change alone does nothing to explain awareness. Everything else being equal, we have no more consciousness of a blue totality as we did of the red. We have only shifted from one undifferentiated whole to another. In order for there to be awareness, we must know there has been a change from red to blue. The two colors must in some way exist together, but how can we have both simultaneously?

We might gain insight as to how awareness arises by considering a well-known optical illusion experienced in the observation of certain visual fields. In the phenomenon known as Troxler's fading, when one fixates on a particular point of a field, especially a field of low contrast and fuzzy borders, the scene quickly fades away into a uniform field. This is because our sensory systems quickly habituate to situations of unvarying stimulus. This is the situation described above. This simple presence of a diverse field is not enough for awareness. The reason we can see is that visual perception is characterized by constant rapid movements of the eyes called saccades. We do not really see a whole scene before us all at once but construct it as the eyes rapidly shift focus between objects in the field of view. As soon as the eyes (or the world around them) stop moving, as when we fixate on a point in a low contrast field, consciousness quickly fades away.

The conclusion we arrive at is that consciousness exists in the transition between differentiated entities. It exists in the rapid back and forth movement, where, within the temporal resolution of distinguishable difference, i.e., within the timeless moment, multiple entities do exist simultaneously, and with them consciousness. It is a quick moment, as per the phenomenon described above, without change the scene rapidly fades out of existence. Buddhist doctrine holds that everything only exists momentarily. That seems to be a good characterization of consciousness. It only exists in the instant of transition.

If everything only exists in the moment, what accounts for the sense of stability of existence? The sense of a stable world with persistent objects is a result of a continuous, fast processing of these moments of integrated difference. Continuous existence or the appearance thereof is due to repetition. Each of these moments of consciousness is immediately followed by another. To return to our visual example above, the saccades of the eyes are constant. Neurons fire on and off continuously. Brain activity is characterized by waves. For example, the alpha and beta brain waves associated with awake and aware consciousness are roughly in the range of 10-30 cycles per second. In other words, consciousness of objects and an enduring world is a matter of flicker, the rapid repetition of the moment of transition where two states are retained. One can think of it like the illusion of the blades of a turning fan that seem to present a solid continuous surface, yet the existence of the blade at any point in space constantly comes and goes. Likewise, motion is perceived as in a film, where the rapid succession of slightly different frames gives the appearance of continuity. Existence is only in the fleeting moment which ever repeats. The timeless moment is the place where the differentiated two become one and give the awareness of consciousness. We will consider time in more detail in chapter 3.

Consciousness, then, is not something that gazes upon the object from the outside but is what it is to be the transition between objects in the succession of moments. It is the being of the body in this transition state. This relation in the moment is what gives consciousness and existence. The sense of a separate "seer" is due to the ever-present relationship loop between the sensory qualities of the object and the constructed self consisting of the identity narrative, desire laden sensation, and the judgments and cognitive constructions imposed on sense data. As noted above, these latter, although unique to the feeling, desiring subject identified with the body, are really objects themselves. Consciousness is what it is to be the movement and transition between facets of differentiated existence.

CONSCIOUSNESS AND THE BODY

Having considered the prerequisites for the possibility of consciousness, we return to the question of its relation to the body. We must not confuse consciousness, i.e., the pure sense of awareness and experiencing, with the particulars of what is experienced. When we feel pain, pleasure, and other sensations, however much we connect them with the body, there is still a sense of detachment from them as objects of observation. Yet we have also done away with notion of a viewer that looks upon the world of inner sensation. Consciousness is in the relation and movement between objects. The next question is how this process relates to the specific nature of the body. At first, it might appear that these ideas are compatible with or even support the notion of consciousness as something that emerges out of particular physical structures and processes. After all, the networks connecting individual and groups of neurons, with their constant activity and cyclical patterns of firing, seem to be exactly what this idea calls for. However, it is not clear what the existence of consciousness requires in relation to physical development. Is the development of certain physiological structures necessary before there is consciousness, perhaps a particular level of complexity only attained in human beings? Alternatively, could the prerequisites for consciousness exist even in basic matter, with differences in experience between entities being not a question of the attainment of consciousness, but of the qualities and complexity in objects of consciousness possible through a particular vehicle?

Above we considered how the perception of a connection between body and mind is derived from the way experience takes the form of a unified perspective from the body. Another factor was the existence of experiences that relate solely to our own bodies and are absent in relation to external objects. These are most notably the bodily sensations and the feeling of valuation and desire connected to them. One way to look at the relation of consciousness to the body is to say that consciousness, or more accurately, the world of which one is conscious, is simply the perspective from inside the body, or in other words, is the being of the body. The question "what is it like to be" something gets at more than just the meaning of having conscious mental states. It should be taken literally as referring to a fundamental ontological relationship. Conscious experience, as the inside perspective of a thing, is what it is to be that thing, to experience through that thing. The world of human consciousness is the being of the body. Consciousness is not an observer that looks upon its objects. This notion was the problem we needed to get around. Qualia of any kind, i.e., all kinds of experience, are what it is to be this body. To feel pleasure or pain, or to experience red or blue, is what it is to be the brain and body, which, from an external "objective" perspective we experience as anatomical and neural structures and their patterns of activity. We are conscious because of the transition between the differentiated-integrated entities in relation as described above. We do not observe this movement from the outside but rather we are it. We do not see, we be. It is what it is to be this body in a particular state. Whether we can say anything about why experience of being has the qualities that it does is something we will address later in the book.

Consciousness experience is the being of a thing. The body is a vehicle of consciousness. What we are aware of is consciousness from or through this particular body. This is similar to Schopenhauer's position that we can access the "thing-in-itself" in the immediate subjective experience of the body. We also understand why he sees this thing-in-itself as the "Will". As we have observed above, a unique aspect of this inner world is the experience of desire. This desire is seemingly at the center of our perspective and relation to the world is at the core of our self construct. It is basic to the relation that creates conscious awareness insofar as any perception of an object is referred back to the self and the questions of "what does it mean to me", how does it relate to my desire, do I want it or want to avoid it, etc.

WHAT HAS CONSCIOUSNESS?

One's own body is unique in that it is the only object that one experiences from both a subjective and objective perspective. We recognize it as the one place where we can relate the "material" world to our conscious experience. However, this does not mean that consciousness itself is reducible to or emergent from the body. Rather the body is a vehicle or perspective of consciousness. There is a connection between the two, but to what extent does consciousness depend on the body or particular qualities of the body? Is consciousness a universal property of being, with the vehicle only serving to create the objects available to it, or does consciousness depend on and only come into existence with the appearance of specific physical developments? For example, does consciousness depend on life? Does it depend on the existence of a brain and nervous system, or on the development of particular structures and processes or a specific degree of complexity within these? Alternatively, is consciousness more widespread? To answer these questions, we must consider the possibilities of consciousness beyond our own bodies.

The only sure consciousness we know is our own. We have awareness in relation to our bodies. We cannot have awareness of the experiences of the objects we perceive around us with the senses or know if they even have any. We cannot know what objects of consciousness they may have. We cannot know for sure if they have any sort of feelings or what they may be. At the same time, we do not doubt that at least some objects are like us in having some sort of interior world of experience. We are most sure about this when the objects in question are other human beings. What is it that gives us such confidence in this case? First, there is the fact that they appear as being so similar to us. We have already made the connection between our experience and our own bodies. We grasp the relation between our eyes and visual experience, the ears and hearing, the skin and touch, etc. We know what sensations are associated with our own sense organs. We know what sensations arise in ourselves following interactions with other objects. We know the experience of pain will follow if we miss the nail and the hammer comes down on our thumb. Science has made the connection between injuries to particular sections of the brain and functional deficits. It would be odd if others had this same equipment, and it did not have similar interior correlates. However, perhaps even more important is the observation of behavior in others. They act as we imagine we would act in response to the same events. The behavior of others is often so in accord with our own behavior in the same situation that it hard to imagine they are not feeling the same interior motivational experience. Another source of evidence is communication. When we speak with someone, their response usually makes us feel that they understand us to some degree. It feels like they can relate our expressed thoughts to a matrix of desire and feeling of their own and that they can appreciate what we are thinking, feeling, and wanting. Long before scientists and philosophers started wondering whether computers could think, people were intuitively conducting their own sort of Turing Test in relation to other bodies and concluding that these others must have an interior world of awareness very much like their own.

However, we also quickly realize that however similar in many ways, the conscious experience of others is not identical to our own. Communications from others also tell us that they obviously do not see the world exactly as we do. They do not think what we think or like what we like. They do not always respond or act as we expect in a given situation. Despite the similarities of each member of the species, they are still not identical. Each is an individual with a vehicle of consciousness which, while very similar to others of their kind in the broad strokes, also displays many differences from each other in the details. An obvious example of such difference would be individuals with extreme cognitive deficits, such as severe brain injury or dementia or psychosis. Conversation with or observation of such individuals quickly reveals that there is something missing or that they have a very different perspective on the world. Sensory deficits such as blindness create a very different world for the affected individual. Visual experience for the blind is very limited or non-existent, but they may gain an acute enhancement of the auditory world and the ability to extract information and meaning from sound of which the sighted are unaware.

Of course, differences are not only a result of affliction and deficit but are the norm for all human groups and individuals. Perhaps the most obvious example would be the divide of the sexes. It is inconceivable that the differences in anatomy and reproductive tasks would not be associated with very different concerns, inclinations and aims and how an individual relates to and perceives the world. Likewise, people are predisposed to particular temperaments and body types that color their interests and desires. Cultural differences, a function of both genetic inclinations and social circumstances, must affect how one perceives and evaluates one's world. Even within the same culture, or even with identical twins, the specific development and experience of each individual forms a different perspective and understanding of the world.

Differences in the physical vehicle of consciousness result different worlds of experience. However, this does not mean that there is a difference in consciousness itself between individuals. Consciousness per se is the existence giving awareness. The pure sense of awareness is always the same. Different vehicles only determine what there is consciousness of, i.e., its objects. Consciousness relates to the brain insofar as the brain allows certain objects of conscious to exist. The specific objects and forms of experience that human beings have may depend on the emergence of certain brain structures, but not necessarily consciousness itself. A blind person is not less conscious, but rather has experience lacking in visual objects. An Alzheimer's patient is still conscious, but the kinds of experience they have and the world of which they are aware are impoverished. Perhaps they can no longer make associations between things, or they can no longer recall past experiences, etc., but they are still conscious of whatever their brains still can differentiate and relate. We must not confuse consciousness with the objects and forms of experience. It is the perspective of consciousness that changes with physical differences, not the property of awareness itself.

Is this always the case? Is there no material prerequisite before such awareness can exist? Can we infinitely reduce the complexity of the brain, or have no brain or no life at all, and still have something we recognize as consciousness? To answer this question, we must move down the chain of complexity and life and assess the plausibility of consciousness at each level.

Consider the higher animals. Using the same kinds of observations applied to arrive at a judgment in favor of consciousness in other human beings, it seems that we must grant consciousness of some sort to at least some animals. First, we note the structural similarities in the bodies of human beings and animals. Most animals have sense organs similar to our own. They have nervous systems and brains similar to our own. Perhaps their brains are smaller and less complex, but qualitatively they are similar to ours. We also see many of the same behavioral signs that lead us to infer consciousness. When they are injured or sick, animals act much as humans do. They appear to show affection. While we are perhaps inclined to anthropomorphize our pets and project intentions onto them that are not there, anyone who has ever had a pet senses some sort of communication with animals and sees something we can only interpret as the expression of emotion, or something that looks like understanding to some degree. Can we really think that all this is all just a matter of mechanical reaction and believe there is "nobody home"?

However, there are of course great differences between the world of a human being and the world of even the highest animals. Their ability to consciously process complex information and to deliberate on potential courses of actions and consequences is limited or non-existent. Animals largely lack the ability for symbolic thought and communication (beyond instinctive gesture or purely chemical processes) and seem not to have the capacity for highly abstract objects of thought. Here again we must make the distinction between consciousness itself and the objects of which it is aware. Consciousness is not explicit self-awareness, or thought, or language, or understanding. It is simple pure awareness, the existence of experience, made possible through the integration of difference through relation and movement. The nervous system activity of an animal seems equipped to provide that in a basic form as much as that of a human. What is animal consciousness like? We can only speculate. The simpler vehicle of the animal brain might only yield basic sensory objects. There are no abstract concepts here. Perhaps there is no constructed self-object for many or all species. We think of animals as being mostly governed by instinct rather than thought, as being compelled to act by their nature rather than being agents of choice. Animal consciousness might be something like being a spectator of life. The animal simply finds itself doing things and feeling things. The cat just finds itself stalking the bird or feeling hungry and heading for its food bowl. Whether these specific speculations are correct or not is unimportant. The main point is to consider that consciousness need not be thought of as identical to the human world of experience. Consciousness per se is not its objects.

If we move down the chain to the lower animals to the insects, it seems from an external perspective that the same basic structures we equate with consciousness in humans and the higher animals still exist, only in a much simpler form. There are still recognizable sensory organs and a brain and nervous systems of a sort. Although with the number of neurons and connections being so greatly reduced from the quantity present in humans, we would expect any awareness insects may have to be very limited in its possible objects. With insects, it is hard to imagine much of the human sense of consciousness. Given their neural limitations, we cannot expect them to recognize us as holistic entities or consciousnesses. What might the consciousness of a bug be? Perhaps there is some awareness with changes of light or contact, a sensing of movement, or of the presence of chemical compounds the insect can respond to and distinguish. The reflex responses these stimuli activate are not felt as coming from choice or agency but are simply there.

So far, we have relied upon physiological similarities and the presence of sensory and nervous systems as supporting a claim for consciousness outside of Homo sapiens. This might imply that some specific material condition is necessary for consciousness to emerge. In some ways, this makes sense. We have described consciousness existing through the relation and integration of diversity, and this is precisely what nervous systems provide. They allow the association of discrete and distant points of stimulation and make possible relation between body feeling and memories and other mental contents. However, we cannot assume that such structures are sufficient or necessary for awareness. There are many physiological processes of which we have no awareness, so something else must be involved in consciousness. In addition, computers and other machines have connection and interaction between parts similar to a neural system yet are not thought to be conscious. Something else is required for awareness. On the other hand, neither can we jump to the conclusion that something like a nervous system is necessary for the existence of consciousness. A complex central nervous system may only serve to make possible a greater diversity and complexity of objects and not be required for consciousness itself. In order to examine this idea further, we must further descend the chain of life to where there are no nervous systems, i.e., to the kingdom of plants.

Do plants have consciousness? This idea gets more consideration in New Age and paranormal writings than mainstream science. Perhaps though, the better part of the disagreement is again the inadequate distinction between consciousness itself and the object of consciousness. Advocates for plant consciousness seem to overextend its meaning and anthropomorphize the world of the plant with talk about plants feeling pain or having emotions. If plants have consciousness, its objects of experience are likely to be so limited compared to a human being's that if one could somehow enter into and take up the interior perspective of a plant, its awareness might seem to barely exist if at all. What might plant consciousness be like? We can only imagine, but the small number and simplicity of connections would mean a very limited simple awareness. It would be the inner perspective of these basic plant physiological processes, the momentary sense of the change of states.

If we understand the notion of plant consciousness in this limited sense and consider plants from the exterior material perspective, it does not seem unreasonable that a plant could provide a vehicle for some rudimentary awareness. While plants do not have brains and nervous systems, they do have analogous activities and structures. They sense and respond to changes in the environment. They use signaling pathways to coordinate their development and adaptation. This need not mean awareness in the sense we use the term in the case of human beings. One can argue that this is just chemicals doing what they must do in particular environments. However, plants are living unified entities consisting of integrated parts with active processes whereby they exchange substances and affect each other. This is at least part of what we associate with consciousness. Is it perhaps then the presence of life, a self-sustaining, unified organism that we should consider as a material prerequisite for consciousness? In order to answer this question, as we did above, we must descend from life and ask if can see any possibility of consciousness at the level of inert matter. We must consider the possibility of a full panpsychism.

Before trying to conceive how consciousness could exist in simple matter, a couple of clarifications are in order. One more time we must emphasize the limited sort of world that would be possible for consciousness through inanimate matter. We must not anthropomorphize it. The consciousness of a rock would have very little to do with the experience of awareness in human beings. Whatever the world from the perspective of a rock is, it is so limited we might not even recognize it as such. All it can do is bask in its being, to exist in its dumb rock nature.

A second question is what precisely is the entity of consciousness? To postulate consciousness as existing in matter or within some inanimate objects is not to imply that it has consciousness qua object. It does not suggest that a teapot has a specific teapot consciousness. Consciousness requires integration and transition through difference. The question of a whether a thermostat has consciousness is irrelevant to a debate on panpsychism. The parts of a thermostat are not centrally connected and do not all relate to each other as an integrated entity. Perhaps there is a sort of consciousness within the bits of metal and wire as they expand and contract or change resistance or voltage as temperature changes, but these relations are local. There is no integrated connection and movement through the device. There is no vibration like repetition of signals to sustain an object. Likewise, it is unlikely that an automobile has consciousness as a totality. There is no relation between the tires and the engine and the steering wheel. Perhaps there is consciousness between the molecules of rubber in the tire or in the metal of the engine block, but consciousness of automobile as an entity seems unlikely. This is not to say that we can dismiss the possibility of a larger scale inorganic consciousness in a mechanical construction, for example, to have a computer that is conscious qua computer. Perhaps the construction of the right sort of neural net with the right sort interactions between the parts could result in some sort of larger integrated consciousness. This might depend on the specific properties of the material substrate so we must leave the jury out on computer consciousness for the time being.

Even to speak of a rock consciousness is overstepping the bounds because a rock is also not a true integrated entity. It is only a conglomeration of elements. If a rock were a unified entity of being, it would mean that a big rock would have a different consciousness that a small one or a round pebble would have some distinct interior difference from a jagged one. Rocks are not integrated entities of consciousness. So what is the entity of consciousness in inert matter? It would likely be at the molecular or subatomic level. Compounds have their being in the relation of their elements. Atoms are bound together and exist through the continuous forces between their constituent parts. Quarks are always confined and cannot appear in isolation. The reigning theoretical framework in physics regarding the most fundamental stuff of the universe is quantum field theory. These fields are separate-connected interacting points in constant fluctuation, which is almost our definition of the basic conditions of consciousness. It appears that consciousness is at the very heart of existence. What would consciousness through simple matter be aware of? We can only guess but imagine it would be the slightest sense of the movement of forces.

WHAT IS CONSCIOUSNESS? (REVISITED)

We have reduced consciousness to its simplest existence, detaching it from the experience of any individual perspectival subjectivity. Consciousness cannot be identified with any specific subjective experience. It is not, for example, a particular orientation or responsiveness to the outer world. It is not the existence of particular human experiences such as seeing, hearing, feeling, or thinking, etc. These are rather the contents of consciousness and made possible by the particular vehicle through which consciousness exists. They are a function of the construction of the human body, of its sense organs and the organization and activity of the millions of neurons and trillions of synapses in the human brain. These experiences are the perspective from the interior. What is present to consciousness is in effect the being of a thing. The world of qualia, i.e., all experience, is existence from the perspective of being. What I am conscious of is what it is to be this body, with these eyes, with this brain, in this operational state, in this location, etc.

As we descend the chain of life and existence, the complexity of connections decreases, and hence the perspective of consciousness diminishes with it, but there is always some being and hence some interior awareness however limited. Stripping away the connection to any particular vehicle, what remains is consciousness itself, the awareness for which and through which objects exist. If that which appears to any particular entity is what it is to be that thing, then this pure awareness is being itself. Consciousness is the existence giving source and the nature of being.

This should not be understood as an idealism that views the "spiritual" or "mental", whatever that may mean, as having some higher or exclusive reality, with the material being derivative or illusionary. On the contrary, consciousness/being must include the seeds of both awareness and object within it. If consciousness is being, it is not merely awareness of a world, but is also the source of the differentiable and differentiating activity which creates that of which consciousness is aware. How can we comprehend consciousness as both the seer and the seen? We come back to the original question of how the two are related. If consciousness and matter are in fact one, how does one become the other?

We can make an analogy to light. We do not see the light that fills a room. It is simply that which illuminates and makes objects in the room visible. However, if we shine light through a prism, it becomes visible in the diversity of its component colors. The illuminating, visibility enabling quality of white light is like consciousness, i.e., the unseen seer, the grantor of existence. As white light contains frequencies of the visible individual colors within it, consciousness contains within it the potentiality for the manifested world and is at the same time the activity that brings it about. It is the potentiality to modulate itself into a differentiated and then integrated whole in the timeless moment. The existence of objects begins as a limiting or separation of consciousness.

There is no awareness without the contrasting objects of which we are aware. Consciousness depends on difference. These objects are both of consciousness and make it possible. Emerging out of consciousness/being, they are also related to and dependent on one another, each taking on its appearance in opposition to what it is not. Continuing with the example of light, if a single wavelength is extracted out of white light, it takes its appearance in relation to the totality of the residual light. It is only with the full separation of the spectrum as can be distinguished by the human eye that colors take on their normal appearance. People with most forms of color blindness will have differences in their color palette across the spectrum. Objects thus depend on and co-constitute each other. Their existence is like the Rubin Vase illusion, where we ambiguously see either a vase or two faces depending on how we interpret figure and ground, or the tessellated images in the work of M.C. Escher, where the content of one figure defines the boundary of another part of the other. Each entity takes on its existence and appearance in relation to everything else in existence that it is not.

The foregoing still does not really answer the question of exactly how mind and matter are forms of the same thing and how one can transform into the other, or how one object emerges out of the source in relation to another to take on a particular appearance. We will examine these issues in more detail in the chapters to follow.

A second major theme of the book is the significance of these issues. Earlier we earlier asserted that this mind-body issue is not merely an academic question but is the abstract expression of the fundamental desire of all of existence. From the above, consciousness and object are two forms of the same thing. Arising out of consciousness, the world is therefore always self-consciousness, although it is not immediately recognized as such. The desire to overcome this alienation and opposition of consciousness and object in both philosophy and life is the subject of the next chapter.

CHAPTER 2

Desire and Purpose

Philosophy is the discipline of the absolute, aiming at the most fundamental essences and principles behind all particulars. To say that the desire behind a philosophic question is prototypical of all desire is to say that what the philosopher seeks in attempting to answer this question is the satisfaction, at the most abstract general level, of a common desire embodied in all concrete individual desires. It means that the specific things that motivate us in life, such as survival, sex, love, knowledge, self-realization, etc., are partial attempts at satisfying this general desire as fitting to the particular concrete forms through which they exist. The question at hand is of the reconciliation of mind and matter. Before considering how the particular desires exhibit the same general desire, we need to understand the abstract question in more detail and the meaning behind it.

What do we seek when we inquire into the nature of the relation between mind and body, or more generally mind and matter, or consciousness and object? We exist, and only exist, in relation to the world. Yet as subject, we feel separated from it. The world opposes us. There is an otherness about it. We are alienated from the objects of experience. The world resists our actions and responds in ways we cannot predict or comprehend. To ask the question of the relation of mind and body is to seek to overcome this separation in the most universal way. We wish not merely to overcome the difference from this or that entity, but from all existence.

We begin to grasp the relation between the subject and the object through the body. Conscious experience correlates with states of the body and its interactions with the world. When we change the position of the body or its contact with objects, our experience changes with it. Thus, understanding begins in the specifics of the mind-body relation. Consciousness has a connection with the body wherein we comprehend it uniquely as both subject and object. Consciousness is what it is to be a particular body, i.e., it is the perspective from the body. Earlier we saw that consciousness itself is not an artifact of a specific kind of body and brain but is the pure awareness in the integration of difference. The specific body and brain determine the kinds of object that can come into consciousness, but these are not consciousness itself. The nature of consciousness has within it that which creates the world and is thus ultimately one with the world. Demonstrating how this is so will be the task of the chapters to follow.

Returning to the original question, to seek the connection of mind to body is to seek to overcome the sense of alienation and separation from the world. It is to unify consciousness and object. Insofar as conscious is the source of all, it is thus self-consciousness and self-knowledge that is sought. In other words, it is to transcend the self, to put consciousness out in the world as object, to be both consciousness and object, realizing self as object and object as self. This is what underlies the consciousness of desire and the fulfillment of desire. Satisfaction of desire is always in some sense self-transcendence and increasing unity of self and world. It is to know the world and self more completely. In this chapter, we will consider how this abstract desire is the underlying meaning of the range of specific human desires.

The means through which the self-consciousness of being comes about is the activity and nature of consciousness. Pure consciousness, i.e., pure being, alone would be awareness of nothing. It would be like an eye trying to see itself. It needs something other than itself. This comes about through self-activity whereby the whole modifies or differentiates itself. Consciousness of objects comes in the relation and integration of these differentiated, limited aspects of being, in the movement between them. The creative, differentiating activity of the universe manifests the possibilities of being, which enter into conscious awareness through their subsequent integration.

This activity also includes the capability to increase integration through the development of more complex forms, as consciousness cannot immediately know itself. Matter evolves to complex molecules, to life, to more perceptive senses, to nervous systems, to increasingly larger brains, etc., capable of higher integration and creating a better mirror of consciousness to itself. A full self-consciousness of being itself would be the spinning out all of its possibilities in the centrifuge of existence, followed by their integration back into a whole. Being becomes aware of itself through consciousness of the relations that unify the whole of manifested creation. To capture the whole of being in the integration of all its possibilities is to have consciousness of being, as opposed to the unconscious state that exists in the original undifferentiated wholeness of being. It is being become conscious of itself.

This is not a new idea. The notion of an underlying unity of subject and object and the realization of consciousness as self-consciousness has a long history in philosophical and theological thinking. The expression may differ, but we see the same thing repeatedly stated in different forms. Thus, Aristotle identifies the "unmoved mover" with pure thinking in contemplation of self, which is another expression of the idea of self-consciousness, with consciousness as self and source of its objects:

> ....thought thinks itself through participation in the object of thought; for it becomes an object of thought by the act of apprehension and thinking, so that thought, and the object of thought are the same....Therefore, Mind thinks itself... and its thinking is a thinking of thinking.
>
> Aristotle, Metaphysics, Book XII

We find similar ideas in Spinoza. Spinoza starts with a presumption of unity in his declaration of a single substance, *Deus sive Natura,* i.e., "God or Nature", from which all individual things flow as modifications or modes of its attributes. For Spinoza, the Mind is the idea of the body, where for each finite mode of extension there is a corresponding mode of thought. The nature of the mind depends on the complexity of the body, which is another way of saying that the objects of consciousness depend on the body as the vehicle and the perspective of consciousness:

> Wherefore, in order to determine, wherein the human mind differs from other things, and wherein it surpasses them, it is necessary for us to know the nature of its object, that is, of the human body...., that in proportion as any given body is more fitted than others for doing many actions or receiving many impressions at once, so also is the mind, of which it is the object, more fitted than others for forming many simultaneous perceptions; and the more the actions of the body depend on itself alone, and the fewer other bodies concur with it in action, the more fitted is the mind of which it is the object for distinct comprehension.
>
> Spinoza, Ethics II, Prop. XIII

For Spinoza, "The mind's highest good is the knowledge of God, and the mind's highest virtue is to know God". He distinguishes three kinds of knowledge, the third of which, the intuitive, being the highest:

> The third kind of knowledge proceeds from an adequate idea of certain attributes of God to an adequate knowledge of the essence of things, and the more we understand things in this way, the more we understand God.
>
> Spinoza, Ethics V, Prop. XXVI

In this knowledge, we grasp the things in their relation to the attribute of God rather than through particular things, or as we have stated it, how things connect at the level of being. As Spinoza puts it, in this intuitive knowledge we come to conceiving things "under the form of eternity".

With Hegel, the idea of a process whereby consciousness becomes aware of itself becomes explicit:

> This vast congeries of volitions, interests and activities constitute the instruments and means of the World-Spirit for attaining its object; bringing it to consciousness and realizing it. And this aim is none other than finding itself - coming to itself - and contemplating itself in concrete actuality.
>
> Hegel, Lectures on the Philosophy of History

The "Absolute Idea" at the end of Hegel's Logic, which is realized through the development of nature and the processes of history in the rationally connected whole of Hegel's philosophy, is the unity of subject and object:

The idea of the unity of the subjective and objective idea is that the concept, of which the concept as such is the object, or of which the object is the concept; - an object which all determinations have converged. This unity is consequently the absolute and all truth, the idea thinking itself.

Hegel, Encyclopedia of the Philosophical
Sciences in Outline

We provide one more example from the 20th century with Jean-Paul Sartre, whose thought brings these ideas into concrete human existence and desire. Sartre opposes consciousness, the "being-for-itself" characterized by a lack of being, to the "being-in-itself" of the object. The fundamental desire of man is to have this being that he lacks, but at the same time to retain the freedom of the "for-itself":

The for-itself is the being which is to itself its own lack of being. The being which the for-itself lacks is the in-itself... It is as consciousness that it wishes to have the impermeability and infinite density of the in-itself. It is as the nihilation of the in-itself and a perpetual evasion of contingency and of facticity that it wishes to be its own foundation.... The fundamental value which presides over this project is exactly the in-itself-for-itself; that is, the ideal of a consciousness which would be the foundation of its own being-in-itself by the pure consciousness which it would have of itself. It is this ideal which can be called God. Thus, the best way to conceive of the fundamental project of human reality is to say that man is the being whose project is to be God.

Sartre, Being and Nothingness

Again, we see another version of consciousness wanting to have itself as object. Insofar as consciousness is also the source of all that it is conscious of, these ideas also pervade theological thought. For Hegel, religion is another expression of the absolute spirit, only lesser than philosophy in being communicated in a figurative pictorial form rather than on its own ground in purely conceptual terms. Religions differ in their outer forms, but at the deepest esoteric levels, we find one common idea that has been called the "Perennial Philosophy". As Huxley describes it:

> Philosophia perennis, the phrase was coined by Leibnitz; but the thing - the metaphysic that recognizes a divine Reality substantial to the world of things and lives and minds; the psychology that finds in the soul something similar to, or even identical to, divine Reality; the ethic that places man's final end in the knowledge of the immanent and transcendent Ground of all being; the thing is immemorial and universal. Rudiments of the Perennial Philosophy may be found among the traditional lore of primitive peoples in every region of the world, and in its fully developed forms it has a place in every one of the higher religions.

> Aldous Huxley, The Perennial Philosophy

This philosophy is concisely summarized in a statement from Indian non-dualist thought:

> Based on the direct experience of those who have fulfilled the necessary conditions of such knowledge, this teaching is expressed most succinctly in the Sanskrit formula, *tat tvam asi* ("That thou art"); the Atman, or immanent eternal Self, is one with Brahman, the Absolute Principle of all existence; and the last end of every human being, is to discover the fact for himself, to find out who he really is.
>
> Aldous Huxley, The Perennial Philosophy

This idea is not specific to any particular religion. Each has an esoteric form where this same sentiment is expressed in some manner. Thus, there is a Christian mysticism, Jewish Kabala, Islamic Sufism, Hindu Vedanta, Zen Buddhism, etc. The idea of non-dualism exists in every approach to the absolute. To be non-dual is to see the self as world and world as self. It is self-consciousness of the absolute. There is really only one idea, so we can claim nothing new. However, having an intuition of this unity is not the same as realizing it. Recognizing that this imperative permeates all desires of concrete existence and finding a path to its realization from the particular world we find ourselves in at a given place and time is the eternal task.

HUMAN DESIRE

There are a number of theories that attempt to understand human needs and motivation. Perhaps the best known is that of Abraham Maslow, who describes a hierarchy of needs starting from those of the physiological and moving to the desire for safety, belongingness, esteem and eventually self-actualization as each is satisfied in turn. In addition to the needs theories of the psychologists, there is another significant body of thought that we may characterize as the developmental. These theories, found in the psychological, philosophical and spiritual traditions, generally outline stages in the development of "consciousness". For examples of these models, one is referred to the work of Ken Wilber, who has examined a great number of such theories and shown that there is great agreement with regard to the general stages and direction of progression across a wide range of thinkers. In general, these theories can be characterized as depicting a process of development in one's identifications, objects of consciousness and orientation to these objects, moving from one's body and the sensory towards a universal non-dualism. While not necessarily couched in the language of desire, we could say that where one is in this development – what they identify with, the kinds of objects and the orientation towards them – determines the nature of wants and the actions of a person.

What follows is a rough outline of significant categories of desire similar to those of Maslow and others. There is some hierarchal aspect to these desires. One cannot be too concerned with self-actualization when one is on the brink of starvation or running from a tiger. However, it is not strictly a sequential development. The lower levels never really go away, and the seeming higher activities may be in the service of the "base" desires. For example, one may be on a scientific or artistic quest either for pure knowledge or for material gain and personal recognition. This works in the other direction as well. For instance, some might take sex as being about nothing more than pleasurable sensation, with all the significance of eating an ice cream cone, while for others it might be symbolic of and reserved for the highest love. Thus, the arrangement of desires given below should be understood as a typical sequence of their unfolding and not a fixed hierarchy. The aim is to demonstrate the notion that there is really only a single desire, expressed in a form appropriate to and possible for a particular vehicle of consciousness. This is the desire for self-consciousness and self-transcendence, moving from the particular to the universal, from the concerns of the vehicle to those of consciousness/being itself.

Life/the Physiological

The desire for life comes first, as without the existence and preservation of the physical vehicle there is no other desire. There are two aspects of this level to consider. The first is the explicit conscious desire for life, and the second consists of the demands and desires of the body. These latter are feelings and sensations such as hunger, thirst, hot and cold, pleasure and pain, etc., that motivate behavior. These are the conscious correlates of homeostatic processes that maintain the body, the feelings that motivate activity to keep physiological structures and processes within the bounds where the organism can survive and thrive.

Why do we want to live? The idea of a survival instinct does not really explain anything. It only moves the desire to a hypothetical entity outside of consciousness: We want to survive because there is this something that makes us want to survive. On the contrary, we are interested in the consciousness experience of the will to live. What is it that we are drawn to in life? It may be easier to consider this question in terms of the negative, i.e., why do we fear and try to avoid death? There may be practical concerns such as the care of dependents, or we may think of the pain and suffering associated with terminal diseases and other life-threatening conditions. However, these are not the fear of the loss of life itself. What is the actual concern? Are we really so attached to this particular body, which as we age becomes more and more a source of discomfort, less functional and less aesthetically pleasing? Are we really so attached to the self-object we have created, the image constructed out of a set of traits and a bundle of memories? It seems we can do without these things. The real fear of death is the thought that I will not be here, or I will not be aware. It is the fear of nothingness; that we will sink into an eternal void. In other words, it is the loss of the sense of existence. However, what is existence? Existence is being is consciousness. As long as we feel we are still here in some way, the particulars of our existence are not so important. It is the cessation of consciousness that we cannot bear. The desire for life is the desire for awareness. Having life at all is the first step towards self-consciousness, the fundamental desire of all existence. The living organism is the physical vehicle that provides the possibility of any self-consciousness. Simply being alive is the prerequisite for and first step towards knowledge of being and the recognition of self in object. Given the burden of maintaining physical existence, if we could somehow gain certain knowledge of the continuation of consciousness after death, there would likely be little of the dread it now inspires. In many cases, death might even be welcomed.

Yet outside of occasions when we come face to face with the reality of death in some way, we generally do not dwell on the fact of our eventual demise. To the extent that our daily thoughts and desires relate to the physical and the preservation of life, they are focused on the demands that our bodies make upon us through sensations such as hunger, thirst, discomfort, etc., which impel us toward activity that serves to maintain and preserve our physical being. If we are considering sensations from the aspect of desire, we are talking about the motivational aspect of the experience, which is to avoid pain or gain pleasure.

A full phenomenology of pain is beyond our scope. Here we can only focus on certain general features of pain in relation to the project of self-consciousness. By pain we refer not only to the specific sensation of pain, as when we drop a rock on our toe or get cut or burned, but also to various states of physical discomfort, tension, pressure, etc., that we find undesirable. Beyond the seemingly ineffable qualia and negativity of the pain experience itself, the fundamental characteristic of these sensations is that they demand our attention. Especially as pain becomes more severe, we are forced to focus on it. It compels us to remember that the well-being of the body, the basis for consciousness, comes first. It is this demand of pain that is the most insufferable about it. Pain is in essence a contraction or diminution of consciousness. It takes over consciousness and pulls us back into body, away from the world and the realization of self-consciousness in the world. As long as we are able to continue in our activities and forget physical discomforts, we can be relatively happy. However, when the severity is such that the call of pain dominates consciousness, especially for extended period, it can become almost intolerable. One can no longer engage the world. Chronic pain conditions and/or extended hospital stays easily lead to depressive states and a questioning of the worth of living.

Physical pleasure is the opposite side of the coin, being that which we toward which we are impelled. However, physical pleasure seems largely not a truly positive attractive force in itself but is on the same scale of pain. What is pleasurable is mostly the release of discomfort rather than a positive good in itself. The pleasure of coming out of the cold into a warm house is the cessation of discomfort as body temperature returns to normal and the expenditure of effort to maintain body heat comes to an end. A meal or drink is largely particularly pleasurable because the sensations of hunger and thirst subside as the body gets what it needs. Perhaps we do not recognize pleasure as primarily being a release from the negative because we normally exist with a certain baseline tension and expenditure of effort to which we are accustomed. If we walk outside and take pleasure at the temperate weather, is it not because our bodies are relieved at being able to lower the tension and use of energy to carry out processes that regulate body temperature? A massage might seem like a pleasurable indulgence, but it is more a removal of muscular tension of which we were perhaps not fully aware. The maximal pleasure in sex comes only after tension has been heightened and then released at the moment of orgasm. The sensations calling consciousness to the body are a contraction of consciousness. When the body is functioning well with minimal effort and discomfort, conscious is free to expand its scope towards a greater awareness of self.

Sex/Reproduction/Love

Initially sexuality may be seen simply as a continuation of the physiological, serving the physical foundation of consciousness in the survival of the body. However, sex does not merely assist in the preservation of a particular vehicle as with other physiological drives but creates a new one. Not only does it create a new center of consciousness, but because sexual reproduction works by genetic recombination, it produces new variations and increased differentiation of being.

Freud placed the sex drive at the center of psychoanalytic theory and therefore at the center of human existence. Sexuality is important, but the notion that everything is "really" about sex is a materialist reduction. Sex is rather a specific manifestation of the more fundamental desire of self-consciousness of being under the aspect of the physical. As with the desire to live, we cannot simply refer sexuality back to a hypothetical reality of matter and instinct beyond consciousness. As with other physiological needs and sensations, we are concerned with how sexual desire is lived in consciousness. Sexual desire has several different aspects. First is the desire for sex in itself, for the activity and the immediate pleasure it brings without any larger meaning. Second is the desire for reproduction, i.e., to want children. Thirdly, sexual desire is closely associated intersubjective relations and the emotions that follow them.

In pure sexual desire, that is, the lust for the act itself and its pleasures, we are not particularly concerned with the reproductive function of sex. In fact, often the last outcome wanted from sex is pregnancy. Nor at this point are we concerned with the full human subjectivity of the sex partner. Relative anonymity is often fine, maybe even preferred, as we can project our fantasies on to the other. What is the desire in this kind of sex? We are interested in specifically in the body. We are after the other's (and accordingly our own) physical existence as generic human beings. We are interested in them as living beings with particular physical qualities and sensations like our own. What we want is consciousness of our own corporeality as object, a placing of our physical existence beyond ourselves into the world.

In sex, we attempt to become subject-object in the aspect of the physical. In the close proximity and engagement of the senses, we annihilate the sense of difference and know the other's body both as object and as our own. We lose ourselves and find ourselves in the body of the other. Physical attraction is at the fore in animal sex. In being attracted to beauty, we are attracted to bodies that encode the truth of the world and reflect its reality. We want bodies in harmony with the world. In intercourse, one literally merges with this objective subjectivity. In the moment of orgasm, we literally put ourselves via our genetic essence into the other, and in the moment of conception create a version of our physicality and subjectivity beyond our own.

The subject of the sexes is too large to go into in detail here, but we can characterize the attempt to overcome the subject-object split as projective in the male mode and incorporative in the female. The male goes out into, penetrates the object, whereas the female removes the barriers of separation from the object and incorporates the other. Desire is enhanced by display that suggests suitability for these roles. Female attractiveness is heightened by appearing as a pure receptivity, as a means through which the male may overcome the separation of subject and object and transcend himself. Male attractiveness indicates the power and strength to act on and overcome boundaries and resistance of both partner and world. Yet in the end, both modes serve the same end. To enter into is to be held in the other, but also to know and hold the other in one's own subjectivity, and vice versa. They both have the end of subject-object reconciliation. Rather than oppositional, they are complementary. Male and female do not oppose but complement each other. This complementary characteristic extends to the biological outcome of sex in reproduction. Nature enforces a fair contract, with each partner contributing equally to the genome of the child.

This brings us to the second aspect of sexuality, the desire for children. As noted above, often the last outcome wanted from sex is pregnancy, so the desire for children is a different thing from the desire of the activity that leads to it. Why do we want children? Typical explanations do not help very much. To call it a biological instinct is again to just explain away and relegate desire to a material urge beyond consciousness. To say that one wants a family or loves children is really just a restatement of the question. Sometimes we hear of the desire to carry on the family name or to gain a kind of immortality through children. Insofar as one's child is in part a replication of one's own body and one's conscious experience is a function of this body there is some truth to this. The desire for children is in some sense an extension of the desire to perpetuate the means of consciousness and self-consciousness. The child is the closest we come to transcendence of our subjectivity in the object. The desire to create and support a life is the desire to support the larger project of existence through creation and perpetuation of the physical basis of consciousness. Not only are offspring a continuation and expansion of consciousness, but in addition to increased numbers, each new child adds a new revelation in the possibilities for being. The shuffling of the genetic deck and the idiosyncrasies of development bring about ever-new conscious experience and a further unfolding of being. People find meaning not only in the physical creation and witnessing of these possibilities, but in the role of nurturing these possibilities to unfold and reach their potential. For many or most, the creation and perpetuation of the physical is their main calling in life as evidenced by the numbers who find their primary purpose in family life.

However, there is something more to both sex itself and children and family than the physical. Both are nearly inseparable from the notion of love. With love, we enter into relations of desire with respect to the intersubjective. In chapter 4, we will consider love and its variations in more detail as part of an exploration of the emotions. Here we will consider the general meaning and significance of the intersubjective with respect to desire.

Social Desire

Social desire here refers not to interest in the practical benefits gained from interaction and cooperation with other human beings, but specifically to the significance that others have by virtue of their existence as subjects. We recognize that they have subjectivity like our own. They have conscious experiences. They have an understanding of a world around them. They have desires, sensations, and emotions. Not only do they see a world, but they also see us. They perceive us as subjects just as we see them.

It is this fact of subjectivity in the other and of being for others that opens up new possibilities with respect to the project of self-consciousness and self-transcendence. We can not only attempt to transcend our embodiment through the lover or child, but our subjectivity itself. Other people can potentially see the world as we see it and feel what we feel. We can communicate our subjective existence and they can hold it in their own. The other seems an avenue to consciousness of self and transcendence of our subjectivity as object. It is this potential for realization of subjectivity through others that motivates the project of social desire. However, the potential in this relation is not without risk. Others can also see the world and ourselves differently from how we see them. Whether accurately or not, they may see us in ways we do not wish to be seen, in effect rejecting and denying our transcendence. We do not have to go as far as the Hegelian life and death struggle between master and slave for recognition to understand that social relations are fraught with conflict between competing subjectivities seeking validation.

Desires of a social nature, such as the wish for love, companionship, respect and preeminence or dominance over others, are versions of a project to recruit the subjectivity of the other in support of the self-consciousness and realization of our own. It is the desire for the other to see as we see and see us as we wish to be seen in an attempt to transcend our own subjectivity through the other. The various social relations are versions of this general project distinguished by the role and expectations placed upon the relation.

We will look at specific relationships in more detail in terms of the emotions associated with them in a later chapter but will provide some general examples here. In relations of love, we attempt to take on the other as self. We expand the boundaries of the self to include the loved one. They become the transcended object version of our self and desire, or at least that is what we want and project them to be. Whether we can really achieve the aims of the project of love is different story. Much of our feeling is based on fantasy and projection where we imagine transcendence is attained through the loved one. The psychoanalyst

Hellmuth Kaiser described the "universal conflict" underlying psycho-pathology as being between the reality of man's essential aloneness and separateness, and the attempt to overcome it through creation of a delusion of fusion with others, carried out via duplicitous and indirect communication.

We pursue a more limited transcendence of subjectivity without such absolute demands in relations of friendship. We do not require of friends that we become their desire. Nor is the relation of subjectivity in this case tied up with sexual interests. In friendship, we find affinity and commiseration. We only ask for a degree of recognition and validation. Friends see or can see the world as we do. They can understand and have empathy for our concerns. We may have mutual interests for which we find objective expression in the relationship. Yet expectations on what friendship is to bring are moderated, and we can tolerate differences more so than we might in love.

Many social relations are formed not in pursuit of self-transcendence but are accidental and formal relations that come about in the course of living in a society to gain the benefits of cooperation. For example, there are casual social relations as we go about our business out in public on the streets, on public transportation, in shops, etc. We also have long-standing and often formal relations associated with employment, organizations with which one has dealings, with neighbors, etc. Here we are concerned less with the subjectivity of the other in relation to desire, but primarily with successfully managing a cooperative relation necessary to some end. Nevertheless, the element of the intersubjective is still present and must be negotiated. We still demand to be recognized and respected by others in accordance with nature of the relationship and our own assessment of our self-worth.

For example, in casual contacts, we expect certain social norms and courtesies to be maintained. Rude behavior is behavior that denies us the basic respect due for our value as human beings. In a work environ-ment, we may accept a degree of deference to others because it is part of a defined role. For instance, a salesclerk or waiter displays a degree of deference to a customer because he knows it is expected and is good for business. An employee yields to the boss's demands because he recognizes the role of the manager as decision maker. However, when the organizational superior forgets that this respect belongs to the role rather than his person and demeans the employee or takes advantage of a power relation, there is cause for conflict. When a relation is of a casual or utilitarian nature, and not specifically about the value of subjectivity, we expect others to refrain from attempting to inject such concerns into it. For example, when an acquaintance brags or displays conspicuous consumption, it comes off as an attempt to elevate their value with respect to ourselves and generates resentment. Social relations are thus a double-edged sword, with potential for both realization and denial of one's subjectivity. Desires of a social nature are another attempt to overcome the separation of subject and object. When our own subjective experience is reflected back to us and we sense we are seen as we see ourselves, there consonance of inner and outer.

In addition to personal relationships, the quandary of the intersubjective extends to relations between the individual and the culture and institutions of a society. Just as relations with other individuals can affirm or deny our subjectivity, so the ways of a culture reflect or thwart the self. A society is not merely a collection of individuals and individual transactions. A society also needs a kind of collective consciousness. By its nature, certain functions must be performed cooperatively and in a uniform manner. There must be understood or explicit norms for behavior and a mythology through which a society's members relate. Just as a person can confirm or deny another as subject, institutions may be in accord with or in opposition to the individual. The way a society operates collectively can feel as fitting with our inclinations or as alien. Laws and norms can facilitate or frustrate our desires. We do not all agree on what these norms and institutions should be. Politics is perhaps primarily about economics and the allocation of resources and is therefore largely at the level of the physical. However, it is also about the values with which we live, and its outcomes determine whether we feel at home in a society or alienated from it.

Self-Actualization

Once basic physical and social needs have been met to a certain degree, the marginal satisfaction gained from their pursuit diminishes. When consciousness is no longer under the dominance of physical discomfort or social needs, the door is opened for a previously unattended lack to enter into awareness. At first, we may not recognize what this new dissatisfaction is, and may attempt to abate it by chasing after what has provided relief in the past, for example by compulsively eating, or pursuing new sex partners and relationships. There is no end to the amusements and distractions that can be gained from new possessions and stimulating experiences, making the pursuit of money and pleasures it can purchase a common strategy to ease the new discontent. However, all this is just a diversion, because what this new uneasiness is really about is the alienation of self from world and meaning and is only resolved by what is often called self-actualization.

What is self-actualization? As Maslow and others have used the term, it refers to a process of becoming what one can be, to "realize" or "actualize" one's capabilities in the world. Self-actualization is thus finding one's inclination and talents through which one is most suited to know and act upon the world and transcend oneself in the object. The drive to self-actualization is another specific instance of a drive towards overcoming the alienation between the self-object and the object world. To know the desires and capacities of the self is to be one with that self. To realize oneself and act successfully upon the world, one must know this world and, in some sense, become one with it. The inner ideas, i.e., the understanding we impose on objects, are in harmony what that we perceive the object as being and doing. We place ourselves in the objects beyond us.

Why is self-actualization not the normal state, but something for which we must work? After all, it seems that we ought to know what we are and what we want, but such is not the case. Conscious awareness only exists through relation. Likes, dislikes, and abilities are revealed through concrete relations. We sometimes need to experience things to know how we feel about them. As we gain experience, we become more capable of judging likes and dislikes without direct experience because we can make inferences from similar things we already know, but for the most part human beings are not governed by pure instinct. In addition, we often do not have the luxury of pursuing and exploring what it is we really want. The biggest impediment is the burden of meeting the more basic needs of existence. Even to attain a moderate standard of living is a challenge for most people. Jobs that are fulfilling generally do not pay well and/or require exceptional skill. Well-paying possible employment options may be limited. Most of our time is taken up by work. Essential chores in our personal lives and rest and recovery consumes most of the little free time we do have. Most people have neither the resources nor time to explore what they might want to be doing with their lives, nor the opportunity or skill needed to do it.

Another consideration is the nature of the self-construct. We sometimes consider this construct to be the subject itself, but as noted earlier, it is actually another object. It is largely a collection of facts and narratives by which we create a self-image. This image becomes the center through which we relate and evaluate new experience. It is partly rooted in the direct sensibility and judgment of the body but not exclusively. We also incorporate ideas and images from external sources, most notably social messages. From the time we our born, our parents give us messages, explicit or tacit, about what should or shouldn't be done, about what we should or should not like, about what kind of person we ought to be. The receipt of these messages and the self-concept we construct based in part on them is conditioned by basic social needs. We incorporate what will seem to make others love and esteem us and will allow the illusion of fusion with the other. This continues at school and then into adulthood through social norms and narratives, peer pressure, products of the news media, entertainment and advertising, etc. This is not to imply that this socialization is all bad. We often lack the instinctive capacity to understand what is harmful or the longer-term consequences of actions. In addition, the benefit of the complex human brain and its capacity for symbolic communication is the transmission of knowledge within and across generations and not having to discover everything anew for ourselves. Without a degree of social trust, we lose the benefit of experience. However, when we mediate our relation to the world through an external social construct, we may lose awareness of our own affect and judgment to a greater or lesser degree.

What is the "real" self that we find and actualize? The self is the truth of the body. To know the self is to know the desires and aptitudes of the physical vehicle through which conscious awareness exists. Self-actualization is to find a way to live where this body is in harmony with, and can most effectively act on, the world. There are diverse aspects of the experience of objects, diverse modes by which consciousness engages the world, and individuals differ in the degree to which they can discriminate the object world through a given mode, i.e., the degree to which they can know and be one with the world through it. They also differ in the abilities to act upon the world and express themselves in that mode. Self-actualization is discovering our best inclinations and talents in this regard and finding a way to live where we can use them to act upon the world and realize our subjectivity in it to their maximum potential. For example, some people are oriented to the activity of the body and using it to act upon and transform the world. Others are primarily drawn towards gaining understanding of the world. Many find their greatest satisfaction in interpersonal connections. The full range of these individual differences in inclination and ability are the subject matter of psychological theories of personality and temperament. In the chapters ahead, we will examine the makeup of conscious experience in detail, and it is differences in the dominance and capabilities of the brain and body systems associated with these various facets of experience that make for differing preferences and talents in individuals.

The Return to Being

We have traced the expansion of self-consciousness, where, as the prerequisite needs for awareness are met and the elementary forms of desire are satisfied, the way is opened for consciousness to develop a more discriminating and complete reflection of self. After ensuring the survival and continuance of its vehicle, the body, consciousness can attend to the possibilities for realization of self in the subjectivity of others. It also becomes free to explore the unique inclinations, tendencies and talents of the body vehicle to develop a more discerning and unified connection to its objects through their exercise.

However, all these relations of consciousness are still limited and personal. Self-actualization is just that – a realization of a particular body and self. Actualization at this level is self-expression, an objectification of particular subjective perspective and a satisfaction of personal desires. The result may be a life of congenial activity, but it only refers back to the desire of a limited individual entity. Yet consciousness is not identical to a particular body but is the source of all particulars. Ultimately, desire is not just for the realization of a specific vehicle or the overcoming of difference from a limited element of the objective but is for the knowledge and transcendence of the deepest self, which is consciousness/being itself. The self-consciousness and transcendence of being comes through the unfolding and integration of all its possibilities. The separation of subject and object is only overcome, and being is only known as being, when all potential objects are known via a relation that passes through the source. The final development is not only the realization of the conscious perspective of the individual, but a movement beyond the finite vehicle of consciousness to realization of being itself.

The consciousness and expression our individual desire is no longer enough. Our little niches of knowledge of the world are incomplete. Desire turns to consciousness and realization of the whole. We ask the question of the meaning of it all. The quest for knowledge moves from compartmented disciplines to more inclusive system and wholeness. On the side of the object, physics seeks the "theory of everything" that explains and unifies all aspects of the physical universe. From the subjective point of view, philosophy and religion are the disciplines of the absolute. Philosophy, while it has its subcategories of limited sectors of knowledge, is essentially knowledge of relation at the level of being. The philosopher's question becomes everyone's question. To ask the question of general relation of mind and matter, of subject and object, is to seek consciousness and knowledge of being itself.

Whatever the differences in the details and the adequacy of specific expressions of the concept of God in the various religions, the idea points to the sense of the absolute. God is the ground and source of all, the eternal One out of which everything arises. In the Hebrew bible, when Moses asks for the name of God, the reply "I am that I am" describes the nature of God as Being. "That I am" is the fact of existence itself, the fundamental ground of existence out of which all things arise. Religious answers to the purpose of human existence all point to the same end: To know God is to have self-consciousness of being. To serve God is to reveal and realize God/Being. Creative activity that unfurls the possibilities of God/Being reveals its nature and then realizes it in consciousness and knowledge of it. To love God/Being is to unify the subjective and objective expressions of being. We have already addressed the "perennial philosophy" in which recognition of the non-dual nature of self and existence is the end to be realized.

With this, we reach the end of human desire and how its forms can be understood as limited forms of a general desire of being. We may analyze and understand these desires because as human beings we have subjective experience of them. However, if we are to make the case that there is a drive within being itself towards consciousness and knowledge of itself, we cannot only consider desire as experienced by human beings. The universe is estimated to be nearly 14 billion years old, with mankind having been around for only the slightest fraction of that time span. The human vehicle of consciousness, and the knowledge of being made possible through it, is the outcome of a 14-billion-year development of "matter" and life. If being itself "desires" to know and transcend itself, we must examine the entire process that led up to and created creatures capable of knowing and reflecting being back upon itself. We must ask if there is anything that looks like an impulse or striving in a particular direction. Are there signs of activity in the development of the universe of what we call purpose?

DESIRE IN NATURE

Is there evidence for desire and purpose in the activity of nature? The reigning scientific paradigm rejects the idea of purpose in the development of the universe. Accepted opinion generally holds to the idea of a material mechanistic universe. What is "real" is the "physical", i.e., what is known through the senses and subject to measurement. Reality operates through deterministic physical laws. While quantum mechanics has recognized the reality of uncertainty and probability in the behavior of physical systems and some have argued for the involvement of consciousness in collapse of the wave function, there is still no admission of the presence of purpose in the universe. Where the development of life is concerned, the modern evolutionary synthesis holds that variation arises in populations through random mutation and recombination. Life forms evolve solely by natural selection. Genetic variations that increase reproductive success spread through a population. The process is ongoing as these evolved life forms compete in turn, with some developing and spreading even greater fitness enhancing variations, thus ratcheting the species towards even more robust and sometimes more complex forms.

Yet why is this doctrine of meaningless mechanical materialism the official faith? To accord a special "reality" status to some phenomena while denying others is as much a metaphysical claim as anything else. What appears to consciousness as the physical is taken to be an ultimate independent reality consisting of matter and forces, concepts that go beyond the immediate data of the senses, so it seems science is not really ready to do away with metaphysics. Yet neither are we satisfied with a strict positivism that yields nothing but a catalog of observed associations and correlations. We believe there is and seek to understand the underlying reality that unifies experience, and this requires more than sense data alone.

Why is there an insistence on deterministic materialism? On the one hand, we can understand it as a methodological issue based on the success of the scientific method. There is no question about the contribution of the scientific method to our understanding of the world. This is precisely because science provides a method to put ideas to the test. Experiment generates data and allows isolation of factors - it is this and not that. Insistence on sense data and measurement serves to largely strip out the "subjective". The measurable appears to be prior to conscious construction. Everyone seems to see more or less the same thing at sensory level of processing. There can be consensus, as others are able to replicate and verify experiments. Quantification also gives a precision lacking in the intuitive sense of quantity. It distinguishes between what feels like an association and what actually is one statistically. It is understandable that there is a strong desire to advocate for and insist upon adherence to the method that has been so successful.

Yet it seems that the argument goes beyond issues of methodology and has something of a religious crusade about it. It is not only that we ought to apply certain standards of rigor before accepting a theory as reality, but that certain ideas are off limits. Only particular interpretations can be given to experimental results. Certain phenomena are deemed unsuitable for scientific inquiry or are denied reality. This has the appearance of a theological purge, perhaps by an insecure Enlightenment worldview that feels compelled to wipe out anything exhibiting the slightest hint of a return of the pre-modern.

This is nowhere more apparent than with the subject at hand, evolution, in the debate between Darwinists and advocates of "Creation Science" and "Intelligent Design". Yet we must separate ideas and arguments from the agendas they may serve. One cannot draw theological conclusions, whether for or against, from the facts of the natural world.

The spiritual and natural are of two separate orders. It seems that for fear of giving ammunition to the other side, evolutionists have been too quick to shut off debate or questioning of the orthodoxy. Surely some of the issues raised by "intelligent design" advocates are valid and were it not for the suspicion of an agenda beyond honest scientific inquiry they might be more readily acknowledged. Are there really no questions regarding the development of the complexity in living organisms? Is it certain that change only results from random mutation? Do random processes create sufficient variation for new species to evolve? Are there not places in the fossil record that suggest a rapid proliferation of new species uncharacteristic of Darwinian gradualism? Can we really explain the origin of life by clockwork mechanisms? Acknowledging problems with a materialist position does not support a leap to theology. There are possibilities between the two extremes.

Returning to the original question, what leads us to think there is desire and purpose in the natural world? First, what do desire and purpose mean? Desire is a subjective experience of wanting, of being consciously drawn to something thought to increase positive feeling or of being repulsed by what is associated with negative feeling. As discussed above, it is ultimately always in some form an attraction towards the preservation and accretion of the self-consciousness of being. Purposeful activity, as conceived of in human beings, is intentional activity with an end in mind. It is directly connected to conscious desire in that it is action undertaken in response to it. Where we are merely buffeted about by external forces or happen upon some result by accident, there is no sense of the presence of purpose. Purpose refers to the willful engagement in activities which, based on the notion of cause and effect, we imagine will bring about a desired state.

When we come upon the objects and events around us, what leads to the sense that purpose has been involved in their creation? Here we speak only descriptively and ask what accounts for the experience without making claims for its reality. First, we do intuitively recognize products of the purposeful activities of man. We have an instinctive grasp of the kind of environments and forms produced by nature and what is not, even if we cannot formally articulate the difference. Statements to the effect that there are no straight lines or right angles in nature might be exaggerations, but there are certain formations that are unlikely to come about on their own, and we are generally pretty good about knowing the difference between products of man as opposed to natural forces alone. When one turns to living things, and considers their complex systems and forms, one can understand the thinking that something very different is at work from the processes that brought about the geologic world. We know physical forces to be crude and uncontrolled. Biological forms seem a little too perfectly adapted to have come about by the forces of physics. This is particularly true with complex systems that require a number of parts to work together. If not constructed with purpose in mind, biological systems can at least be said to bring particular results and act "as if" they exist for the purpose of keeping organisms alive. Homeostatic mechanisms go into operation when an organism transgresses certain boundary conditions and stop when its state returns to a healthy one. It is this sense of perfect functionality and ability to bring about particular states, along with the intuition that such forms are not consistent with the activity of purely physical forces, that incline us to believe in the presence of intention. It seems an odd reversal to say that these complex mechanisms just happened to come about by chance, and because of compatibility with physical laws of the universe just happen to maintain the operation of living organisms. Life appears to actively strive for survival and in some respects is in opposition to the laws of physics. It actively fights against entropy and finds a way to proliferate in every conceivable ecological niche and the harshest conditions. If the universe allows life to survive and thrive, it seems that life and consciousness must be a part of its basic nature as much as any other force.

The establishment position is that the development of new complex systems and new species can and does come about by randomly produced small incremental changes. Changes with even the slightest fitness advantage can become dominant in a gene pool over larger time scales. In this way, complexity can be gradually shaped and does not have to come about all at once. Specific examples, such as the development of the eye, have been offered to demonstrate how even the smallest (and therefore feasibly random) changes, could give some small adaptive benefit, thus allowing the slow incremental shaping towards complexity that the theory demands. Other mechanisms, such as the "re-purposing" of pre-existing structures and processes, have also been proposed. However, these demonstrations seem to be more arguments for feasibility than actual evidence. It is one thing to construct an example of how something might have come about and another thing to demonstrate that it actually did happen that way. Evolution may work like this, and perhaps it largely does, but is it the whole story?

If desire is shaping existence and there is directedness to activity, then we would expect to see growth in a discernible direction over the history of the universe. Specifically, it would reflect progress towards a particular end, i.e., the movement towards self-consciousness and self-knowledge. If we take a top-level view of the history of the universe and life, is there anything that looks like a trend? This would not be proof of purpose, but it would be consistent with an understanding of the activity of the universe as an unfolding of its nature towards a realized self-consciousness.

The reigning explanation of the origin of the universe is the Big Bang theory. According to the theory, the universe began some 13.8 billion years ago with a rapid expansion out of a singularity. It expands into, or rather creates space. There is no definitive explanation of how this event came about. Some models have suggested quantum fluctuations as a possible explanation. Others have proposed cyclical universes or multi-universes, but this seems only to push back the question: If there were earlier universes, then how did they arise? However, once we get beyond the initiating event and the early "Planck epoch" the theory provides a remarkably fine-grained breakout of the event phases of the early universe down to minute fractions of the first second. In that short period there is continued rapid expansion and cooling, with the differentiation of fundamental forces and the beginning of elementary particles. What meaning can be placed on these early events? In the beginning is the singularity. It is the pure "in-itself". There is no self-consciousness because all is one. There is no "place" to create and juxtapose separate entities. However, already there is this potentiality of activity, this impetus to burst forth, to create a place where things can be. The early activity is a rapid differentiation of the One, creating the elementary particles that we know as the basic building blocks of all existence. The quantum fluctuations at the beginning result in a universe that is not uniform across space, creating a diversity of conditions in which forces play out and the universe has opportunity to be what is within its possibilities. In particular, what follows out of this is the creation of larger, complex matter structures. As expansion and cooling continue, after around 370,000 years, the recombination era begins, with protons and electrons becoming bound in neutral atoms. Slowly clouds of hydrogen collapsed to form stars and galaxies. Heavier elements are forged through stellar conditions. And somewhere around 4.6 billion years ago our own sun was formed and shortly thereafter the Earth.

The next significant development, not too long after the Earth was formed, is the beginning of life. Life on earth is thought to have begun at least 3.5 billion years ago, with some evidence for an origin as early as 4.3 billion years. As to the origin of life, we can only speculate on how it came about. Experiments such as Miller-Urey demonstrated that certain organic compounds could be synthesized from inorganic substances by subjecting them to conditions thought to represent the environment of the early earth. However, no one has been able to synthesize life in the lab, and life's origins remain a mystery. Rather than emerge out of purely mechanical process, it is just as likely that, like the unexplained energetic activity of the quantum world, life in some way exists at the core of being and only needs the proper conditions to manifest. Life on earth began to emerge early enough, perhaps as soon as conditions such as liquid water were present.

What is life? There is no canonical definition, but most refer to a set of attributes such as homeostasis, organization, metabolism, response/adaptation and reproduction. However, we can best make sense of the overall meaning of these properties by considering their results.

Ultimately, all these processes serve to serve to maintain the continued existence of the organism whether directly or through making copies of itself in reproduction. Life behaves as a self-contained anti-entropy machine. Life processes make it possible to acquire and process energy and material resources that allow the organism to withstand the physical forces of the universe that would break it and also allow it to repair damage. This preservation also proceeds by organisms making more of themselves via reproductive processes. It simply looks like life "wants" to exist and acts to this end.

For our purposes, the more important question is what life adds with respect to the realization of self-consciousness? The significance of life is that it brings about the possibility of large-scale complex integration and moving parts. As we considered earlier, with elementary "mechanical" matter, consciousness will be no more than what is possible in direct binary atomic/subatomic interaction. Life brings into existence the structures and processes that allow diverse and wide connectivity in an interactive manner. It brings the possibility of modeling the world internally. Not at first of course, as early life probably adds little to the proto consciousness of matter. However, it provides the building blocks of the mechanisms will make possible consciousness of a fine-grained world object and a sense of self-consciousness. In the development of life, we see a trend in this direction.

It did not happen quickly. Life may have begun early in the earth's history, as soon as physical conditions allowed it, but significant development was long in coming. From the first single-cell, prokaryotic bacteria and Achaea it took perhaps another two billion years to reach eukaryotic life, and then another billion or so reach true multi-cellular organisms to any significant degree. It is only with the Cambrian explosion some 3-3.5 billion years after life's origin that we begin to see something that reflects the diversity of life today. Whatever set off this phenomenon, environmental change or the development of some internal process, life becomes prolific and diverse at this time. If there is no imperative to life, it certainly acts that way, finding a way to exploit every imaginable ecological niche with myriad adaptation strategies. It is at this stage that we can begin to trace a trend of development supporting greater self-consciousness. Of particular relevance to consciousness is the development of perceptual and nervous systems.

By perceptual systems, we refer mainly to the initial processing of stimuli provided by the sense organs and perhaps up to the early processing of the signals transmitted to the cortex. This early processing provides the possibility of knowledge of the differentiation of being. The Big Bang began a differentiation out of the singularity of being, but the development of sensory systems is what begins to make possible a significant consciousness of it. We can trace developments along a number of parameters. First, there is the development of multiple sensory modalities that we can distinguish and experience simultaneously. Here we think of the five classic senses of sight, hearing, taste, smell and touch, which from an objective perspective we relate to different kinds of physical phenomena. A second differentiation is the development of sub-parameters within these modes. For example, we distinguish light in terms of both color and brightness. There are a number of different tastes and odors and body sensations. A third development is the sensitivity of response: How much of a difference in an underlying parameter is necessary to differentiate response (e.g., how large of a change in frequency is needed to distinguish colors?). Other examples along this line are developments in spatial and temporal resolution: How small of a difference in space and time we can discriminate. These developments have resulted in greater and greater response to the world and its possibilities in differentiated form.

If perceptual systems provide a reflection of differentiation in the universe, it is the development of nervous systems that makes possible the integration that creates objects of consciousness, eventually understood as self-consciousness. Perhaps nervous systems had their origins in the adaptation of action potential mechanisms present in relatively early life. Plants use various signaling pathways to respond to the environment. Early animal precursors were nerve nets, a loose system of nerves with no central control that could propagate response throughout the body. In time neural cells segregated from other tissues to form the nerve chord and clusters of nerve cells, the ganglia that control particular functions. This was followed by a process of cephalization, a concentration of the sense organs and nerve ganglia at one end, beginning the formation of the head and brain. The brain becomes the central receiver and coordinator of stimulus inputs and controller of response. The evolution of the brain is characterized by the development of species with ever-larger brains, and not just in relation to body size but adding capacities beyond body control. Brains become more compartmentalized, with specialization of function in different areas, and more complex, as in the convolutions of the cortex.

Expansion of the experience of objects and of an integrated world parallels physiological development. At the start, in the early precursors of nervous systems, there is perhaps little accretion of consciousness over matter. Nerve nets, without a central organization would provide a barely conscious propagation of signals setting off simple chemical/electrical responses to environmental change. As nervous systems evolve with the formation of ganglia the process of cephalization, a central organization begins, which allows coordination of input and more complex response. In time, complex neural circuits evolve that can coordinate stimuli and allow capabilities to process and respond to activity in a visual field, for example, or adapt to characteristics of space and physical forces. In effect, organisms start to become capable of relating the parts and internally modeling a world. Response, while it may still be largely "hardwired" and reflexive, or at most result from simple associative learning, becomes more adaptive in that it can take into account multiple coordinated inputs. Human beings, with their large brains of over 80 billion neurons and trillions of connections, bring the simulation and knowledge of the world to entirely new levels. The ability to freely adapt is a key development. No longer is response merely instinctive and automatic. The capability to learn goes far beyond classic conditioning. The ability to make connections becomes conscious and seemingly limitless. Activity becomes creative. This is related to the development of symbols and language, which are the tools of forging new complex associations. In addition to gaining the ability to have far more complex objects of consciousness, we also gain new classes or levels of object. If before, our ability to recognize objects and navigate the world effectively was encoded in unconscious circuits forged in the trial and error of natural selection, we now have the ability to make conscious objects of these underlying structures, i.e., the possibility of abstraction and the creation of concepts. Objects become recognizable as being particular types of things or as being similar to other things. We have reached the complex world of everyday life, but there is one final development: The recognition of ourselves as objects. We attain self-consciousness. We become aware of ourselves as a collection of properties like any other object. We make up narratives about it; we imagine it acting in the world. Yet we also recognize it as having a subjective aspect and as being separate from the world. With that, we reach the original question of our relation to this world and our alienation from it.

We have traced a development from the origin of the simplest matter to highly complex consciousness and knowledge of this world with awareness of itself. Skepticism that this development could have come about through a strictly mechanical process is understandable. Yet neither can we simply leap to the assumption of a transcendent creator. However, if neither materialistic determinism nor gods provide an adequate explanation, how can we understand the possibility of purposefulness or direction in the development of life?

As set forth earlier, consciousness is the nature of being and always exists. It does not emerge out of a development of the physical. Rather the forms of the physical determine the objects available to consciousness. These objects are actually consciousness in differentiated form and awareness of them is therefore self-consciousness. However, the recognition of this only comes through a long process of development where the object gradually becomes adequate to consciousness itself. Conscious awareness is a function of the vehicle through which consciousness exists. The world available to consciousness depends on the extent to which being is differentiated into its potential limited forms and on the extent to which a vehicle develops that is capable of integrating this fragmented being. At the start, consciousness has no awareness of anything. To grasp itself from a state of pure being would be like an eye trying to see itself. Consciousness needs a mirror. It cannot set out from pure undifferentiated being and purposively create the conditions for self-consciousness. To do so would be to presuppose the knowledge it desires. The early activity of consciousness is not like the purposeful action of a human being with knowledge of the world and a comprehension of how to act upon it. These are precisely what being in itself lacks. Consciousness of a world, and hence of itself, develops with the differentiation of consciousness and evolution of the vehicle of consciousness.

How then is anything like self-direction possible in the evolution of life? Again, consciousness itself, the capability for awareness, is at the core of being before any development. While this consciousness does not come with immediate knowledge of itself, as soon as there is any manifestation of being through its differentiation, then there is some awareness, even if only the slightest inkling, and with it also the attraction towards consciousness of self. Consciousness cannot plan operations upon the world at this stage because it does not know what the world is. It can only make use of what it has at each point in time. In its essence, consciousness exists as the movement between differentiated-integrated parts. It exists as pure activity, and in the beginning, it is this activity that consciousness has at its disposal. This active tendency allows it to shake itself up and throw out infinite variations of self and new forms. It is perhaps blind activity at first, but with each variation, more of itself is revealed. Some variations will be consciousness enhancing, attracting more of the same activity. As certain patterns of activity are held to, a baseline of higher awareness comes into existence that can guide further activity, and so consciousness begins to bootstrap itself up. It moves closer to the kind of purpose that we credit human beings with having.

This is actually not so different from evolutionary theory. In the modern synthesis, variation arises mostly through spontaneous random mutations. To call an event random is only to say that there has been no discernible pattern or explanation. Yet spontaneity and randomness are not necessarily the same as purposelessness. Consider an analogy to the process of creativity at the conscious human level. When faced with a novel problem, "trying everything" is a typical purposeful strategy. We brainstorm. We consider ideas that worked in similar situations. We use trial and error or attempt brute force solutions, etc. The specific solutions we arrive at might come about by luck, without a rational deliberation on cause and effect, but the general process is still intentional. In evolutionary theory, the idea is random change subjected to the struggle for survival, with whatever sticks becoming the baseline for the next generation. The difference here is the idea that developments are not entirely random but are shaped by an attractor of desire. Because the organism does not know exactly what it is aiming at, the process might be characterized not as "intelligent" but as "stupid design". Consciousness may not know how to get to where it wants to go, but it can churn up new forms and knows when awareness has increased. With each accretion of consciousness, there is more awareness and more forms upon which to work. Life reuses and varies creative mechanisms that have worked in the past. When complexity of the brain becomes such that desire can be set in conscious relation with knowledge of cause-effect interactions, and when the mind becomes capable of evaluating possible actions and outcomes, nature arrives at conscious purposeful action.

This should not be understood as support for the idea that the mind can control the development of the body. Perhaps at some advanced level of development this might become possible to some degree, but for the most part the human race is a far from where intentional thought can influence the physical at this level. The intentional consciousness of everyday life that moves muscles operates at a different level from that which codes the development of the body. It is to be expected that the process of change to successful organisms would be very slow and conservative. Survival of the physical vehicle is a prerequisite for any higher self-consciousness. Most mutations are harmful. Change of physical structure and operation at the whim of conscious desire is unlikely to be a successful evolutionary strategy.

As life forms and awareness grow, how could additional awareness enter into the process and become a factor in further developments? From the start, life is characterized by homeostatic processes that maintain it. At the level of everyday human consciousness, the subjective correlates of these processes, pain and pleasure, motivate intentional activity aimed at bringing the body back within hygienic bounds. Where these activities fail, consciousness of physiological stress might instigate similar activity at the cellular level. For example, it might elicit a "more of the same" response, or a duplication or re-application of some other existent process. Exactly how life could occasionally "hit upon" a new idea is uncertain, but at this level, the biochemistry of the response is not far removed from that of the genome. Consider another analogy to creativity processes at the conscious intentional level. Researchers in the field distinguish conscious directed problem-solving activity, which is purposeful activity, from an "incubation" period, where conscious effort applied to the problem ceases and an unconscious, non-directive mode takes over. In this mode, sometimes new connections relevant to the problem arise without conscious intention. Suddenly the answer we could not think our way to through conscious effort pops into consciousness on its own. How exactly does this subconscious process work? Perhaps in turning away from directed consciousness we leave aside conscious preconceived constructions and allow looser concrete associations, characteristic of primitive perception and physiological response, to form. The answers might come seemingly without conscious intention, but the process is still guided by consciousness. Significant discoveries do not come to just anyone, but to those who are very knowledgeable of a subject and have spent many hours consciously working on its problems. The guiding hand of consciousness is still connected to the unconscious processes. Evolutionary processes might work in a similar way, where need is recognized at a physiological level of consciousness over which we have no awareness or control.

These ideas might seem to have something in common with the Lamarckian theory of inheritance acquired characteristics, and both do admit effects related to the experience of the organism. While

Lamarckism is out of favor, research in epigenetics and related areas has demonstrated that a kind of heritability stemming from environmental influences is possible. These heritable effects are currently understood as changes only in gene expression rather than actual alterations to the DNA sequence, but there have been studies suggesting they may eventually be encoded in the genome. Such effects require evaluation over the time scales afforded to evolution and in more sustained stress conditions before they can be written off as only temporary.

Perhaps one can continue to hold to the idea of strictly random changes shaped by natural selection to explain the evolution of life. Reasonable sounding scenarios have been constructed to show how even small changes could provide meaningful fitness advantages and eventually move towards complex adaptations in an incremental manner. However, demonstrations of possibility are not evidence that evolution did occur in this way. The accepted paradigm leaves unsolved the problem of the long odds of certain complexities coming into existence by chance as well as the question of how structures and processes that so precisely support survival come into existence. It requires us to accept what seems to be an odd reversal of causality. Rather than organisms striving to survive and developing mechanisms to serve this end, these systems are to have come into existence solely by chance and they happen to result in survival. The universe simply unfolds its possibilities as it must in accordance with natural laws. However, the opposition to entropy exhibited in life seems to demand at the very least some principle in nature beyond the laws of physics and chemistry as conceived of under materialism.

Again, why the insistence on mindlessness? If it is for fear of a retreat to pure speculation or theology and a retreat from the discipline of the scientific method, then by all means demand that ideas be put to the test before accepting them as truths. However, materialism seems to insist on something more than that. It requires belief in its own god, its own transcendent absolute beyond man. In this case, rather than an omniscient consciousness, the absolute is a zombie world of hyper-real substance and forces acting in accordance with deterministic laws.

However, whatever science does or knows comes through consciousness. Whatever observations it makes are products of consciousness and can only be what consciousness makes possible. The sense of the physical and of forces is not an absolute in-itself, but an appearance through consciousness. In the end, consciousness must be accounted for and be a part of any "theory of everything".

CHAPTER 3

The Creation of a World – Part 1 (the Objective)

In this chapter, we return to the relation between consciousness and object, shifting from the considerations of its general nature in Chapter 1, to the specific appearance of the world through the vehicle of the human body. After describing the general characteristics of this world, we consider how its attributes arise in relation to human perceptual and nervous systems. We will break the experience of consciousness down to its simplest elements and their correlates in simple physiological structures and processes. These "elements" are the irreducible qualia upon which all experience is based prior to the speculative activity of the mind that constructs complex objects to understand the world. They are the basic parameters of consciousness that create and limit the basic ways we can know the world. As the common constituents of experience, they are what makes possible the relation and integration of experience. As the most basic elements, they are also the earliest emergence out of the wholeness of being and are thus the path back to being.

THE NATURAL WORLD

We wish to account for the world of everyday life, the naïve pre-reflective experience of a real world around us that we all have and take for granted. What are the characteristics of this world as we know it? The world is a world of objects consisting of various qualities. Simple qualities such as color and shape come together to form compound objects that appear as distinct coherent entities. These objects appear to exist independently of that which perceives them. They appear to have solidity and heft. They offer resistance to our attempts to understand and control them. These objects exist in space and time. They exist in quantity, having magnitude or existing in plurality. Each object exists in associations and relations with other objects. They are like or unlike others in quality. They relate in time, space and quantity. They affect and change each other. Objects are more than individual instances of perception. They have a constancy and identity that goes beyond the specific appearance that changes with each perspective. We find in them something that is the same underneath each individual appearance. We recognize an object as something we know and have seen before. We recognize them as being particular types of things, as having general qualities in common with other objects.

In opposition to this consciousness of an external world of objects is the sense of a subject, something that is aware of, or "has" objects, and exists apart from them. We identify with this awareness. We are a self, an "I", which is associated and identified with a particular body through which it experiences the world. Our knowledge of objects and their significance to us is relative to the state of the body. The subject has experiences that belong uniquely to it, and which do not exist in the perception of external objects. These are primarily the sensations and feelings of the body, emotions, and thoughts. It is through feeling that we also gain the fundamental experience of desire. These feelings of the body come with a sense of value. They are of good and bad. They motivate us to seek out or avoid particular interactions.

UNDERSTANDING CONSCIOUS EXPERIENCE

These characteristics describe our general experience of the world, but how does this world come about? How it is possible for a world of objects to arise out of the wholeness of being? The first question is of the general conditions for awareness of a world. What are the basic pre-requisites for awareness? Secondly, how does the world take on its specific form? As discussed earlier, human conscious awareness exists through the physical vehicle of the body. Exactly how do the particular forms of subjective experience relate to the structures and activities of the body?

Once we understand how we got here, the next question is what exactly the nature of this experience is and of what does it consist. In what ways can we experience the world? For the most part, we do not easily distinguish the difference between what the world presents to us in its most simple sensory immediacy and the interpretation we impose upon it. The everyday world is a world of action on complex objects in complex environments. We take for granted what we have learned, mostly unquestioningly and semi-consciously. If something new comes along, we relate it to things and relations with which we are already familiar. The everyday mind works by analogy, and most commonly by analogies built of analogies built of analogies. We do not consider the roots of experiences and what they consist of at most elemental level. What we see is what we think we see. We impose ideas on the world. We do not grasp their ultimate connections in being. In order to understand consciousness and its relation to the object then, we need a clear and complete understanding of the roots of experience. We can liken conscious experience to the operations of a computer and its software. In our everyday lives, we are like the end users of a software program. We use the menus and functions presented in natural language, but most of us do not have any idea of how they actually work. The next level down is the programmer using a high order language. He creates the end product for the user with his knowledge of the language's data structures and processes but is still working with complex objects at some remove from the instructions to the hardware. He may be able to do his job with little understanding of how the language actually relates to operations at the machine level. We can go another level down to the even more general assembly language, and finally trace back to the 1's and 0's of the machine code, which in turn relate to the physical circuitry of the hardware, the real roots of the program.

The objective here is to take conscious awareness back to its origins. The study of the physical vehicle provides some assistance here from an external perspective, but we are interested in the internal perspective of conscious experience. There are only so many ways that we can experience, a small number of parameters or elements of consciousness. There are only a limited number of ways we can predicate a subject or make judgments. We need to understand conscious in terms of its lowest elements, whereby any object or event in consciousness can be described as a set of values on these elemental parameters of consciousness. After we have understood the basic conditions for the development of conscious experience, the next step is to uncover the basic dimensions of experience and understand their properties.

This brings us back to the ultimate question of the relation between subject and object and the attainment of the self-consciousness of being through the integration of differentiated existence. To integrate is to relate the pieces, the diverse objects of the manifested world. Relation depends on having something that unifies the terms of relation. There must be some parameter they have in common, some shared element through which they both exist. The importance of these elements of consciousness is that they are the medium of relation that makes integration possible. They are also the roots of lived first person experience. Every object is experienced and known through the same set of parameters. They allow us to know the world in terms of grounded immediate experience. In addition, these parameters are also the categories of the earliest differentiation out of being and will be the approach back to it. Following the identification of the roots of consciousness in these elements, the task will be to unify them in turn and to collapse the separation of subject and object back into the wholeness of being, but now a being that knows itself in conscious awareness.

IN THE BEGINNING

What makes consciousness of a world possible? In the beginning there is being, that is, pure undifferentiated consciousness. As with Hegel, we find that simple being is essentially the same as nothing. In its wholeness there is nothing to be aware of. The first prerequisite of awareness is differentiation. There must be something in contrast to something else. What exists only exists in relation to other things. Light only exists in opposition to dark, positive against negative, interior in contrast to exterior, etc. Objects co-constitute each other and preserve the whole in their totality. From an objective perspective, we equated this state of the primal oneness, the pure potentiality of awareness, with the singularity at the origin of the universe. The Big Bang is the first differentiation of the universe. As noted earlier, the question of what it is that differentiates and how it does so is the fundamental question regarding the relation of consciousness and object. To understand the nature of awareness and how at the very outset it becomes the stuff of the "physical" world is to grasp the unity of mind and matter and is for mind to know itself. We must defer this ultimate question until we have examined the world that consciousness has provided. For now, we can only assume that consciousness has something in its nature that allows it to create variation within itself, separating into limited aspects of itself.

The generation of difference, however, is only the first prerequisite. It is a necessary but not sufficient condition for conscious awareness. Differentiation alone does not create a relation of consciousness and object. It is only a separation into parts. Without connection between them, each piece is just another isolated singularity. We are no better off than we were when we started. To have consciousness we must "know" there is difference. Difference must be juxtaposed and unified. There must be integration of the parts. As described earlier, consciousness manifests in the transition between its objects. Difference and consciousness exist in the moment. The potential for integration exists from the start due to the co-constituted nature of differentiated objects. Each is inherently connected to the other. However, this initial awareness is quite limited in that these connections are immediate and simple. They can only yield the negligible consciousness of the atomic/molecular level of matter. To approach the consciousness of the world we know as human subjects, a highly complex connectivity and movement is necessary. What makes this possible are the processes of life.

Life is characterized by integration. It is an organized whole, a complex assembly of molecules whose components work in a coordinated fashion to carry out the processes recognized as definitive of life, i.e., metabolism, homeostasis, adaptation, reproduction, etc. This coordination requires a certain connection and communication between parts, thus even in life's simplest forms it exhibits a degree of integration. Life, as we have noted, is a seeming anti-entropic process that acts as if it has an end of preserving and proliferating itself. The above-mentioned processes serve to build, maintain, repair and copy the living organism. These functions require resources in the form of both physical materials with which to build and as energy to execute these processes. Thus, at the heart of life are the integration of parts and the movement between them that are the characteristics of consciousness.

Acquisition of the resources needed for survival depends on the ability to identify, locate and get to them, so the development of systems that respond to the environment and communicate with a motor system that allows mobility within it, are critical to survival. These are the perceptual and nervous systems we also relate to the development of conscious experience. Because the senses and nervous system provide the basis for experience, we must examine them in more detail.

THE SENSES AND NERVOUS SYSTEM

A. The Senses

The senses are the initial point of connection to the world. Sense receptors respond to variation and change in the environment around them. The senses create in effect an internal reflection of the differentiated environment, at least to the extent to which they can respond to it. The organism integrates the raw inputs of the senses to construct the objects of consciousness. From the perspective of consciousness, the senses provide the elemental qualia of the five classic senses of sight, sound, taste smell and touch. The term "elemental" as used here refers to the initial inputs of the senses, i.e., the immediate differentiation of the environment to which they respond. However, secondary nervous system processing of this immediate sensory input begins at very early stages of perception. If we want to get to the roots of conscious experience, we must separate out higher processing from the elements upon which it operates. We can clarify the distinction between elemental qualia and complex higher experience by analogy with the activity of a painter. The only thing the artist actually puts on the canvas are the colors that come out of the paint tubes. Paint is the medium of the artwork and is like the initial input of the senses. All the other qualities of the painting that turn it into a recognizable representation derive from how the artist puts the colors together in patterns of difference. This is what the higher order neural activity provides. This secondary processing has its own elementary qualia, and we will consider these later.

Pure sense data are essentially ineffable qualia. They serve primarily as media, i.e., carriers of information, with little or no intrinsic meaning. There are perhaps some deeply rooted unconscious instinctive responses. For example, particular colors might have some instinctive meaning developed in relation to natural phenomena. Perhaps green might evoke some instinctive response because of its association with vegetation, or blue with water and sky, or red with blood and sexuality, etc. For the most part, however, colors get their significance in relation to other colors, in the patterns of difference they reveal that allow us to identify and locate objects in space.

For now, we defer the question of why and how particular sense qualia appear as they do (e.g., as "redness" or "greenness", etc.). In chapter 5, we will address the so-called "hard problem" of consciousness and consider why and how physiological processes relate to particular subjective experiences. Our immediate purpose is to identify the elemental qualities of the sense experiences on which higher cognitive processing operates.

1. Visual Experience

From a scientific perspective, visual experience discriminates differences in light in the environment. From this perspective, light is understood as a wave (although also exhibiting a particle nature). If mind and matter are dual perspectives of the same thing, we should expect that the qualities of light appearing to consciousness would relate to the basic attributes that vary in waves, and this is the case. The primary parameters of waves are wavelength/frequency and amplitude. Differences in wavelength are distinguished in the visual system via differential responses of the cone cells and are experienced subjectively as color. Amplitude, or intensity of the stimulus, is coded by the rate of firing and appears to consciousness as the quality of brightness. While the perception of color depends on more than simple wavelength alone, for example, appearance is affected by the mix or purity of wavelength (saturation), admixtures of achromatic "colors", intensity of the light source, etc., these factors only create color variants in consciousness. Thus, we can consider color and brightness to be the basic elements of visual consciousness. They are its raw media, the paint that goes on the canvas. What we get from vision beyond that is a result of higher processing that extracts patterns of difference from or becomes associated with these elements.

What we are conscious of depends on the vehicle of consciousness regardless of whatever may actually be "out there". What we experience is a function of what our perceptual and nervous systems respond to and how they process it. For example, we are not able to visually experience the entire range of electromagnetic radiation that scientific instruments reveal. We only respond visually to a very limited band of the electromagnetic spectrum. Neither can we see the transverse waves of the magnetic field. Thus, our ability to know the world and to attain self-conscious of being depends on the evolution of the human body. If we are subject to effects without a corresponding conscious awareness that allows us to make sense of them, then the opposition to the world cannot entirely be overcome. This prompts the question of whether at this time; given the current state of human physical evolution, it is even possible to realize a project of complete self-awareness of being.

2. Auditory Experience

Hearing, like light, is also based on waves. In this case, mechanical pressure waves through a physical medium, usually in the form of air compression waves. As with vision, the basic qualities of hearing relate to the properties of waves. Sound waves are internalized by their setting off vibration of the tympanic membrane. Hearing thus starts with creation of a physical copy of the wave in the body. In this case, frequency and amplitude eventually reach conscious awareness as the elemental experiences of pitch and loudness. Timbre is another characteristic of sound which, like color saturation, is mostly a function of the complexity of the waveform and its changes over time. Also, like vision, the significance of sound is largely in its patterns rather than its raw qualia. Certain sounds or types of sound may elicit instinctive responses, but most of the meaning human beings derive from of sounds comes from their relations, with language and music being prime examples of this.

3. Gustatory Experience

Taste differs in being a function of the perceptual discrimination of chemical composition rather than wave properties. The internalization of taste starts with a small number of different taste receptors that respond differentially to specific chemical classes. Five basic tastes have been established: sweetness, saltiness, sourness, bitterness and umami. Presumably, the development of receptors that distinguish these particular classes is due to their relation to key nutrients and to substances detrimental to health. For example, sweetness is associated with the presence of sugars, thus signaling energy foods. Saltiness relates to sodium. Bitterness is related to alkaloids and is associated with toxic compounds. The sour taste is a response to acids, which can be dangerous in themselves or a sign of spoiled/rotten dangerous foods. Umami is a response to glutamates, related to proteins. In contrast to the visual and auditory, where meaning derives from association, taste elicits a valence of desire. We immediately like or dislike tastes.

4. Olfactory Experience

The sense of smell is also chemically based. It is not well enough understood to break it down to "elemental" odors, and there appear to be a much greater number of distinctive responses and kinds of receptor compared to the handful in taste. Olfaction has many functions and plays a greater role in parts of the animal kingdom. Among its functions is a relation to taste and the evaluation of nutrients, and it has a role in social and sexual identification and selection.

5. Somatosensory Experience

While the fifth sense is usually referred to as "touch" in common usage, the topic here is much broader than tactile perception of external objects. Not only is there consciousness of contact, but also experiences relating to changes to the state of the body itself. The subject is better described as somatosensory perception: the whole of experience derived from sensation at the surface or within the interior of the body. The somatosensory is more complicated than the other senses and is actually a collection of diverse sub-senses.

The specific sense of "touch" is an elemental quality experienced in response to physical contact. The ineffable quality of touch is contact, but tactile experience is complex in nature. We can understand this better if we consider the qualities that describe tactile experiences. For example, one of the properties revealed in touch is smoothness/roughness. The impression of smoothness or roughness is based on the perception of change in contact. The receptors at one point feel more pressure than those at another. Judgments of roughness or smoothness also depend on the use of movement. We get a better sense of the change in contact by moving our fingers along a surface. Movement also reveals roughness or smoothness by revealing differences in resistance to movement. As the movement and changes get larger, we engage in "haptic" perception, the active exploration of surfaces. Here the senses of contact and movement work together to determine the form of an object in space. Movement also enters into discrimination on the hard-soft continuum. Does the object "give" when we press into it or do we feel a greater contact pressure and resistance? Variations in the change of contact and resistance to movement enter into the perception of many other tactile qualities, e.g., stickiness, slipperiness, fluffiness, etc. Touch has a dual aspect in that on the one hand, we use it to explore and interpret the world, but to touch is also to be touched and so comes with a value to the body. This inner feeling aspect of the somatosensory is called interoception.

Interoception refers to the sense of internal states of the body. It includes a diverse set of feelings that are not easily broken down to a definitive set of elementary experiences. Many of these feelings serve to provide signals regarding the needs of the body and prompt behavior to attend to them. Thus, interoception includes feelings such as hunger, thirst, warmth, coldness and pain for example. It also includes other feelings of discomfort such as itches, irritations, and of illness. Interoception provides the perception of body states such as tiredness and arousal. Because the interoceptive sensations are related to homeostasis of the body and immediately motivate behavior, they appear to have an instinctive intrinsic valuation in themselves, in contrast to our understanding of other senses as serving primarily carriers of secondary information.

Proprioception is the sense of movement and body position. We also include here the vestibular system that provides the sense of balance and spatial orientation. This latter is provided by the semi-circular system, which responds to rotational movements, and by the otolithic organs that are involved in the perception of linear accelerations. The basis for the sense of the position of the body and limbs, of movement and bodily effort is largely accomplished by mechanical "stretch receptors" such as the muscle spindles that detect changes in the length of the muscles and the Golgi organs that detect changes in muscle tension. The feelings of "stretch" and "tension" are important elemental experiences. We already saw an example of the latter above with the place of resistance to movement used in the judgment of textural qualities. They are also the basis for the sense of "mass" and "force, basic properties in physics. This will be addressed in more detail later in the book.

B. The Nervous System

Through the senses we internalize, and in effect become, the differentiation manifested in the environment. However, as noted, they largely function as media, carriers of information in their patterns of change with little intrinsic meaning. A multitude of unrelated receptors would not get us very far towards higher awareness. They would merely replicate the unknowing wholeness of being, as isolated monads with no connection or interaction. It is only in the connection of difference and the transition between separate perceptions in the moment that we have awareness, and it is through the relation of elemental sensations that we attain awareness of higher objects of consciousness. This connection and relation is provided by nervous system, the basis of which is the neuron.

While determination of the precise physiological mechanisms relating to specific forms of experience is the province of neuroscience, certain well accepted basic principles of the field are sufficient to provide a top-level accounting for most of the elements of subjective consciousness in relation to neural structures and activities. These basic properties of neurons are as follows:

1. Neurons either fire or they do not. It is all or none. Neurons are digital as opposed to analog.
2. Neurons may fire at different rates. Firing rate codes for the intensity of the stimulus.
3. Neurons connect to other neurons via the synapses. Connections can be direct, i.e., one has a synapse that ties to another, or indirect. For example, A connects to B which connects to C. Neurons have multiple connections. A single neuron may have thousands of synapses. The particular logic or architecture of connections makes possible and bounds the flow of experience.
4. Neurons affect and are affected by the other neurons to which they are connected. These effects can be either excitatory or inhibitory. In the former, the effects of a neuron firing, i.e., its associated chemical changes and release of neurotransmitters at the synapse, make the neuron at the other end of the synapse more likely to fire. In the case of inhibition, the outcome of neuron A firing is to make neuron B less likely to fire. In addition to the mere fact of connection, the particular chemistry of the neurons and synapses affects the conditions for firing.
5. Neural connections can be hierarchal, meaning that whether or not a neuron fires may depend on the inputs of a number of neurons that feed into it. Hierarchal connections provide a mechanism for developments such as complex objects, contingencies, and the recognition of essence, as we will get into below.

6. Neural activity is also affected by what are called "neuromodulators", which work not by direct transmission at a particular synapse, but in a diffuse manner referred to as volume transmission. These neural modulators can alter the synaptic chemistry over a large area of the brain, creating effects that are more general. Examples are neurotransmitters such as norepinephrine, which has the general effect of increasing arousal and alertness, priming the brain and body for action. Dopamine has broad effects related to motivation and reward behavior, as well as general motor system and cognitive functioning. Serotonin affects mood and numerous cognitive and physiological processes.

Just as we recognize the initial inputs of the sense organs as providing raw qualia of experience, so must we consider neural activity as providing another form of the same. It is perhaps more difficult to fix a firm idea in the mind of these qualia than it is for a sensory quality such as color, but nevertheless the outputs of cognitive processes yield distinct subjective experiences in the same manner. A thought feels like something. A judgment has a specific experience. If we say X is the same as or different from Y, for example, that determination is a distinct experience. It is hard to picture these experiences in our minds or describe them as we can imagine a particular color for example, but they are just as much a part of experience. As with the immediate data of the senses, we must also reduce these "mental" experiences to their most simple elements.

CONSTRUCTING THE LIFE-WORLD

The world originates in the unconscious wholeness of being, and through its differentiation and subsequent integration develops to the conditions for self-consciousness. Differentiation is associated with creation and unfolding of the "physical" world. A wider, more holistic integration becomes possible with the evolution of life. With life comes the existence of coherent organisms, an integration of parts working together through the harnessing of energy. The development of sensory systems allowed organisms to respond to and in essence internalize and model the differentiated world. Internal connections and communication, provided in higher life forms through nervous systems, made possible an integration of sense data, creating the conditions for awareness of objects in consciousness.

With these developments, an elementary awareness of objects becomes possible. They gain existence through integrated difference. However, this is not sufficient to get us to the objects and world of our everyday consciousness. Initially, what could these objects be? Without additional processing, they are no more than an assortment of varied raw qualia of the diverse senses, changing as the world changes around them, but with no larger meaning. As described above, our experience of the world has certain general characteristics. Objects exist and appear as independent of the perceiver. They have qualities and are coherent entities with distinct identities. They are recognizable. They have constancy in their identity and appearance beyond the specific sensory qualities of any individual perception. We understand objects as existing as types or in classes, with some characteristic(s) that makes them the same in some way. Objects exist in what we know as space and time. They exist in relation to one another in these frameworks and in other ways. They affect each other, exist together or apart, are identical or different. Their qualities, states and relations change over time. Thus, there are a number of interrelated questions that must be resolved to get to the most basic consciousness of objects.

General Characteristics of Objective Existence

The feeling of existence is the consciousness that originates in difference. We are aware through change. Something exists in contrast to something else. With existence comes the notion of quality. To be is to be a specific something in opposition to another specific something.

Each differentiation has a distinctive subjective experience. Most entities are not merely simple qualities like a blob of a single color in contrast to other colors. We recognize objects of the world as being discrete coherent wholes consisting of a set of qualities. They might have color and form and consist of a specific configuration of parts. What accounts for the sense of a coherence of qualities forming a distinct entity? It arises through a specific kind of association. The qualities exist together, move together and maintain certain relations to one another. They are "attached". Later we will look at the possible kinds of relation, the ways in which things can exist together, but for now we are concerned with the notion of association itself, existing with, as a fundamental category of conscious experience.

Association has its physical counterpart in the basic principles of neurons described above. We can understand the sense of a discrete entity as a binding together of associated inputs through the hierarchal aspect of neural connections. The state of a particular neuron "up the chain" depends on the conjunction of inputs from neurons that feed into it, for example, neuron A fires only when B, C, D and E fire. Neuron A serves as a binder of the lower inputs, creating a unique physical state for a collection of associations and thus a unique conscious experience of a specific entity. This of course is only a simple example, to explain the basic mechanism. In reality, even simple objects are highly complex, involving the relations of millions of neurons. Nevertheless, the construction of real objects is only an application of these basic mechanisms on a large scale.

The details of the physiological basis for this process works are beyond our scope, but in general, when neuron A repeatedly excites neuron B, the connection between them is strengthened, making the firing of neuron A more efficient in on bringing neuron B to action potential. As a common paraphrasing of what is called Hebb's rule puts it, "Neurons wire together if they fire together". Associated stimuli thus become a unit. This comes about through the changes in the chemistry of the connecting synapses and sometimes in the longer term through the creation of new synapses.

When and Why Are We Conscious?

Before continuing to trace the development of the perceptual object in consciousness, the idea of association in consciousness and its neural counterpart is a good place to consider the question of when we are consciously aware and what function it serves. The integration of differentiated being is the path to the consciousness of being, and the ability to form associations, i.e., to learn, is at the heart of integration.

We can distinguish three primary processes through which the development of association comes about. First, there is the development of hardwired reflex circuits. A stimulus elicits an immediate and automatic behavioral or physiological response. This is the knowledge of the world encoded in the body through the processes of natural selection. It is acquired unconsciously through evolution across generations. Closer to the idea of learning, because acquired through the life experience of the organism, are processes such as classical conditioning. Here the association is made through the pairing of a neutral stimulus with another that has usually has some connection to pain and pleasure. The learning here is still unconscious.

The third process, and our interest here, is intentional conscious learning. This is the kind of learning we do in school, in learning a new task or skill for work or leisure, or in negotiating some situation in life. This learning typically does not take place because of an immediate visceral payoff as in classical conditioning. For example, touching a fire is immediately followed by pain, and so we might automatically develop an aversion or fear to fire without consciously positing the idea that fire is dangerous. On the other hand, there is no direct payoff in learning how to read. In the end, there may be many pleasures that follow directly or indirectly from this ability, but the only thing driving the activity is the will to learn. We can pair nearly anything with anything or create the most complex set of associations without there being any immediate relation to desire. How are such associations possible?

When we intentionally learn in this sense, specific actions and techniques are applied. These activities afford insight into the nature of learning and the function of consciousness. When we learn a skill, for example, we "practice", or attempt it repeatedly. However, to be successful, we must practice in a particular way. We must have an idea of a particular desired outcome. When a musical instrument makes the right sound, or a tennis stroke puts the ball in the right spot on the court, we are forging a relation between the feel and control of body movements and external perceptions. Notably, we are conscious in this process. In time, we may reach the point where we do things automatically, seemingly without paying attention or thinking about it at all. For example, once we have learned how to drive a car and know a particular route, as long as the trip is uneventful, we are barely aware of the countless judgments and adjustments we have made along the way. We play our instrument or engage in our sport without even thinking about what we are doing. In fact, being too self-consciousness may trip us up. However, when we are learning, we are aware. Concerning the question why we are conscious or what function consciousness has, it seems that consciousness is essential to the forging of new relations of a certain kind. We are conscious in the creation of relation. Consciousness is the place where we bring together things that are unconnected by physical desire and forge a relation between them. Once established, the relation no longer requires the mediation of consciousness. The response can become unconscious or semi-conscious. Meaning and awareness are no longer necessary. The process becomes reduced to mechanical association.

The same applies to scholarly learning. Simply listening to a lecture is not enough except for perhaps the simplest ideas. Learning does not happen by itself, at least not for complex topics. We must read and review the material. We must willfully bring concepts to mind, consciously relating them through concrete examples and integrating them with ideas we already understand. If we want to recall, we must practice recall. This is why advice for learning often recommends not just the review of material but questioning oneself, engaging in the act of retrieval. Conscious activity is the forge of new associations.

We find the creation of relation occurring in any situation where conscious awareness is present. Suppose we are doing a mathematical calculation for example. Unless are autistic savants, most of us cannot instantly multiply large numbers in our heads. We must consciously work through a process to perform such an operation. Why is conscious activity necessary? Because what we actually are doing is relating specific numbers to a procedure. In summary, conscious awareness has evolved as a kind of substitute or addition to instinct and automatic conditioning. Rather than being limited to a fixed hardwired repertoire of response, or by automatic associations conditioned by immediate visceral effects, the juxtaposing, the association forming ability of consciousness makes possible infinite and complex relations and connections. To the question of what consciousness is good for, the answer is that conscious awareness is what makes it possible to flexibly and creatively bring together stimuli into new relation beyond the hardwiring of instinct and simple mechanical processes, creating the possibility of highly complex objects and concepts.

Object Independence, Constancy and the Problem of Universals

Returning to general appearance of the objective world, we noted that one of the fundamental characteristics of this world is that the objects in it appear as being independent and alien from the subject that perceives them. What accounts for this impression? In part, it derives from changing appearance of the object as we move with respect to it, unlike, for example, the after image following exposure to a bright light that stays the same and moves with the direction of our glance. The physical also offers opposition. The perceived qualities of solidity and heft are experienced as a resistance to movement and manipulation of the object. As noted above, these appearances are rooted in the somatosensory sensations of contact and muscle tension. Objects posited as belonging to the physical world and independent of the subject appear with varying degrees of unpredictability and uncontrollability in our interactions with them.

Another general characteristic of external objects is that they are more than just collections of sensations. Each is a distinctive thing or type of thing. It has an identity. It has a specific set of qualities making it recognizable as that particular thing and which by association may also attach it to a wider set of meanings. Further, it retains this identity despite the differences between concrete perceptions that come with different perspectives or environmental conditions.

The most basic sense of "identity" refers only to the judgment of sameness or difference of qualities. Along with difference, this sense of identity has its origins at the roots of consciousness and is one of the most fundamental determinations of consciousness. We become aware through difference, and with the proliferation of difference we come to distinguish the identity or difference between entities. To have an identity, or to be a particular something, is to exist in identity to a specific set of qualities. To recognize something is to know we have seen it before, which implies memory. Memory, as described above, is a function of strengthened neural connections. When we see an object that we have seen before, the sensory perception activates the entire chain of associations tied to it, including an identifier such as a name that binds them together. The sense of identity/difference detects the extent of match between the current perception and the set of associations connected to a defined object.

A larger problem though is how it is possible to recognize an individual perception as being a particular object or type of object at all. Any singular concrete appearance of a thing is almost always different from any other one. Each comes from a different perspective. If entities consisted of nothing more than collection of specific concrete sensations, there would be no way to recognize a particular object or to establish general classes of object. This problem of finding object constancy in individual perceptions and of assigning objects to abstract categories is the ancient problem of universals.

When we recognize objects, they are more than just the recall of specific sensory stimuli. If concrete sense values were all there was, our perceptions would be largely meaningless. Every individual perception, even of the same object, is nearly always from a different perspective. The physical signature of something even as simple as its color registers differently depending on the lighting source and level of illumination. A picture frame viewed straight on yields an image with right angles. Viewed from the side, the angles are obtuse or acute. Yet we recognize and understand these perspectives as referring to the same object which in its immediate tactile appearance is a right-angled rectangle. A ball moving towards us from a distance takes up a tiny fraction of the visual field. When in front of our face it dominates the field. Yet we know both to be the same object of the same size. If all we had were concrete perceptions, every perception would be a different object. We could only recognize exact matches of sensation. Associations made with one view would not carry to another.

There must be some underlying sameness or likeness to know that two views are of the same thing. We accomplish this partly by coordinating perspective and appearance. We learn to associate and coordinate the appearance of a series of views with perspective to interpret them as belonging to a single entity. Interpretation of sense data depends on overall context. In the example of form given above, we grasp that shapes and angles change with perspective in a predictable way. We judge the size of an object not only by the extent of its dominance of the visual field, but also by its relation to the objects around it and through cues to its distance from us.

More fundamental than the issue of how we grasp a stable object despite an ever-changing series of appearances, is how objects have recognizable properties at all. We know and describe objects through their qualities: a thing is a particular color, shape, size, or has a particular function, etc. However, the issue is not just to explain how a set of properties is joined together to form an identifiable individual or type of object, but how even simple general properties can exist. The problem extends down to the most elemental level of experience. Even the simplest properties are already understood as general classes. To describe an object as "green" for example, is to not only point to a specific hue, but refer to a group of colors and shades that are distinct yet also the same in some way.

What we are really considering here is the problem of universals, which we can define broadly as the question of the meaning of ideas such as properties, abstractions, essences, concepts, and classes, etc., and how are they possible. Qualities are known through their individual concrete existence but are also understood as partaking of something general beyond their specific values, where they are experienced as belonging to a class of things. They are understood as having concrete specific values, but also as having something in common with other individuals in the class. What exactly are these shared qualities and how can we account for their meaning in relation to the physical vehicle through which they are experienced?

For sense qualities, essence can be understood as the result of a reduction mechanism, where a specific set of diverse stimuli, and only those stimuli, result in a common response. For example, imagine a simple light sensitive receptor that responds only to the presence or absence of photons. Once a certain threshold of light is present, the cell will fire, whether it arises from the dimmest flash of a firefly or the brightest sun. A range of light conditions will result in a common physical state and with it the same appearance in consciousness. However, with such a simple receptor, there is only one experience of light. There are no individual instances to contrast with a general class. Suppose, however, that the perceptual system evolves to become capable of discriminating more than just the presence or absence of light and gains the ability to respond differentially to light intensity. Physically, this might be accomplished by differences in the firing rate. Now there is no longer a single experience of light. Individual experiences of light can now be distinguished due to variations of luminous intensity (subjectively experienced as brightness), but still share the general response to light and thus be recognized as belonging to a class of experiences with a common "essence".

As a sense mode develops a more finely grained differentiation of some physical property, the experience becomes more diverse and complex and develops more sub-classes of experience. For example, in taste there are five basic receptor types, resulting in not only five basic tastes but also the possibility of many more different tastes in their infinite combinations and proportions. The physical basis for distinct basic taste categories, i.e., the reduction that creates a common essence binding individual tastes together, follows from the existence of the atomic/molecular substrate common to all matter. Everything is made of up of a limited number of elements in specific combinations and arrangements. Foods differing in the whole of their specific atomic composition and appearing as different things may contain common specific elements or compounds to which only specific taste receptors respond. For example, many different fruits contain the forms of the same simple sugar compound, $C_6H_{12}O_6$. A taste receptor that responds specifically to this underlying common chemical structure (and perhaps others similar to it) provides a basis a common taste class we recognize as sweetness. As with light in the example above, a single basic taste may also constitute a set of experiences that differs across members of a more general family of substances. For example, substances differ in the perceived intensity of sweetness. The response depends on how well the compound fits the sensitivity characteristics of the taste receptor.

Taking this idea to a further level of complexity, consider the experience of different colors. The issue here is not of understanding the physiological processes by which we respond to and discriminate specific wavelengths of light, nor of how those processes come to be consciously experienced as the specific qualia of color. Rather, the question is how it is possible to have distinct color categories. The visible spectrum of electromagnetic radiation is continuous. We can distinguish perhaps 150-200 distinct spectral hues, but taking saturation and luminance into account, the number of colors the human eye can discriminate is perhaps in the millions. Yet we group colors into only a handful of basic categories. Our elementary color categories are more or less limited to the six or seven colors of the traditional spectrum, the achromatic "colors" of white, black, and grey, and perhaps a small number of anomalies such as "brown", for example, that are treated as basic colors. We easily sort the thousands or millions of colors we can distinguish into a few basic categories.

At first glance, color categorization seems similar to taste in that we do have separate color receptors in the three types of cone cells, which respond differentially to wavelength. Yet while differences in the relative mix of cone responses might be sufficient to account for the number of colors we can distinguish, it is not readily apparent how this provides a basis for our specific color categorization schemes. Human beings normally have only three cones, so the number of individual receptors does not track with our basic color categories. Further, if we examine a graph of cone response to wavelength, we see there is much overlap in the response range of each and no discernible pattern in the mix of response that would form distinct physiological states corresponding to the distinct color categories of consciousness. For example, we see a "pure" yellow in approximately the 575-585nm range, yet there does not seem to be anything special in the cone response patterns at these points that would privilege them to define the boundaries of a distinct color category.

However, the existence of the three cones is not the whole story. Opponent process theory showed that that the input of the cones is processed at a more complex level. According to this theory, the responses of the cones are processed through a system of opponent pairs. Data from the cones feeds into separate green–red and blue-yellow opponent channels (along with a third "black-white" channel related to the perception of luminance), where the output is one color response or the other depending on the relative strength of the cone response. For example, if the input from the mid-wavelength "green" cone is stronger that the input from the long range "red" cone, the response of the green-red channel is green rather than a mix of green and red and likewise for the blue-yellow channel.

This provides physiological correlates for the four psychologically primary colors of blue, yellow, green and red. We see these "pure" colors at the points where the two wavelengths of "other" channel are near equal in response and cancel each other out. For example, at around 580 nm, the blue-yellow channel fires yellow and the green-red channel is at a neutral point, effectively canceling out green-red response and resulting in a pure yellow. Combinations of these binary states account for the other major spectral categories as well. A red response on the red-green channel plus the blue on the blue-yellow channel yields violet. Red with yellow is of course orange. It's a little trickier on the green side since it seems that we usually do not name specific color categories between green and blue and green and yellow. However, the traditional seven color spectrum does make a distinction between blue and indigo, and psychologically we do perceive a distinct change centered around 485-495nm in a spectral diagram. Nowadays, with its importance in computer graphics and printing, we are more likely to recognize the "blue" of the traditional spectrum specifically as "cyan". In the RGB color model, cyan is defined is as an equal blue-green mix, so it seems that the physical state where the opponent channels signal a both green and blue responses does have a distinctive psychological counterpart. The range between green and yellow does have color terms such chartreuse and lime, although it seems that we tend to identify these more as shades of green, rather than as a distinct color class such as orange or purple. It may be that to some degree that the colors we define depend on pragmatic usage. For example, we know that cultures differ in the colors they name. There is not a lot of chartreuse in the world. On the other hand, we do separately name the non-spectral color of brown as a distinct category. Technically brown is a sort of a darkened orange, although colors included in the brown family range from offwhites and beiges in its lighter, low saturation tints, to the tans and khakis in the middle, to the chocolates and coffees in its darker forms. Shades of brown are very prevalent in nature, seen in soil, wood, stone, skin and hair tones, etc. However, the main point here is that there are discrete physical states that provide a basis for the distinct categories of subjective color experience.

Sensory qualities are only the beginning of what makes up the identity of a distinct recognizable entity. As we have noted, the senses mainly serve as media to carry information in their patterns of difference. Most of what makes up the identity of an object is a product of the higher neural processing that extracts patterns of difference from the raw sense data. As an example of how this processing creates general categories through which the classification and relation of objects becomes possible, consider the property of form.

Along with color, form is another basic property through which we recognize and classify visual objects. Objects are not merely blobs of color. They have distinct boundaries. These borders separate objects from the rest of the world and give them form. Form makes up part of the identity of the object. We more often recognize objects based on form rather than color. Forms are like colors in that they are recognizable categories in themselves. We recognize objects as having common qualities such straight lines, or as being round or rectangular. We recognize general form properties in concrete existents and so make comparisons between them. We also recognize that individual visual images, despite differences due to changes in perspective or lighting conditions, can refer to the same object. For example, a circle viewed from the side appears as an oval on the eye, yet we understand it as circular because we grasp the relation between appearance and perspective. We are so good at this that most of the time we do not realize what we really "see". A novice artist drawing a vase from the side will make the top more circular than it should be. The beginner's instinct is to draw what he knows the object to be in its tactile reality rather than its two-dimensional projection on the retina. While it is relatively easy to define what makes for a simple regular form like a circle or square, and to conceptualize physical mechanisms that account for the perception of such forms, it is not as easy to understand the means by which the generalization and recognition of irregular forms, e.g., "guitar shaped", becomes possible. Here it would seem that we make use of more complex processing, binding together multiple simple shape concepts and relations between parts. There are two questions: First, how do we account for the emergence of objects experienced with form-like properties in consciousness, and secondly, how to we attain consciousness of form universals?

Outlines do not exist in nature, yet we easily pick out distinct borders separating one object from another, as if they had lines drawn around them like a cartoon image. When we draw, the first thing we do is trace out borders. However, the only visual information we receive from the world is difference in light. Perhaps this is sufficient to account for the perception of juxtaposed areas of different colors, but it would not provide the clear sense of a border between distinct objects. How do color contrasts become the strong experience of line? Earlier we noted that secondary visual processing of data received from the sense organs begins almost right at the start. In vision, this starts with the "center/surround" structure of cells in the retina and brain, whereby inhibitory processes work to enhance the contrast at the point of change. The next step is the integration of individual cells. The cells of the retina and visual cortex do not exist in isolation. They are connected to each other and to hierarchal neural structures to form a visual field. The integration of contiguous cells with activated center/surround inhibitory effects creates the sense of a distinct edge. With the basic principle for the formation of lines established, we can consider form in more detail. The work of Hubel and Wiesel on the detection of edge orientation is well known. They found that certain cells responded to very specific orientations of lines (e.g., vertical, horizontal, particular angles, etc.). These effects arise from contingent hierarchal structures, where a cell only responds when a set of cells in a particular orientation are excited.

With these and similar mechanisms, the brain models general shapes such as straight lines, curves, squares, triangles, circles, etc. A continuity of line creates a border, separating the shape from the world. Specific patterns of change in orientation define particular shapes. A straight line maintains dimensional orientation. A curve changes orientation in a particular continuous manner. The boundary of a square changes orientation at a different angle than that of a triangle. The number of orientation changes and the quantity of space covered between changes also determine shape. Distinct breaks in orientation create the number of "sides" of a figure. The proportion of sides is another defining factor. A square must have four equal sides, while a rectangle need only have opposite sides of the same length. A circle changes orientation at a specific ratio, etc. Thus, each concrete array of sense data holding a particular pattern within it activates a common physical state and with it a specific subjective consciousness, allowing them to be recognized as common members of a class.

We have just introduced a number of terms, which, while taken for granted in everyday language, need explanation. Characteristics such as continuity, orientation, number and proportion have a much larger significance than their role in defining form and are attributes of the more basic categories of space and quantity. At the origins of perception, there are only a limited number of elemental parameters through which we can experience and know the object world. These have their parallel in the most simple and basic sensory/neural physical structures and activities. Everything we know is a compound of these elemental experiences. They are important because integration depend the existence of common dimensions on which things can be related. These parameters are the unity of experience. As the most basic elements of experience and unity, they are the earliest emergence out of the wholeness of being and are the path back to it. The next task then is to define these elementary parameters of experience.

THE ELEMENTARY PARAMETERS OF CONSCIOUSNESS

Space

As we begin to see above, the sense of space is central to consciousness. Things exist in space and are largely known and related in terms of spatial characteristics. Objects partake of space. Space is an elemental parameter of consciousness, one of the fundamental categories of experience. Language is filled with references to space. The question of "where" is one of the basic interrogatives. A large percentage of relation words, the prepositions, describe spatial relations. Verbs of activity are dominated by actions involving movement through space or changes to an object's footprint in space. We use spatial terms in metaphorical ways to describe things that are seemingly not spatial. For example, people are "close" when they are emotionally connected. When we compare things for likeness, we say they are "close" or "in" the same ballpark. We speak of social spaces, mathematical spaces, cyberspace, etc. The larger usage of spatial terms suggests that space has a more fundamental relationship to consciousness and being than other basic parameters of experience. We will consider this idea in more detail later.

Space is fundamental, but what is it? We have an intuition of what we mean by space, but it is not easily defined. Unlike qualities such as color or sound or taste, there is no concrete object to which we can point as an example. Perhaps the Greek *khôra,* introduced into philosophy by Plato, is a sort of pointing in its original meaning as the area of the polis outside the city proper. It is where the city is situated, its context. Space is where stuff is. That is circular though, as "where" is the meaning of space. Perhaps the best approach to space is to consider the specific attributes through which we experience it:

1. Points and Fields – Space consists of distinguishable parts. It is divisible into individual units or points, seemingly almost infinitely so. However, points or parts only exist in contrast to a whole. Space is thus also a unity of points, a plurality that also makes a whole. Space exists as a field. Points connect to and relate to each other in some way. It is the fact that points are differentiable yet relatable that makes everything else possible.

2. Dimension – We relate locations in space via dimension, an orientation they have to each other. Like space itself, it is hard to define dimension, but we can grasp it through its concrete manifestations. Our natural understanding of dimension is of the three dimensions through which we grasp the world, i.e., vertical, horizontal, and depth. We can immediately relate dimension to the asymmetries of the body, distinguishing the direction from

the left and right side, head to toe and front to back. The vertical dimension is also anchored with respect to the force of gravity. Dimensional values provide the information needed to define a particular location in space. Location and dimension are relational terms, as space itself does not have and fixed center. In everyday life, we orient and locate objects in relation to other objects and landmarks. Even latitude and longitude coordinates, which serve as universal reference points within the context of the earth, are relative. They are defined with respect to the earth's axis of rotation and an arbitrary reference point (i.e., a prime meridian).

3. Quantification – Quantity is an elementary parameter in its own right but is also an attribute of space. Space is quantifiable. It exists as quantity from the start, being a severable whole and consisting of a seemingly infinite number points or regions. These divisions of space are countable. We can take any part of space as a whole and use that as a reference unit to count the space between points. Thus, objects can exist in a quantity of space, having a measurable length and width. We also measure distance, the amount of space between locations. Quantities can exist as differentiable regions of space. We can count ten areas with distinct blobs of color. Because we can create units, or partial wholes of space of any size we wish, the idea of proportion or scalability is inherent the measure of space. Region A covers ten units of space and region B five. Or we can define the relation using the compounds as units and say A is twice the size of B. Spaces can be compared in terms of general quantitative relations such as larger, smaller, or equal.

4. Contiguity/Continuity - If we can recognize distance between points in space, we can also distinguish where there is no separation, i.e., where points are immediately adjacent and in contact. We can expand this concept to the idea of multiple connections. A is contiguous with B, B with C, etc., forming a continuous line.

5. Boundary/Division - A continuous differentiable set of points serve as a means of creating a boundary that divides space. We can define regions of space in relation to the boundary line.

6. Separability/Enclosure – We can extend continuity and boundary further to the point where the boundary is completely continuous with itself such that a region of space is completely closed off and separated from the rest of space. This creates the relation of interior and exterior.

Returning to form, the properties of any given shape are simply the patterns of change in raw sensory experience in reference to the framework of space. For example, a square originates from a continuous differentiation (boundary/continuity) within the same dimension (giving a straight line), which at some point, and without loss of continuity, changes dimension such that there is no further movement in the original dimension (i.e., a right angle), then continues an equal amount of space as the first line (quantity/equality), before changing again back to the origin of the first dimension, etc.

Spatial relations between objects are relations with respect to these parameters. For an object to be "next to" another means there is little or no quantity of space separating them. An object is inside or outside in reference to a spatial boundary. Above/below, ahead/behind, to the left/right are orientations to dimension. Locations are assigned by anchoring spatial characteristics to specific frames of reference, either local or more general. For example, I can refer an object to my left or right, behind me, above or below, etc., using the body and its asymmetries as a frame of reference. We can make the orientation somewhat less specific and personalized by using landmarks in the local environment as points of reference: "the table is in the kitchen", "the post office is across from the school". Then there are the even more general frames of reference such as latitude/longitude coordinates as mentioned above. Ultimately, all locations and directions are based on the basic spatial parameters of dimension and distance, continuities and enclosures.

How do we account for the experience of space in terms of the physical vehicle of the body? The physical body models and is an external perspective of the consciousness that is the being of the body. The visual consciousness of space parallels the field structure of the retina and visual cortex. Individual cells are like points of space, which in their connection provide a spatial field. This basic structure carries the other spatial qualities within it. Continuity and boundary are a reflection of presence or absence of gaps in activated neurons. A detailed accounting is beyond our scope, but the discoveries of grid cells, place cells, and head direction cells also provide insights into the physiological modeling of space.

Ultimately, the sense of space is rooted in the somatosensory. The visual provides a representation, but space only has meaning in relation to our movement through it: To move to locations, to approach or be approached by objects, to manipulate objects. We do not directly get the third dimension through the visual image, which is flat. We grasp space through movement and use visual cues to make judgments about location in the third dimension. These visual cues of distance are well known to perceptual psychologists and include phenomena such as:

1. Object size - Closer objects with the same form take up more of the visual field
2. Interposition – a recognized object that doesn't show its full form is understood as being "behind" something else
3. Texture gradients - More detail is seen in closer objects
4. Binocular disparity - the slightly different perspective of each eye varies in a way that is predictable with distance
5. Oculo-muscular cues – The body feeling of how the eyes are turned to focus and the accommodation of the lens can be correlated with distance
6. Shading – patterns of light and shadow and correlate with the third dimension
7. Motion parallax –the relation of a moving object to background objects

All these factors correlate and are associated with change in distance, to create an experience of a three-dimensional space. The body has its own "field" characteristics and its own set of sensations that it uses to comprehend space. We assess change in position through the stretch and tension sensors. We grasp distance through the quantity of effort and intervening consciousness experienced in reaching a location. The asymmetries of the body itself provide an anchoring point for the dimensions. From an external perspective, the semicircular canals of the vestibular system look like a three-dimensional carpenter's level in the head. They provide a somatic parallel to the lived sense of dimension. Grasp of the vertical dimension can also be related to the sense of effort with respect to gravity. The coordinated whole of multiple visual and bodily cues is lived as consciousness of space.

Time

Time is the parameter of "when". We intuitively grasp what is referred to when someone speaks of time, but again it is hard to articulate exactly what it is. Attempts to define time tend to be circular, making use of terms (e.g., duration, sequence, progression through past, present, future, etc.) that depend on or are merely restatements of the phenomena they wish to describe. Operational definitions might be useful for science but really do not get at the essence of time.

What then is time? As with space, it might be best to start with a consideration of its attributes. The perceived properties of time are nearly identical to those of space:

1. Divisibility/Wholes – Like space, time breaks down into individual seemingly infinitely divisible moments. Yet we can also grasp the notion of a time span, a set of moments making up a unified whole.

2. Dimension – Time exists in dimension, on a continuum. In this case, there is only one. Time is understood as a flow from past

to present to future. Time also differs from space in its one-way aspect. We move into the future but cannot go back to a previous point in time. Like space, it is seemingly infinite.

3. Quantification – Time is understood as being quantifiable. We can count moments of time and measure the magnitudes of intervals of time. We can create time units of our choosing.

4. Continuity - We can think of events and blocks of time as continuous or separated in time.

5. Boundary/Enclosure - We can divide time into segments. Time boundaries can be open ended, simply marking off what is before or after a particular point or event, or we can completely separate and enclose an interval of time, e.g., an event occurs between particular dates.

6. Temporal Relation – Events are located in time in relation to one another. The basic relations on the single dimension of time are before, concurrent or after. Like space, position in time is always relative to some reference system. The narrowest frame of reference is the relation of two individual events ("She arrived before I did"); while the most general frame of reference is that of clock-time and calendars which relate to fixed natural events.

What accounts for the experience of time? Is it an ineffable elementary parameter of consciousness that we can say no more about, or is it a construction of the mind explainable in terms of non-temporal phenomena? Or is it somewhere in the middle, perhaps originating in a simple temporal intuition, but developed into a larger concept through analogy with other categories of consciousness?

When we closely examine the experience of time, it seems that our actual immediate sense of time is quite limited and that we mostly infer time from non-temporal cues. One demonstration of this comes from the well-known experiments of Michel Siffre and others, where subjects spent extended periods in caves without clocks or the presence of any indicators of the passage of time. The result was that after a short period, vast differences arose between the subject's estimation of the passed time and time as measured by the clock. However, we need not go to such lengths to grasp the point. Try to estimate the passage of even a minute without carrying out an internal count or without other cues to the length of time. Even in the short term, it is difficult to sense the amount of time that has passed, and it gets worse as the period of time grows. We cannot get by without the use of external timekeepers, such as clocks, watches and calendars. We will say more about these below. The judgment of time is subjective. It flies when we are having fun, but painful events seem to drag on interminably.

The neurological correlates of the consciousness of time are unclear. Depending on the task, the body employs a number of timing mechanisms operating at different time scales, ranging from milliseconds in physical coordination and understanding of speech, to the daily circadian cycles and beyond. However, these mechanisms often operate outside of conscious awareness, and it is not clear how or if they contribute to the lived sense of time.

Like consciousness itself, the sense of time originates in difference. Time exists at the boundary of the moment of consciousness. It is the consciousness of change - the awareness that a state has passed into or out of existence. The actual sense of time is the resolution of the consciousness of change, the minimal sense of existence before something different enters into awareness. We directly sense the duration of the moment. We will not attempt to precisely quantify what this moment is or what accounts for it in the brain, but it must be short, on the order of a tick of a clock. The concept of working memory is similar to the notion of consciousness itself. Working memory is the ability to hold information temporarily in mind such that we can operate on it and make connections between its contents. It too is of short duration. In one model of working memory, the "phonological loop" that temporarily stores sound-based representation is thought to hold only about one or two seconds worth of speech. Whatever the precise time unit is that we can actually sense, it must be very short.

This simple consciousness of the moment is the origin of the intuition of time. Through the application of various internal and external non-temporal cues and devices, we construct the larger concept of time along with the ability to manage it. Because of the limitations of the pure sense of time, we need timekeepers. The clock is main device we use to track and objectify time, but consider what clocks actually do. Clocks depend on the counting of events we assume will consistently take the same quantity of time to complete, allowing us to define a unit of time. We immediately grasp the tick of the clock, the second, as a consistent fixed quantity of time. We also have an elemental sense of grouping or addition, a category of the quantitative (addressed below). Combining the two, we infer and accept the concept of a larger duration of time that we do not directly sense. We sequence events in time in relation to number. In the longer term, we often manage time by spatializing it, as in calendars and timelines. It seems then that the construction of time has much to do with the notions of space and quantity.

In addition to these formal time keeping devices, we judge time in reference to natural events and the structure of events in our lives. Nature reveals the passage of time and our place in it through the alteration of day and night and the transit of the sun across the sky. The change of the seasons does the same on a longer-term basis. The structure of our lives also provides cues to the passage of time and our place within it. We live by schedules. We get up at a fixed time, engage in particular activities at specific times, and do things we know take a set amount of time, etc. We judge the time by our place in this sequence of events.

We know time not only through these external cues and devices, but also in relation to internal experience. The larger sense of time is partly constructed in relation to memory. The contents of memory differ in quality from events of the present. Experiences in memory are detached from the sensory stimulation of a present event. For the most part, an event or object recalled from memory consists of the gist of what happened rather than all the concrete details. This quality of experience tells us that the thing or event called before consciousness belongs to the past. Likewise, we can through imagination evoke similar images detached from the senses to project what has not yet been but will happen in the future. However, it is not only a matter of the quality of experience. As events recede into further into the past, the ability to evoke images and details fades away. Eventually we may have little more than a set of assertions about what happened in the past. We know "that" something happened but have few if any experience traces of the event. Much of our notion of past events and where they are in time is just a set of asserted facts and narratives, with few or no images of the events behind them. Thus, the past becomes only a set of sequenced assertions.

In conclusion, it seems that the actual direct intuitive experience, or actual sense of time, is actually quite limited and originates in the consciousness of the moment. All the rest is constructed in relation to the categories of space and quantity as well the quality of experience.

Quantity

We have seen above that quantity is involved in our basic intuitions of space and time. In fact, it cuts across all parameters of experience. Things fill up more or less space. The classification of shapes depends on the number and relative size of their parts or their ratios of change through the dimensions. Time is quantified into countable units. We use quantitative terms in comparative judgments. Things are "more" or "less" alike because of either the number or magnitude of differences. Sensory experiences are assigned quantitative value. A light has greater brightness, or a thing weighs more or than another does. A sensation is more or less painful. Movement and becoming are described in terms of rate of change. This cutting across experiences characterizes the basic parameters of consciousness. They constitute the framework through which everything gets its existence as a set of specific values on their continua.

Everything has a quantitative aspect to it, but what exactly is the sense of number? Again, there are two questions. First, what does the consciousness of quantity consist of at the most elementary level, and second, what structures and processes of the physical vehicle make it possible for consciousness to have mathematical objects. As noted earlier, most of the objects of everyday experience are complex and we generally have little awareness of the elementary qualia of consciousness from which all complex experience derives. With quantitative consciousness, when we think about the discipline of mathematics with all its branches and its difficult and complicated subject matter, it seems to cover a vast number of phenomena. Yet the actual quantitative sense arises from only a few elementary intuitions.

Quantity is at the heart of being. Existence begins with difference. One thing comes into existence in contrast to something else. Where there is existence, there are always at least two, A and -A. With increase in differentiation without any change of quality, the distinct consciousness of number begins. There are two of the same things. Quantity separates from quality as an independent characteristic of existence that cuts across all other parameters of existence.

The system of numbers takes off from here. However, the actual number sense, i.e., the immediate consciousness of specific quantities, is quite limited. We do not experience precise numbers beyond a certain point. Psychologists studying the subject refer to the ability to make immediate judgments about a quantity of items as "subitization" and have found that we can only make such judgments immediately and accurately up to about four items. The speed and accuracy of judgment drops off quickly as the quantity increases beyond that. Experiments with infants have also shown what seems to be intuitive grasp of certain basic addition and subtraction operations with these small numbers. It seems we grasp the whole immediately up around four items. After that, we must perform a counting operation. Perhaps the next few numbers beyond four can be assessed relatively easy and accurately because only one operation between small groups is necessary, but the ability to quickly grasp specific quantities quickly tails off.

After a certain point, absolute numbers have no immediate "sensed" meaning. We have no sense of "853"as opposed to "850", or even between "19" and "17". We cannot look at a large pile of marbles and immediately know the total. We only use and understand quantities from their place within a number system that we grasp analogically through a small number of basic quantity intuitions. One of the most fundamental is the "many into one" idea. We intuitively grasp the idea of putting a thing and another thing together, making a set called "two" that now also becomes a "one". From here, we apply the same basic joining operation as 2+1 to make the set called "three". Thus, we arrive at the general concept of a number system based on the repetitive operation of joining units into one: $N_x = N_{x-1} + 1$. We do not have an immediate intuition of each of the numbers in the system, but we grasp their meaning as an extension of the basic subitized quantities and the grouping operation that we do directly sense. We accept the results of calculation on faith because each step in its procedures is grounded in these basic intuitions. These few basic experiences are what the sense of numbers really consists of.

Consider the procedure of doing long division or multiplication. We have an intuitive notion of multiplication as a sort of counting. We are adding particular units a certain number of times. However, no number sense is used in applying the procedure of multiplication. For small numbers and individual digits, we only recall numbers out of a memorized times table. When we multiply large numbers, we apply a sequential process: Apply the times table operation to the bottom and top numbers of the first column. Write the number below. If it is two digits, put the left-hand number in the second column, etc. Nothing specifically quantitative is involved. We are merely following a sequential procedure. We could apply the same process to a group of letters. Division is the same, applying the principle of subtraction. We break the whole back into a quantity of equal sized pieces. We directly grasp this only at the quantity level of subitization. Division of higher quantities is an act of faith based on analogy to the immediate subitization level experience and confidence that the division procedure is a valid extension of it.

The basic intuition of number as recursive set is supplemented by fundamental relational intuitions that complete the number sense. These are represented in everyday language through the quantitative modifiers and determinatives such as equals, more, less, greater, fewer, all, some, many, few, a lot, none, etc. What we sense is relation rather than absolute quantities. Perhaps we can think about this most clearly in terms of the visual field of space. The visual field does not have numbers assigned to it. The specific extent of the retinal field covered by a particular object does not have absolute value in itself. What matters is relative size of objects in the field. Proportion is what we really know. If the reference is not too dated, consider the basis for the operation of a slide rule. A slide rule performs most kinds of basic calculations we can think of, from multiplication and division, to roots and powers, trigonometric functions, logarithms and exponents, etc. However, all that exists on the slide rule is a set of markings in particular spatial/quantitative relations to one another. Numbers are after all relational units. Beyond the intuition of many into one, numbers have no absolute meaning. Numbers derive meaning from their place in the overall system of units. A unit is whatever we have made into a one. We can have one electron, one atom, one molecule, one world, one galaxy, one universe, etc. It is a concrete reference point around which the system revolves. Quantity is about the relation of units.

Like the numbers themselves, the relations of quantity consist of a few fundamental intuitions. The notion of equality lies at the heart of consciousness in the detection of identity and difference. We can immediately tell if two sets of objects within the subitization range have the same quantity. Within a certain degree of resolution, we know when two objects are identical or different in size. Also elemental is the relation of greater and lesser. Without knowing anything about specific quantities we can look at two objects or collections of objects and know which is larger or greater in quantity. The idea of proportion can be understood from these basic intuitions. Consistent with the subitized counting quantities we only grasp exact proportions to a limited degree. For example, we can identify halves. Recognizing a 1:1 ratio is quite easy because the two parts are in a simple relation of equality. Recognizing 2:1 or 3:1 ratios is relatively simple because we can easily see that the larger part divides in two or three equalities. Once we comprehend the basic idea of iterative equalities, we can analogically apply the process to any numbers. However, as the quantity increases, we no longer have the direct intuition of the numbers and must apply counting procedures through the rules of a system of units.

While at some point we lose the ability to sense exact numbers and proportions at some point, we are capable of classifying quantitative dominance in terms that, while vague, still give more precision than the simple categories of more and less. We use terms such as "few", "some", "many", "most", etc. The criteria by which choose one or another are fuzzy but seem to reflect some sense of the counting task or of basic proportions. For example, "few" generally refers to a small plural quantity, perhaps within or just outside the subitization range, i.e., an easy counting task. "Many" is the feeling of a quantity beyond the precise intuition of number and perhaps reflecting a kind of significance or influence. "Most" reflects the judgment of "greater than" status at a minimum, and perhaps even a sense of "dominance" as a norm or controlling influence.

What then does mathematical consciousness come down to and what of the physical vehicle of the brain/body makes it possible? In summary, the most primary elements appear to be as follows:

1. Quantity originates in at the beginning of consciousness in the difference that allows consciousness. We "sense" up to four numbers, the range of subitization.
2. We also innately apply basic operations of addition and subtraction to these quantities.
3. Larger numbers are derived by recursive analogy to the numbers and simple processes through the idea of many into one and the concept of unit.
4. Quantity exists on a dimension of magnitude. The basic relation of numbers is that of being greater, smaller or equal to one another.
5. Because numbers are created in a system of relation to one another and because they are units rather than absolute quantities,

their underlying meaning is in proportion. The consciousness of proportion in general is also based on analogical extension of the basic relations above.

Because the origins of the quantitative are found in the deepest roots of conscious experience, it does not seem that any great elaboration of the parallel neurological processes is necessary. The formation of sets can be understood in terms of basic hierarchal neural associations. The identification of equalities and inequalities is the same task as the consciousness of identity and difference. Given that computer arithmetic/logic units are just wired circuits with logic gates, it seems we can easily account for the few actual numbers and basic operations carried out through the brain with its similar connective structures and firing contingency chemistry. As cognitive scientists learn more about the micro-functioning of the brain in performing quantitative tasks, future mathematics might become a more empirical enterprise, a "neuro-mathematics", where the work of mathematicians as practiced today is supplemented by the study of the physiological counterparts of mathematical consciousness.

What is mathematics as an academic discipline, as opposed to the use of number in everyday life? We will defer the question of the onto-logical status of mathematical objects until later in a general discussion of knowledge, but here we consider the general question of what we are doing when we do mathematics. The comments above about a relation to neuroscience fairly points at its meaning. In doing math, we are making conscious objects of the underlying neural structures that we use in quantitative activity. We make conscious explicit objects of the secondary abstracting processes of the brain. However, mathematics goes far beyond the simplest elements of the quantitative sense and involves itself with building these simple relations into larger structures and in making connections between diverse manifestations of quantity. The basic elements we have considered are much the same as what appears in formal work on the foundations on mathematics. For example, set theory and recursion theory are elaborations of the notions of "many into one" and analogical scaling up of simple operations. As we have noted, even much of what we do mathematically in everyday life is not strictly quantitative but is a matter of following procedures. The work of mathematics lies precisely in developing and proving the larger connections and structures entailed by the basic elements. The major tool of this is logic, the other critical element to the foundations of mathematic. We defer a discussion of logic to the following chapter, where it will be considered as part of a more general discussion of thought.

Becoming

Becoming is the change of existence. Consciousness requires change in that it depends on movement through differentiation. In order to have awareness, either the world must change around us, or we must move through its diversity. An active principle is thus a prerequisite for existence. The specific consciousness of becoming is entwined with time, memory and the recognition of difference. We know time through change and recognize change as occurring in time. Something was or was not in a particular state but is no longer. We recognize a difference between states.

Whatever we are conscious of and how we are conscious of it finds expression in language. Words and grammatical structures pertaining to being and becoming are fundamental to language. The most basic unit of expression, the clause, consists of a subject and a verb asserting either a state of existence or a change of state in the past, present or future.

Everything present to consciousness is in a state of being or becoming. As an open word class, verbs do not provide an immediate specification of the categories of the consciousness of change. Becoming cuts across the parameters of existence and they in sum define the activity. Most verbs are complex and packed with multiple specifications. For example, to say that something moves is generic and only indicates a change in space. However, to say that one walks, runs, swims, rides, flies, dances, eats, etc., also informs us about the characteristics of the activity, such as the agent of movement, its rate of change, what is changing, the medium through which moves takes place, the vehicle of movement, the purpose of movement, etc. What an object of consciousness consists of, and what about it can change, are its values on the set of parameters through which consciousness apprehends the world. An object is a set of values on these finite parameters. They are the basic elements or categories of experience that we are defining in this chapter. Thus, each object has an existence status, a set of sensory qualia, a way of existing in space and time, attributes of quantity, a set of internal and external relations (addressed in the next section) in which it exists, etc.

Each parameter has its own form of change. Change under the category of being is the activity of creation or destruction, i.e., the passing into or out of existence, or of transformation, i.e., the change of qualities. The former is a binary transition between existence and non-existence, and reflected in terms such as becoming, creating, producing, making, destroying, annihilating. Change in quality is transformation. Change under being is understood through the judgment of identity/difference over time: There is awareness that current state of existence is unlike what was.

Change in space is movement. An object shifts from one point in space to another. As space is continuous, movement is generally ex-perienced as a continuous change of location in space. We do not really perceive movement: We infer it. The perception of movement depends on memory and the succession of states. What gives the particular sense of movement is the consciousness of a particular series of views. There is a smooth continuity of change in space. The visual appearance changes along with perspective in a predictable way. All consciousness of move-ment is in effect like the motion in film or cartoon animation. At some point gaps in the succession of views becomes too great. The sense of movement goes away, and the experience becomes one of change of being: Something merely appears or disappears at a given location. Changes in each of the properties of space an object exists through has its own specification in language. Thus, to rise and fall or approach and recede are a further specification in spatial movement with respect to dimension. To separate or contact describes movement in relation to continuity. Entering and exiting refer to changes with respect to the property of spatial enclosure. The quantification of change in space pertains to both objects themselves and their relation to other objects. The former is the quality of size, the footprint of the object in space, and its change referred to with terms such as expansion, contraction, enlargement, shrinkage, etc. The space between objects is distance and its change is described as getting closer or further apart.

Changes in quantity are primarily of increase and decrease. In pure quantitative terms, it would be the number or amount of something that is in transition. As an elementary parameter, quantity intersects with the other parameters as in the example of space above. However, quantity also relates to changes to time (e.g., we lose or gain amounts of time), and to sense qualities (for example, a color becomes less bright or more green; a pain intensifies or abates (it feels like there is more or less of it, etc.). Changes in time relate to the one-dimensional flow of time and the quantification and boundary of time. Something is done earlier or later in time, (moved up, delayed, postponed), takes more or less time (got longer or shorter), is occurs or is placed within an interval of time, etc.

The activity of becoming itself can be taken as an object exhibiting transformation of its own qualities, i.e., change of the change. For example, rate of movement in space can get faster or slower, i.e., it accelerates or decelerates. A movement might change in direction or destination, or in the mode of transport. Becoming itself exists within and through the other parameters of existence. Action occurs in some place and time but is not necessarily the change of its object in space and time. An action may be described in quantitative terms, e.g., it occurs a certain number of times or proportion of the time but is not change to the quantity of the existent (it necessarily does not make more of a thing or make it larger, etc.). The details of a movement's qualities can be packed into the descriptor of the action itself, i.e., in the verb, as in our examples above, or through adverbs that qualify the action.

Adverbs are described as belonging to categories such as place, time, frequency, degree, and manner. This list is largely in accord with the parameters of experience we have already noted. Here, however, they refer to the change itself vice the object of change, in its relation to the other elements of experience. Adverbs of place tell us where something happens, i.e., locates the movement in space. Those of time assert when it occurred. Frequency and degree specify a quantitative aspect of an activity, how often it happens or its intensity or extent.

The category of manner refers to the "how" of activity, meaning not the method but rather the style or qualities of the action. Some manner terms refer to the object categories discussed above, but others reflect parameters not yet considered. Adverbs of manner elaborate on the broader relations and effects of actions. For example, some pertain to the sensory effects of the action, for example, people talk noisily or quietly. Another set characterizes activities in terms of force and energy. Things are done "energetically" and "powerfully", or "wearily" and "weakly". Actions are performed "gently" or "roughly", "violently" or "softly", etc. Thus, part of manner is what the activity takes into account and what it affects.

Many adverbs of manner reflect "subjective" parameters. The subjective will be explored in detail in the next chapter, but we can briefly consider its relation to action here. Actions may have a relation to emotion: To do something angrily, anxiously, calmly, cheerfully, etc. The action is driven by emotion and/or displays behavioral correlates of emotion. In the same way, activities may manifest a state of desire: To act "eagerly", "enthusiastically", "reluctantly", etc. Another dimension is how an action reflects one's judgment processes and attitudes towards the world. For example, one acts "thoughtfully", "wisely", "patiently", etc., or "impulsively", "recklessly", or carelessly". One behaves "boldly", "bravely", "confidently", or "fearfully", "anxiously", "shyly", "cautiously". Actions may be qualified with respect to desire and how well they accomplish their intended purpose. A thing is done "perfectly" or "poorly", "competently" or "ineptly", "gracefully" or "awkwardly". We specify judgments and actions with respect to clarity and openness of knowledge, describing them as occurring "doubtfully", "clearly", "mysteriously", "openly", "stealthily", "unexpectedly", etc. Finally, actions are modified to specify their intersubjective effects, i.e., the meaning and impact of actions with respect to social and moral relations. We can do things "cruelly", "faithfully", "fondly", "honestly", "innocently", "justly", "kindly", "generously", "obediently", "politely", "unethically", "rightfully", "rudely", "selfishly", "conscientiously", etc. These descriptors specify the action in terms of its orientation to other subjects. We will examine these "subjective" categories such as emotion, feeling, thinking, desire and intersubjective relations in more detail the next chapter.

Relation

The final parameter of objective consciousness is relation. We have already addressed many relations in the course of the analysis above. For example, to attribute spatial properties to an object, such as a location or orientation, is to assign it a position within the parameters of spatial experience with respect to other objects. To date an event is sequence it with respect to other events within the single dimension of time. Quantities and magnitudes get meaning from their place within a number system and the relative judgment of larger and smaller. In reality, relation is all there is since all that exists does so only though relation. Even qualities of sensory qualia depend on relation, as each exists and takes on its appearance in contrast other sense qualities.

Despite the dependence of existence on relation, we tend to think of objects as things in themselves with objective qualities of color, form and size, for instance. The object seems to exist in itself as a set of qualities or of parts aligned in particular relations. These we may call internal relations. They are qualities and relations of essence, i.e., that which makes the object what it is, or if not essential qualities, are those the object has in its state of existence.

In contrast to these defining qualities and relations of being are external and accidental relations. These are relations an entity happens to have with others, whether by design or chance, by virtue of its own state or properties. For instance, a thing exists in a particular orientation or location in space with respect to another. Two events have relative positions in time. One is larger or more numerous with respect to the other. A thing moves in relation to something else. These relations may not have any bearing on the being of the object. On the other hand, external relations can also be defining properties of an object in essence or existence. For example, a substance is identified as a "catalyst" precisely because it accelerates a chemical reaction, i.e., exists in a particular affecting relationship to other substances.

Relation itself is thus another basic parameter of conscious experience. Below is a summary of elemental relations as they relate to the other parameters of consciousness:

1. Being

    a. Existence – A thing's state with respect to the consciousness of existence. Something is or is not.
    b. Inherence – The sense that a quality belongs to a thing. These are properties that it has in essence or existence. Something is or is not this or that particular thing or has this specific quality.
    c. Identity/Difference– The relation between objects under the aspect of inherence is the comparative relation, or the judgment of identity and difference. This is the consciousness of whether or not things are the same.
    d. Association – The relation where qualities or entities exist together is some way. It cuts across the parameters of existence. For example, a set of sense qualities might define an object: It is A *and* B *and* C. Alternatively, entities might exist together in the same place and/or time. They might engage in activity together, etc. This relation is largely what is expressed in the "and" of natural language. A exists with B. It is represented in formal logic by the

logical conjunction, defined as the condition where all operands under the conjunction are true. Also included here is the "or" of natural language and the logical disjunction. While the everyday language usage of "or" is sometimes not quite the same as disjunction of logic, both are based on the idea of an association of alternatives. These concepts will be considered further as part of an examination of thought in the next chapter.

e. Affecting relations - This refers to the sense that one thing can change another in some way or that they exist in some dependency. In natural experience this is what we think of as causality, although here we are concerned not just with the confluence of temporal events, but also the underlying relations of necessity that make those results possible. Thus, also included here is the material conditional or implication of logic, i.e., if A then B. The senses in themselves do not perceive causality, but the mind in its most elemental existence seems to contain the notion that one thing can affect another, and immediately imposes this idea on the data of the senses. One billiard ball strikes another and it moves. In our natural understanding, we assume that the moving ball is an agent that exerts some causative force upon the second ball. Yet as Hume explained, we have no justification for believing that this relation will continue to hold. The attribution of causation is merely an inference from the "constant conjunction" of events. The mere assertion of causation in itself does not explain how such interaction is possible. For example, Newton's law of gravity precisely explained the attraction between bodies as a function of their masses and distance between them, but it provided no understanding of how this action at a distance occurs. The idea of a force of gravity" is just a label for the notion of a "something" that makes objects fall or move in particular ways. What it really is or how it works we do not know. The use of jargon evokes then sense of an "in-itself" of some exceptional reality status, but the term gravity is only a pointer to a specific appearance to consciousness. How should we understand the possibility of one thing interacting with and changing another? The proper understanding of causality is not of one distinct thing acting upon another, but rather as a change of existential relation between forms that are always co-constitutive in their differentiation out of being. As noted earlier, all objects of consciousness exist in relation to other objects. They are not independent. An object is always an interaction. Figure is always opposed to ground. The qualities of any particular existent are always a function of the environment around it. A clay vase sitting on a table appears to be a thing in itself with fixed qualities, but it is only what it is within a specific matrix of forces. The force of gravity wants to flatten it but is opposed by atomic forces within that hold it together. Set the vase on Jupiter or change the temperature sufficiently and the balance of forces changes, turning it to formless mush. Causality is a change of necessary existential relation.

The notion of an agent acting on another thing, i.e., causing it to change, comes from the form of the appearance. A thing appears as a causal factor or agent of change because it is the element that enters into the current state of our center of interest, or because the change resulting from interaction is more visible in one term or the other. We forget that change does not occur in one direction only. Every action has an equal and opposite reaction. The parties to a relation must change each other. We think of the sun as causing the planets to orbit around it. However, because the effects of the planets on the sun are so much less noticeable, we do not naturally consider that they are also affecting its movement.

The occurrence of a causative event is the formation of a new interaction between objects that are always existentially co-dependent. A true knowledge of cause would be to understand the existential relations between forms and how they emerge out of being as such. Observed causation is the manifestation of an underlying contingent relation. It is the expression of the conditional, if A then B, in temporal events. Exactly how and why forms emerge out of being with particular appearance and in necessary relation to one another is a question we must defer for the time being.

f. Accordance/Opposition – Associated with the fact of existential co-constitution and the affecting relation is a second relation that specifies the existential significance one entity has to another in becoming. We will call this relation the continuum of opposition and accord. Entities exist in opposition to other entities. Their existence depends on this opposition, and without it, they annihilate one another. Negative numbers offset positive numbers. Hot and cold neutralize each other. Matter is annihilated by antimatter. These relations exist on a spectrum where at one extreme an entity negates or makes impossible the existence of the other, while at the other end is the case where one is necessary for or even necessitates the existence of another. In between are varying degrees of opposition and reinforcement. These relations are the meaning of basic categories such as possibility/impossibility, necessity/contradiction, etc. At the one extreme is that which contradicts or annihilates the object: Two things or states cannot exist together. This is the impossible. They contradict, i.e., they are existential opponents. Possibility is that which is not contradictory. If something is not absolutely precluded by existential necessity or definition, then it could exist. Once the threshold of possibility is crossed, the relation is defined by degrees of support or opposition. The next place on the continuum is the range of strong opposition, i.e., a force that goes against and greatly weakens a particular existent or trend but does not preclude it. For example, a strong headwind hinders forward progress but does not stop it all together. Moving up the scale, opposition weakens in degrees until the point of neutrality. Neutral objects have no existential consequence to each other. Beyond the neutral are degrees of accordant relations that support and reinforce existence. A tailwind adds to forward progress. The addition of a chemical perhaps strengthens bonds and makes an object more likely to survive. Money donated to a cause makes it more likely to succeed, etc. At the far positive end of the spectrum are relations that not only reinforce the entity, but also are necessary for its existence. The final point on the continuum is where A is not only a condition for but necessitates B. These relations are in effect the laws of being that we use in making judgments about the world. They are the basis for determinations of what can and cannot be.

2. Space

a. Dimension - Spatial relations exist on each of the sub-parameters of space. Objects are described in relation with respect to dimension: above/below, left/right and front/back.

a. Continuity – Objects are together or separated in space: next to, beside, abutting, attached, on, against, touching, etc., or apart, away from, detached, etc.

b. Quantity – Certain spatial relations between objects are quantifiable: 1) the extent of space filled by objects can be quantified and compared – X is larger/smaller than Y; 2) the space between objects is quantified as a distance relation. Dimension and quantity together give location.

c. Boundary/enclosure – Objects relate in space with respect to boundaries and enclosures: A is inside/outside of B, A and B are on opposite sides of the fence, etc.

3. Time

a. Time has the same general characteristics as space except for being one dimensional rather than three and in being directional. The primary relation on this dimension is that of being before, concurrent, or after. As with space, events can be continuous or discontinuous in time, can be quantified as taking up or being separated an amount of time, and can be related with respect to being inside or out of an interval of time.

4. Quantity

a. The basic relation of quantity is greater/lesser/equal. Because numbers are constructed out of a minimal number sense (subitization) by a simple recursive process, and because any application of number is based on a changeable unit, the true relation of quantities is one of relative value, or proportion.

5. Becoming

a. Relations in becoming refer to relations where A changes with respect to B. They imply a current state or origin, a process of change, and a vector of change, i.e., it is moving towards or has reached some state. The primary dimension of this relation is that of identity and difference. If a thing changes in relation to another it is a movement (literally or figuratively) towards or away the state of origin/end. Becoming on the dimension of being and inherence is to become more or less like a thing in qualities. Movement in space with respect to another thing is to get closer or further to its location in space. Quantities increase or decrease with respect to one another, becoming closer or further apart in value. Change in relation to itself is the difference in the qualities of the movement, for example altering the rate of change (acceleration/deceleration), direction/vector, manner/qualities of change, etc.

This concludes our preliminary consideration of the elements that make up the conscious experience of an objective world. What appears to consciousness appears as relations and values on these basic parameters. In summary, they consist of the following. First are the qualia of the senses, which constitute the initial basic differentiation of the world. The differences and patterns provided by the senses are processed by higher levels of the perceptual and nervous systems to create the additional cognitive qualia through which we know the world. These include space, time, and quantity with their sub-parameters and relations. They also include the general categories and relations of being consisting of the consciousness of existence/non-existence, of inherence of qualities, of change and motion, of identity and difference, of association/conjunction, and of relations of existential dependency and effect.

This is a preliminary consideration because the purpose of this inquiry is not merely to clarify conscious experience or find its physical coordinates in the body. The final goal is to return to the essence of consciousness itself, to its unity and source in being. These elements are the most general parameters of conscious experience but are still a differentiation of being. They represent a general, early differentiation and do provide a basis for a large degree of integration of the manifested world. However, they still reflect a fragmentation of the whole, and if the end is to know being, they must be unified in the source. We will come back to this question later, but first we must continue with a similar investigation into the phenomena of the inner world of the subject.

CHAPTER 4

The Creation of a World – Part 2 (the Subjective)

In reality, all experience is subjective in that every phenomenon appears to a subject from a particular perspective of consciousness. Yet natural consciousness presents a division between what appears to be an external world of independent objects and a subject that is aware of this world and has experiences belonging uniquely to it. The previous chapter addressed the consciousness of external objects. Here we consider the consciousness of the internal world of the subject:

1. Sensation/Feeling
2. Value/Desire
3. States of Consciousness
4. Subjectivity/Intersubjectivity
5. Thought
6. Emotion

SENSATION/FEELING

Sensation and feeling are part of the sensory consciousness covered in the previous chapter. Here we are concerned with those particular sensory experiences perceived as belonging specifically to the subject. Some experiences never appear as belonging to an external object. For example, we can look at or touch an object and attribute qualities to it such as color, hardness, or smoothness or form, but any pain resulting from that touch belongs to the subject alone. We might infer another person's pain but do not directly feel it. We might feel distress or even evoke a feeling of pain in ourselves through imaginative empathy, but that is our own pain, not theirs.

What is unique to these sensations is the perception that they belong to our bodies. They are first person experiences of what is within and at the surface of the body and are identified as belonging to the self. Also unique to these sensations is that they have an immediate valence of desire, existing on a spectrum of value: They are good or bad, wanted or avoided.

Being related to the body, the largest part of subjective sensation is associated with the somatosensory system, especially the interoceptive sense. This includes the range of feelings such as pain and pleasure, hot and cold, hunger and thirst, itches and irritations, pressure, arousal and fatigue, etc. We also include here the proprioceptive and vestibular sensations, that is, the sense of body position and movement, of tension and stretch, balance and spatial orientation. We cannot say too much more about these experiences, since like color or taste they are mostly irreducible sense qualia.

The dividing line between subjective and objective is ambiguous. For example, the sense of touch has a dual aspect. On the one hand, it provides knowledge about the qualities of objects out in the world. We touch and explore objects to discover seemingly objective qualities such as their form, texture, hardness and mass. On the other hand, to touch is also to be touched, and thus it creates feeling for the body and a valuation of desire with respect to that feeling.

Vision is mostly a sense of the objective. It is a projective sense, creating a world outside us. To look at our own body is to take an objective stance towards it. While visual sensation can evoke subjective reaction, as when some sight elicits a feeling response, this response is usually not part of immediate visual perception itself but due to the associations it calls forth. The sense of the aesthetic is also ambiguous. We speak of beauty as a property of the object. For example, we say that a woman or a scene is beautiful, not that we feel beauty, and there is research to support the idea that the sense of beauty does relate to objective characteristics such as proportion and symmetry. Yet it also evokes a reaction of desire. Beauty and ugliness are assigned value. One is good and the other is bad.

Sound is similar to vision in referring mainly to the object, although perhaps more ambiguously. It emanates from an external source, and its characteristics such as tone, loudness and duration are objectively measurable, yet it isn't a tangible object. Sound may elicit some immediate feeling or physical reaction in response to very loud sound or to certain human or animal vocal expressions, for example, but most of any subjective effect following from it is due to associations it evokes.

Taste and smell also have dual aspects. They do provide information about the object, and we do think of tastes as being qualities of it. However, their sensations seem more in and for us, evoking subjective reactions of desire and bringing pleasure and disgust.

VALUE/DESIRE

What is different about subjective sensations and feelings is that unlike external objects, they are not experienced as merely a set of neutral facts regarding what is. The subjective has value as an inherent aspect of experience. That is, the subjective comes with a feeling of wanting or not wanting, liking or disliking. Subjective feelings are good or bad. They exist on an axis of desire. Just as an object exists through sense qualia in space, time, quantity and relation, the subjective includes a parameter of valuation in reference to the body and self. Every feeling and object has a relation to the self and its desire.

Desire, as described earlier, is in all its forms ultimately about the self-consciousness and self-transcendence of being. Here we are concerned with how it is experienced. Desire and value provide the drive for and purpose of action. The processes of thought, which will be discussed in detail below, provide the "what" of the world. They lead us to the determination of facts, i.e., of what is or is not the case. However, facts have no significance in themselves. They only have value in their relation to desire, i.e., their consequences for feeling and want. This valuation initially comes from bodily sensation and affect. Some sensations are intrinsically value laden, for example, the pains, discomfort, and pleasures that regulate the well-being of the body and work to preserve the physical vehicle that is the ground of all experience. Emotion, which we will examine in detail below, is the assessment of the world with respect to desire. There is no life of pure logic without emotion. Reason and logic by themselves can only tell us what is or can be. They provide no basis for choosing a particular end. That is a function of desire.

In fact, desire does not care about reality. It is pure want. It doesn't care about logical possibilities, what can and cannot be. It doesn't consider cause and effect. It isn't interested it mitigating circumstances when it is disappointed and doesn't worry about whether gratification now will result in much more pain later. It simply wants what it wants and wants it now. Desire only sees its immediate ends and flails out at anything that stands in the way of its satisfaction.

On the other hand, human beings are capable of recognizing the longer-term consequences of actions and are capable of controlling their behavior when in a state of desire. This ability to see beyond immediate passions and to check desire means that desire and actions can be detached from and even contrary to, the immediate desire of the body. We check our impulses and endure physical discomfort and pain in the service of a larger desire. The detachment of desire from simple body feeling makes possible the drive to higher, more complete levels of the self-actualization of being. As addressed earlier, it is precisely when the demands of the body have been met that we become free to pursue the more complete unities of the subject and object. At the same time, this detachment from feeling also allows desire to go astray and makes possible the shifts and displacements of desire in incomprehensible ways, as described by psychoanalysis, to objects that cannot possibly meet the demands placed upon them.

STATES OF CONSCIOUSNESS

We live in what we experience as different states of consciousness. The notion of states of consciousness is used in a wide range of contexts, ranging from description of everyday cyclical states of waking and sleeping; to medical evaluation with regard to variations in alertness and responsiveness to stimuli - ranging from comas and vegetative states to normal waking consciousness; to affective states and moods; to trance and hypnotic states; and to and spiritual and meditative classifications of consciousness. What is a state of consciousness?

First, what is the meaning of "state" in general? We refer to the notion of "state" in many contexts in addition to consciousness, such as physical states, body states, emotional states, desire states, relational states, cognitive states, sensory states, etc. A state is the concrete set of qualities and relations in which a thing exists at a given time. An object of consciousness exists as a set of specific values on the basic parameters of existence through which we apprehend it. For example, a thing has particular sensory qualities; it has a magnitude, a place in space and time, etc. It exists in certain relations, etc.

We speak of states because the specific values of these parameters can change without altering the identity of the particular object. For example, an object can be in an affecting relationship or not simply by its location. Or environmental interaction might result in a change of specific sensory qualities of an object, as when water transitions from solid to liquid to gaseous states with variations in temperature without changing its atomic identity. Life, being activity, exists in a fluctuating range of states. The body is flexible and can have many orientations in space. Metabolic and homeostatic processes constantly change the activity and experience of the body and its engagement with the world.

The question then is what are the flexible parameters of consciousness itself, such that we can speak of different states of consciousness? States of consciousness refer to general orientations of consciousness to the world, reflecting the kinds of objects that are present to consciousness and the relation of consciousness to them. The emphasis is on the objects of consciousness. As noted earlier, conscious itself is the always the same awareness. What vary in different states of consciousness are the qualities and kinds of objects available to consciousness and its orientation to them.

Consider as a baseline the state of normal alert, awake consciousness. This is in fact what we have been analyzing in all of the above. It is the state where there is a world made present by the senses, experienced as a "real" external world consisting of objects existing in space and time. What accounts for the appearance of the world identified with the normal waking state of consciousness? The world of this state seems real due to the quality of experience afforded in the current activation of the senses. Real objects appear to have solidity and mass. They appear through a system of views across perspectives in predictable ways. Real objects adhere to particular restrictions and rules. They interact and affect each other in a specific and consistent way. In normal waking consciousness, we can think about things and events and rationally evaluate their meanings and consequences. We can execute processes where we integrate events with the contents of memory or imagine scenarios of actions and events and follow through their outcomes with cause and effect thinking.

As we shift to "lesser" modes of consciousness we lose the ability to construct objects of consciousness in some or all of these ways. Hypnotic and trance states are characterized by dissociation, where the normal integration and flow between different aspects of experience is temporarily reduced. In drowsiness and lethargy, we begin to lose connection to the outer world. We lose awareness of and become less responsive to the senses. We find it difficult or lose the ability to operate on thought objects. In dreaming sleep, we lose connection to stimuli of the outer world. Its content might enter our dreams in some fashion but not in a way that we recognize its reality. Dream objects are internally generated images not consciously directed by will. Dream images come and go without any rational connection. In fact, rational thought experience disappears. Psychoanalysis describes dream content as exhibiting the characteristics of the "primary process". Freud described dream thoughts as translated into images and saw dreams as being like a rebus or picture puzzle. The dream state is characterized by very different objects than those of waking life, with some aspects of the waking objects lost (e.g., the inputs of the senses and thought) and others moving to the fore (internal images) and experienced in a different way. In deep or dreamless sleep, the objects of conscious diminish further. While awareness of this state is significant in contemplative traditions, under normal circumstances we seem to have little awareness at all when in this condition. Further, we are less inclined to respond to external stimuli. Finally, in coma states, there seems to be no response to stimuli and there is no waking. If there is anything of what we consider to be conscious awareness, it is minimal.

Returning to the normal waking state, there are many nuances of consciousness within it that reflect differences in the objects available or the orientation to them. In a hyperalert state, attention is narrowly focused on certain sensory stimuli. For example, if one hears an unexpected noise in the house late at night, all attention shifts to the perception of sound as one seeks further clues to the cause. Other thoughts disappear from awareness. We can contrast this to daydreaming or preoccupied states where one is barely aware of the outer environment. In mood states, conscious object relations are colored in a general way. When we feel anxious or paranoid, we view objects through the lens of potential threat. When we are happy, all the world is inviting and filled with potential. When we are sad, we can barely engage the world.

Finally, there are states identified as "advanced" or "enlightened", characterized by greater integration of conscious contents and the awareness of more subtle objects, and finally non-dual states where we become aware of the ground of all awareness and there is no separation of consciousness and object.

The differences in these states are all a matter of the kinds of objects or orientations to objects available to consciousness, but they do not reveal new parameters of consciousness. They are alterations of the experiences of normal waking consciousness.

SUBJECTIVITY/INTERSUBJECTIVITY

We have largely already addressed the notion of the subject and self, so will not spend much time on it here. As noted earlier, the term "self" is used in several different senses. First, there is the sense of something that has experiences. This is the closest to the true notion of subjectivity. Objects of consciousness exist for something. However, objects don't merely exist. They exist in relation. Not only to each other, but also to the center that holds a set of relations and associations regarding them. They refer back to the source of feeling and desire. Feeling is intrinsically value laden and motivational. We want to get near or get away from the object. The center which holds these associations and feelings is the self.

On the other hand, we also speak of the self as an object. The subjective experience is rooted in and tied to the perspective of a particular body which can also be taken as object. We observe the experiences and feelings of this perspective and create a set of relations and facts pertaining to it. We think of this self as we would other objects. We create a narrative around it based its origins and experiences, its feeling and desires. I am this. I have done that. I like this or that. We take on this object self as an identity.

The objective self is not necessarily opposed to self of immediate experience and affect and may in many ways come to supplant it as a center of experience. As described above, socialized values, in opposition to affect, also can be incorporated into the objective self and become part of the center of relation that determines action. One can come to identify with this image rather than with affect. This is what leads to need to "find oneself" or to "self-actualize".

Another concept of the self is the spiritual usage as in the Hindu Atman. Here the self is recognized as the ground of consciousness beyond the individual, the non-dual oneness with everything. It is the reconciliation of subject and object in which the source, being/consciousness, is conscious of, and identical to itself as object.

In addition to the immediate sense of being a conscious subject that has objects, another important aspect of this topic is the recognition of subject as object in other human beings, that is, the notion of the intersubjective. We perceive others as a center of conscious experience which includes awareness of a world of objects, feelings and desires, and thoughts. We understand them to have subjective awareness similar to our own, which includes seeing us both as objects and as subjects that see them back. In chapter 2, we considered the significance of this state of affairs to the fundamental desire of being. In other subjects, we recognize the possibility of transcending our subjectivity in the world. Yet this is a double-edged sword. Others can affirm and realize our subjectivity, but they can objectify us in ways we don't wish to be objectified.

Consciousness of the existence of minds in others starts in comprehension of the dual relation to our own bodies. On the one hand we are conscious of our bodies in an objective way, i.e., we can look at them, touch them, etc. However, we also recognize a relation of the body to feeling – what happens to this body, our body, is associated with the experiences of pleasures and pain – and to our objective perceptions. What we see is a function of the particular perspective of the body. It is a quick step to relate those subjective feelings to the perception of another body. Whatever the truth of "mirror neurons", there must be some kind of analogical and projective process taking place in the understanding of others.

We infer and gain knowledge of the mind of the other not only through the perceptions of action on the body, but also through the whole of our observation of their behavior. Others seem to respond as we would in a particular situation. When we speak, they answer back in ways that seem intelligible to us, as if they understood the meaning of our speech. They speak in ways in which we can relate and fathom their meaning. We imagine the possibility of a different perspective of consciousness through another body.

THOUGHT

Thought consists of the processes and internal experiences of mind through which we assess what is true of the world. Through the activity of thought, we come to a determination of what the world is or will become, of what the state of things means with respect to our interests and desires, and of which possible actions will best serve our desires.

a. Cognitive Qualia

Before getting into thought processes, we should consider what thoughts actually are. As an experience and object of consciousness, to have a thought is to experience something. A thought feels like something, just as we have an experience of "redness" or "roundness" when viewing an apple. It is relatively easy to understand what someone means when they refer to a quality of the senses. They can point to an object of a particular color or call attention to a particular sound as it happens, but there is no external reference when trying to describe the experience of thought itself.

Some mental contents consist of images. We have no problem with these since they are abstracted versions of sense experience without the sense organs. However, it is more difficult to describe the experience of the judgments of thought. For example, what is the quality of experience associated with the judgment that something does or does not exist, that it is identical to or different from something else, is larger or smaller, possible or impossible, consistent or contradictory, etc.? Yet these judgments have a particular experience associated with them. These mental contents are qualia in the same sense that we use the term in reference to sensory qualities, even if they provide a different kind of experience. As with the sensory object experiences in the previous chapter, we are seeking the elements of cognitive experience, the simplest qualia of assessment and judgment which have no constituent components.

b. Thought and Language

There has been much debate about the relationship of language to consciousness and thought. Following the conclusions of chapter 1, it should be clear that consciousness itself does not depend on language. Consciousness is the ground of existence and not reducible to any mode or object of awareness. The real question is what language brings to the kind of world available to consciousness. Specifically, what is its relation to thought?

We must define our terms precisely. We have described thought functionally, as a process through which we determine the facts of what is and can be. However, this is not sufficient to characterize what specifically makes for thought. If that was all, a simple physiological response might be considered to be a thought. A reflexive reaction to a particular chemical compound or environmental condition is a kind of determination of the presence of said substance or state. However, we would not consider a thought process to have taken place in this circumstance. It is precisely when we act automatically that we are said to have acted "thoughtlessly". Thought also involves a weighing of possibilities and consequences. It thus involves a mediation of consciousness where alternatives brought together and evaluated.

What is the role of language in this process? First, what do we mean by language? We distinguish language from communication, something which exists throughout the chain of life, but which outside of humans is limited, fixed and instinctive. What distinguishes language is the use of symbols, i.e., arbitrary sounds, visual images, and other media, that represent something else. The question then is whether these representations are necessary for thought and/or what do they add to it?

As we go about our everyday lives, it seems that we constantly act without language. All the time we make decisions without making use of an explicit symbolic dialog. However, at the same time, we would have to say that many of these actions are not completely automatic and unthinking. We sense the existence of a process, however fleeting and semi-conscious, where we weigh realities and possibilities in a manner characteristic of thought. If a car stops short in front of us on the highway, we must quickly react, yet our response can't be entirely mechanical. Every situation has different variables and there must be flexibility of response. Given speed and distance, can we stop in time to avoid collision? If not, is there an open lane on either side into which we can move? If we have to hit something, what will do the least damage? In situations like this, we don't carry on an internal verbal conversation, yet there is the sense of a consideration and evaluation of possibilities. If not a symbolic representation, what is it? The contents of consciousness in this mode are sensory images and their associations. Experience has given us a feeling of the relation between speed and braking distance, and we immediately sense the consequences of being too close. Other possibilities immediately pop into consciousness which are accepted or rejected in turn. So, the process seems to work through simple sensory images and associations and their evaluation with respect to desire.

Here we can begin to see what language adds to the process. The evaluation of situations as those described above depends on concrete associations. What comes to mind is limited to what is possible with simple conditioned or reflexive response. At best it is little more that the instinctive behavioral repertoires of animals, perhaps with some ability to weigh outcomes. What language does is to make possible the creation of infinite numbers of complex objects and the ability to evaluate their significance, far beyond what is possible with simple association and instinct. Language provides an inexpensive, infinitely flexible supplement to reflex circuits and conditioned response. It allows a break from instinct.

In written form, a word is a concrete visual stimulus. It consists of a particular sequence of letters, i.e., shapes. Letters are combined in sequences, also understood through spatial and quantitative elements, to form words. Written visual forms are associated with an acoustic stimulus, which is also recognizable through general elements. These concrete acoustic and visual stimuli generally have no meaning in themselves. What they do is serve as a binder of other stimuli. They make possible the connection of disparate group of items into a whole. Separate qualities become linked through their common association to the same word. In effect, words serve to create and name a set. In turn, each word/set can be bound to others in combinations and relations to create complex concepts. Language allows the construction of complex connections without hardwiring or the chemistry of classical conditioning. The connections possible with language are infinite and can be as large and complex as we need them to be. This is the connection between language and conscious thought. Without language, we would not have the ability to assemble a wide-ranging collection of mental contents into a complex idea. When we name something, we create a set of associations which we recognize as a distinct entity. Once a name is attached, it can be integrated with any other object or relation linked with that name.

Language doesn't create or enable thought itself, but makes complex thought possible. It does not determine but is a reflection of what we can think. It arises out of and reflects the same parameters of all conscious experience. We find verbal expression for whatever we can experience. The parts of speech and grammatical structures of language exemplify the elements of consciousness described in the previous chapter and those we will consider here.

c. Conscious and Unconscious

Before getting into the cognitive processes themselves, we should clarify the difference between conscious and unconscious processes. It is not really accurate to say "unconscious" since, however small, there is always some degree of consciousness in everything. Consciousness in the present context means aware consciousness, where we actively pay attention to the object in front of us and we know that we are aware of it. Earlier we put forward the idea that this sense of consciousness is characteristic of processes associated with the creation of relation. Consciousness is the place where things are brought together, and a relationship is forged. It is in consciousness that we integrate new objects with those we already possess. We assess their similarity and relation to previously experienced objects and events. With these associations we can evoke scenarios to imagine how new events might affect us. We integrate them into a scheme of desire. In learning a physical task, we must relate the internal will and feel of the control of movement with desired effects in the world. The correct actions do not come to us automatically. We must willfully execute a process where we connect the bodily feeling to the perception of the outer result. When we are engaged in this process, we are in a state of conscious awareness.

This is not always the case for every stimulus and task that comes before us. As we have noted, once relations become established and tasks become routine, we are sometimes barely aware of what we are doing. An established relation is one where a chain of associations has been forged to the point where particular inputs result almost automatically in certain outputs on a mechanistic, material basis. As an analogy, consider how a computer works. We do not imagine that a computer "thinks" in the sense of the experience of our own thought processes. A computer generates conclusions automatically based the physical properties of electrons and the structures of the circuits they flow through. Pavlovian conditioning is much the same. Certain events create changes in the chemistry and structures of synaptic connections. Once associations are forged in consciousness, they can be reduced to a direct material basis such that under most circumstances a further consciousness assessment of possibilities is no longer necessary. When we are driving, for example, we constantly make decisions – slow down, turn here, stop at the light, etc. – but if we are experienced drivers and know the route, we barely give an explicit thought to it. Sometimes we arrive at our destination with our minds filled with other thoughts the whole time and scarcely remember how we got there. This is because driving has become habit; it has moved to the realm of concrete association. It is only when the unexpected happens – for example, if there is a detour and we need to find another route, or the car in front of us stops short and we need to find a solution to avoid hitting it – that we are called back to full attentional consciousness. Tasks delegated to the unconscious need not be simple. These habitual scripts can be quite complex. Earlier we made an analogy to computer subroutines. Sometimes only simple decision making is needed, and we flip back to our other thoughts so quickly that we are only semi-aware of having applied conscious thought to the issue. The same applies to the processes of thought we will consider below. When we speak of assessment and judgment processes, it does not necessarily imply the presence of conscious reason and full awareness. We often rely on judgments and assertions that we have already accepted as "fact", and which have fixed rules to determine response without the need to consciously weigh alternatives. It is the nature of human cognitive functioning that, when possible, it will delegate the management of tasks to automatic mechanisms, freeing consciousness to deal with the novel.

This conception of the unconscious as that which is at the level of concrete associational processes also explains much of the phenomena associated with the unconscious of psychoanalysis. If an affect has not been integrated at the conscious level, it remains at the primitive level of concrete association. Anything similar to concrete stimulus associated with a trauma experience easily becomes connected to it, thus the easy "displacement" of the "cathexis". Mechanical association with anxiety can trigger an avoidance response (i.e., "repression") without the need for a conscious process of rejection. Thus, there is no need to posit a "censor" that "knows and doesn't know" as in Sartre's critique of Freud. The unconscious conditioned association interferes with the processes that allow integration in consciousness.

d. The Cognitive Process

The term cognitive as used here refers to the series of processes and activities by which we come to know and evaluate the objects of consciousness and develop appropriate responses to therm. We will consider cognition functionally as an overall process, starting from the insertion of objects and events into consciousness awareness, to the determination of their existence and identity, to the assessment of their meaning and implications, and finally to the evaluation of potential actions in response to them.

1. Attention

Before any thought or evaluation can take place, something must reach awareness. The start of this process is the senses, which provide the initial inputs from the world. Yet how do these inputs enter into conscious awareness? Most of them do not. The senses are constantly stimulated, but much of their content goes unnoticed. If our eyes are open, we are surrounded by a visual field that changes with every movement of self or world. Yet if we are lost in our own thoughts or focused on a particular object or task, we may barely be aware of the visual world around us. We are also continuously present to a world of sound, and of physical sensations of touch, and the feeling of internal states of the body. These sensations are always there, but in the background, with little or no conscious awareness of them. What is it to pay attention and be aware of something?

When we pay attention, a particular object or mode of experience is present to conscious. We are aware of it. It is there and we know it is there. To pay attention is to hold an object in consciousness awareness. Attention effectively is awareness and is perhaps what we usually mean when we say we are conscious of something. This is somewhat different from how we have defined consciousness in general as any kind of subjective experience and not just this self-reflective focus on a particular object.

When we attend to something, a particular content of conscious is held in awareness to the exclusion of others. This is in contrast to the pre-conscious system that stands ready to respond to salient stimuli and raise them to conscious awareness. As we have noted, the human sensory and nervous system apparatus is built to respond to difference and change. When something unexpected or associated with danger or desire occurs, we are prompted to pay attention to it and consciously assess its meaning. This unconscious "alert" system is not merely fixed and reactive. We can also prime ourselves to notice a specific thing. If

I have forgotten where I parked my car, as I scan the rows of parking spaces, I set myself to respond to qualities of interest. The presence of a particular color or type of vehicle in the field of view draws my attention.

In attention, we stick to the object. Earlier we compared the sustained existence of an object in consciousness to the perception of solidity in the blades of a moving fan, with the continuity of appearance being a result of a repeated return of the same state. In attentional awareness, we maintain a loop of consciousness that returns to a fixed content. An object of awareness becomes a relational center, as we bring forth associations, implications, and potential responses pertaining to that object. We can also attend to a specific sensory mode rather than an object. For example, if we hear a noise in the house late at night, we are all ears, fixating on the auditory to detect additional sounds and find clues to their meaning. Awareness is holding an object front and center and contemplating relations in reference to it.

The fact that we must focus on a particular object to the exclusion of others tells us something about the mechanisms of conscious experience in general. It suggests that the processes that make it possible for objects to appear before consciousness are singular. We are conscious of one thing at a time. We do not really "multi-task". When engaged in multiple activities of thought, we are not actually doing them in parallel, but via a process of rapid shifting between them.

2. Memory and Recall

Evaluation of any new content of consciousness involves integration with previous contents. A simple object brought before consciousness by the senses will have little meaning if it does not already exist in a network of associations or has no similarities to the known. To recognize an object is to relate it to a set of associations and facts we already hold. We recognize an arrangement of sense qualities as having particular properties, uses, effects and implications for desire. The contents that link to the present stimulus exist in memory. Memory holds the traces of prior experiences and what we have posited as "facts" about the world. Recall is the activity by which we retrieve this information and call it before consciousness. What is the experience of the contents of memory and how do call them into conscious awareness?

We began the discussion of the nature of memory and learning earlier in the context of the attribution of qualities and identity to objects. The physiological mechanisms of memory are beyond our scope and the precise details are not crucial to the analysis here. The current consensus is that memory largely depends on changes in the chemistry and/or number of synaptic connections in networks of neurons as a result of association in firing.

What is a memory phenomenologically? It is not a full duplication of an experience. Some individuals may have the ability to recall events and objects in high sensory detail, possessing "eidetic" memory, but for the most part, the experience of the memory is far from sensory experience in the present. Memories are what stick. They consist of the general neural correlates and effects that remain without the live sense stimulation. They are mostly the abstract categories of the experience by which we know and recognize objects, and not the concrete details. In time, we lose more and more of the detail to the point where there is little or no actual memory of the past experience itself. We know *that* certain things happened, but they mainly exist only as assertions of what was. We accept that some event occured, that I did something, that I have been to some place, etc., but we recall few, if any, actual images of the events.

What is the act of recall? Some memories spontaneously come to mind, perhaps because of an association with something in current experience or concerns, or sometimes with no immediately identifiable reason. We also are often capable of willing the contents of memory to consciousness in association with some current concern. However, beyond the conscious act of deciding that one wants to access a particular piece of information, the process through which it comes back to mind is largely unconscious. We pose a question and somehow knowledge comes back to us. We have no awareness of the retrieval process. The fact that the process is unconscious suggests that it depends on concrete associations, with a search procedure mechanically carried out by the brain. Recall is similar to creative processes where there is an unconscious "incubation" period that takes over from conscious effort.

3. Imagination

Not only do we recall the details and associations of past experiences, but also apply our knowledge to new situations and use it in new ways. This is the activity of imagination. Imagination is similar to recall in the experiential quality of its contents. However, in imagination, these contents are not merely a reproduction of objects or events we have experienced but are the combinating of such contents and basic elements of experience in original ways to create new objects and narratives.

Imagination in some part works through the willful evoking of particular contents into consciousness, although exactly how this happens is a mystery. Ideas and images also often come without conscious effort, perhaps triggered by some association. As noted above, in creative activity and problem solving, there is a combination of the conscious effort and unconscious processes. We may be stuck on a particular problem, but once we have an idea of what we are looking for, we can seemingly direct the unconscious association process in particular directions to produce relevant ideas.

While we might think of imagination mostly in connection with artistic and other creative endeavors, it is also an important part of everyday life. It comes into play in wish fulfillment fantasies and entertainment, but also has a critical function in any decision making. Any time we face new objects or a novel situation that needs handling, it is through imagination that we generate possible scenarios to assess their potential implications and optimal responses to them. Imagination provides the material on this assessment process works.

The fact that we must apply conscious effort to carry out such a process illuminates the nature of consciousness and thought. Conclusions and decisions having significant impact or pertaining to novel events are usually not arrived via at through automatic unconscious processes. Even mundane daily tasks often require a conscious consideration of the possibilities and contingencies. The necessary information needed to reach a conclusion regarding implications and actions may exist in memory, yet it is still necessary to consciously imagine scenarios and call to mind potential outcomes. We must consciously call forth and think through the particulars in order to judge which result is most likely. Having information encoded somewhere in the brain is not enough. We must consciously evoke relevant contents of memory and consciously run through their possibilities. Of course, this is not always the case. When we know the object well and its variables and effects are limited in number, the process can be automatic or close to it and not require the application of the conscious resources. We make thousands of decisions like this each day, barely aware of them. However, even simple tasks often have unique details that must be brought into relation, even if the task is concrete and specific. Suppose I have an appointment to keep. I have to call to mind where is it, how to get there, how long it takes to get there, what time do I need to leave, what do I need to bring, etc. While all the facts may have been there all along in memory, I must consciously put the parts together. It is in consciousness that such relations are formed. Once these relations have been established, we need not give the task as much conscious attention in the future.

4. Thought

Thought proper is the activity by which we assess the reality of the world. It is the process through which we arrive at a set of determinations regarding what is or is not, what may or must follow from the state of things, and what actions we can and should take in response to it.

Thought and knowledge ultimately refer back to desire: What does the presence of some object or the occurrence of some event mean to me? Will it make things better or worse from the perspective of desire? Is an object or occurrence useful to attaining the ends of desire or will it lower satisfaction? In this regard, thought is also the process of assessing how I shall act. How do I go about bringing about a particular end? I need to understand the facts about the world – what the situation is, what is possible and what is not. I must take into account the conditional relations that exist between objects and between self and objects. I must envision possible outcomes, not just in their immediate effects, but the indirect and long-term consequence of actions. I also must consider that the effects of an action at any step along the way may be contingent, and thus many potential outcomes must be considered and weighed in relation to their likelihood and impact on desire.

This aspect of uncertainty colors the outcome of our deliberations. At the end of the thought process, we come to certain conclusions regarding the object of interest. It is this or that. It will have this or that effect. This action will be the best way to cope with it. The result is the assertion of a set of "facts" that become the basis for action in the present or future. However, because of contingencies and unknowns, we cannot always, and usually do not, have certainty regarding these facts. We may not have, and it may not be possible to have, certain knowledge of and or control over all the variables. We may have only observed a phenomenon in a limited context, or outcomes may be a matter of chance, or depend on the uncertain reactions of others, etc. Therefore, explicitly or not, we must qualify the certainty of our facts. In addition to the determination of identities and realities, we also judge the truth value of our assertions on a scale of certainty and probability.

To assess and judge is to accord an existential status to something. In the most general terms, it is to arrive at an assertion of what something is and its relations to other things. It is a determination of what is and therefore what can be. While we will look more closely at the kinds of possible judgments below, the basic questions answered through the thought process are what something is, i.e., its properties, its relations to other things, especially its effects and potential effects on them, its impact on desire and then the courses of action available and their probable results.

Regarding the subjective experience of thought and judgment, thought is like any other object of consciousness and consists of elementary qualia. Thought has distinctive subjective qualities in the same way that sensory objects have qualities such as "redness" or "sweetness". It is perhaps harder to communicate the meaning of such qualia. Unlike color, where if I want to communicate "yellow" I can point to a banana or a lemon, the experience of a particular judgment is harder to get at. There are no concrete sensory correlates to which we can point. Imagine a simple cognitive test where an experimenter presents a shape and asks which of a series of shapes is identical to the first one. We can do this quite easily, but how do we know we have made a match? There is an experience of "these are identical" in the same way that we make the judgment that "this is red." It is perhaps more difficult to firmly grasp the feeling of this judgment than to know a color, but there is a specific quality of conscious experience that is the determination of being identical. The sense of identity and difference is an elemental intuition at the roots of consciousness, a basic parameter or category of experience to which we can assign a specific value. The goal of this section is to identify and understand these parameters of thought, to define the set of the lowest elements of thought consciousness from which cognitive experience is composed.

The question of judgment is ultimately the question of what is and what can be, so in order to find the answer to what judgments are and what is being judged we must return to the basic properties of being. First, we noted that consciousness, and thus what can exist for it, is rooted in difference. One thing exists in opposition to another. Thus, the consciousness of difference is at the heart of being and the judgment of identity/difference is the most fundamental distinction we can make.

Not only do things exist in difference, but also in contrast to other things. They are what they are in opposition to what they are not. Figure depends on ground and vice versa. Objects are related and co-constituted. "A" cannot exist where the co-constituting conditions of its existence do not exist. If these conditions are not there, it cannot be. Something cannot exist and not exist at the same time. This is the meaning of the judgment of contradiction and impossibility: There cannot be both A and –A.

Determining the state of things with respect to these basic conditions for existence is the essence of the thought process. The determination of identity and contradiction can be applied to all parameters through which an entity exists. That is, we apply the basic judgment mechanisms to each of the parameters of conscious experience and assert a specific value or identity in each parameter. Thus, we consider what sensory qualities an object has – its color, its form, etc. We inquire into its particular location and relation to other objects is space. We determine its quantity or size. We ask in what relations it exists or can exist in, for example how or if it may affect another object. Not only do these parameters have specific values that can be affirmed or rejected in defining a particular object, but they also have specific existential conditions that mutually exclude each other. For example, a thing cannot be both red and green at the same point in space. It cannot be at two places at the same time, or be both inside and outside, or both to the left and right. It cannot have two magnitudes. If a set of measurements leads to that result, something must be wrong. "A" cannot be in a conditional relation to "B" if "A" is present and "B" is not. If this is the case, then the assertion of such a relation is contradictory and invalid.

The most basic judgment is that of identity, either to recognize an object as being a particular thing, or if it is unknown, to define it as a set of properties. In both cases, it is a matter of setting the entity in question in relation to knowledge we already hold through a process of recognizing identities and similarities. Recognizing something as a member of a class is a making a simple determination of identity. We judge that the qualities of the object match those in a set of properties defining a particular entity. For an unfamiliar object, the aim is to define a new entity, although the task is fundamentally the same. We still must integrate it with what we already know. We might identify the general elemental properties that belong to it such as specific colors or forms or might recognize complex similarities to other compound objects. The ability to create analogies is central to this process. We extract simple or complex properties in which an unfamiliar object is similar to something else. This also allows us to extend a range of associations and meanings to the new object. However, all of this is really only the application of a fundamental judgment to identity and difference.

After basic identity is established, the next concern is what a thing or event implies and what consequences it may have. This requires an assessment of extended associations and relations, i.e., the chain of "cause and effect". What will it do? Ultimately our concerns are tied back to desire, which means that the assessment of "what is" must be integrated with "how do I feel about it". This involves imagining potential outcomes and feelings resulting from them. The final step is determining action: What should we do about it? This uses the same process as the assessment of the consequences of events, only here we imagine and evaluate possible courses of action to conclude which might bring about the best results with respect to desire.

We considered the meaning of causal and conditional relationships earlier. The natural understanding of cause sees it as the application of a "force", where a causing agent acts upon and does something to another thing. We have argued that cause must be viewed in the context of the existential dependence and co-constitution of all existents. Regardless of which underlying metaphysics of cause is correct, our interest here is of what appearance to consciousness accounts for the determination of causal relation. The determination of cause and condition is essentially a judgment of the "constant conjunction" of Hume: B always follows, or appears, with A. The judgment of cause is then the feeling/confirmation of identity to this condition. There are two parts to it: 1) A exists in conjunction with B and therefore reflects identity with the condition of association in being, and 2) it happens every time, thus the judgment also pertains to the category of quantity. Every element in the set of "A type events" includes B. To assert such a relation is to assert that if A appears, B will appear (the judgment can also be qualified as in "it may cause", but we will address these qualifications below). If we find an event in memory that does not conform to this condition, we must reject the assertion. The question of why such a conjunction occurs is a separate question and leads to the larger issue of how causality is possible, i.e., or how one thing can affect and co-constitute another.

If the kinds of possible judgment are few and simple, the process of thought is not. Thought and decision-making processes in actual life are usually not a matter of comparing one simple thing to another or of grasping immediate cause and effect relations. Rather, events are complex, possibilities are many and knowledge uncertain. Direct interactions can have consequences at a distance: A affects B, B affects C, affects D, etc. With alternative possibilities at each step in the chain, the number of outcomes requiring evaluation rapidly proliferates. Uncertainty of outcome adds another level of complexity. Thus, to understand the activity of thought, we must understand how we apply elementary judgments in the context of complex objects and their wide-ranging possibilities and implications. Here recall and imagination join together with judgment to bring forth possibilities and evaluate their impact with respect to desire. Yet how do we make judgments at a distance on complex scenarios?

The process by which we do this is formalized in logic. Logic, as we are concerned with it here, consists of as the rules for valid thought, or more specifically the rules of valid inference. It is the means by which we join propositions and move step by step to reach conclusions regarding their implications. Therefore, we need to look at the activity of logic in detail to understand how it works and the judgments on which it depends. Rather than doing logic here, we are asking what it means to do logic in the context of being and consciousness. What are the elementary qualia of mind on which it is based? A second question is why we use logic. What does it say about human consciousness and thinking that we find it to be useful or necessary? Our method will be to investigate the language of logic, i.e., the elementary symbols and operators through which it is carried out, and to consider what they mean and how they are used.

The Language of Logic

Here we take a step back from the doing of logic and meditate on the meaning of its elements that we normally take for granted. We start with the symbols that represent the content of logical analysis. These are the propositions, the uppercase letters (P, Q, etc.) which represent the relations of concern. They are relations, as any existent must be, in the general form of "X is Y". The fact that we replace statements with letters demonstrates that logical operation is not about the truth of the individual proposition, which is asserted as true or "as if" being true. Rather we are concerned with its relations to other propositions, i.e., its compatibility or contradiction. We need not know anything about the content of "P" to execute a process of logical reasoning. The logical judgment process only knows and cares about identity and negation. The process is a means to tell us if we have violated the proscription against the existence of "P and not P", whatever P is.

A proposition is represented more explicitly within a logical grammar by breaking out its subject and predicate. For example, the proposition "an apple is a fruit" is written as "Fa", with the subject in lower case letters and the predicate upper case. This provides a more detailed logical expression of a concrete assertion, but a greater advance is made with the use of variables. Variables, represented by lower case letters (x, y, z, etc.), allow us to symbolize more abstract objects. "Fx", i.e., "x is a fruit", for example, allows us to speak about fruit in general, and thus introduces abstract categories. Along with the quantifiers of logic, variables make it possible to not only predicate some objects as fruit, but to speak to the specific qualities that make something a fruit or to assert an existential state pertaining to all fruit.

The Universal Quantifier, "for all x", asserts that some proposition applies to all members of the set. This can be a statement of necessity in essence or existence. In the former, it asserts a defining property of a thing. It cannot be that thing without it. For example, everything that is a square has four sides. Alternatively, as a statement of existence, it only specifies the reality of a particular state for all members of some category. For example, the statement "every employee attended the meeting" only specifies the actual status of all employees with respect to a particular event. What does the judgment "for all x" actually mean, or rather how is it determined? It is an assertion of some state of being and a determination of identity/difference made upon elements in the domain of the assertion. The assertion that all snakes are venomous would be invalidated by finding something identified as a snake that does not have venom. That is to say, we experience difference between the existence of the non-venomous snake and the assertion of all snakes being venomous.

The existential quantifier, meaning "there exists" or "for some", is an assertion that there exists some actual individual instance of our variable class. The universal quantifier defines an object, i.e., to be this thing, it must have this particular quality or relation. The existential qualifier says there is some existent that embodies it: At least one of these things or conditions exists, i.e., has actual being. We come to accept the assertion by finding an existing example of the entity in question, thereby having the consciousness of identity to it. The two quantifiers are related in their negations. To say that it is not the case that all x's are P is to say that there is some x that is not P, and to say that there is not some P that is x is to say all x's are not P. Thus, the universal and existential are not independent concepts but are in some sense co-constitutive of each other. They also have a relation to conjunction and disjunction. If a proposition in the form of "For all x" is to be true, it must be true for each and every x, which is the meaning of conjunction: x_1 & x_2 & x_3, etc. For the existential qualifier, any x existing as asserted makes the condition true, that is, the truth of disjunction: x_1 or x_2 or x_3, etc.

The use of parentheses finds its way into logic because they are foundational for thought. They indicate a precedence grouping, specifying that the operations inside the brackets are performed first. More fundamental to the precedence is that fact of grouping itself. It makes a plurality into a unity. This making one out of many is one of the most elemental bases of thought. For example, grouping is the idea of abstraction, of universals. The individual instances are part of a collection under the name of the abstract concept. Grouping is also fundamental to the quantitative. As we noted earlier, the grouping operation is what allows the elemental quantitative operations to be extended into infinity. Addition may be a simple binary operation, but when two can replace one and one, we can get to three with only the binary operation of $1 + 2$. The grouping sense allows recursion. Grouping is also fundamental to the process of logical inference, as we will see below in regard to the syllogism.

Negation is also fundamental to thought because it expresses the consciousness of identity/difference. Either something is the case, or it is not. Negation is the basis for all judgment. To assert something as fact is to assert a relationship of identity: The state of concrete existence of the terms of the relation is in identity with the assertion of the proposition. The opposition of being and not being, and the proscription against being both at the same time, is the basis for the judgment of consistency and validity.

Conjunction, the "and" operator, expresses the elementary relation of association. Things are together in some parameter of existence. Conjunction allows consciousness of compound entities made up of multiple qualities or relations. In logical analysis we are concerned less with the fact of conjunction but whether all our propositions are in identity with the condition for it, i.e., both A and B must be the case. If they are not, we have asserted a contradiction to the being of conjunction and the argument falls. Conjunction, the recognition of association, is elemental.

Disjunction, the "or" operator, is about alternatives. Logical disjunction requires any one or all of the operands to be true for the statement to be true. In disjunction, a condition must be met in some, but not a particular way. If conjunction specifies a condition of necessity, i.e., all must be the case, disjunction expresses the notion of sufficiency. The truth of any of the possibilities is enough to make the disjunction true.

The disjunction of logic is not quite the same as the "or" of everyday language, where it often has the meaning of mutual exclusion: One alternative is in opposition to the other. A or B can be true but not both. Logic has a counterpart to this in the Exclusive Disjunction, true when one and only one of the operands is true. This condition can be expressed in terms of simple conjunction, disjunction and negation, so we may question whether this is an elementary judgment of consciousness. Apparently Kant thought it was since it appears in his tables of judgments and categories: "The disjunctive judgment contains the relation of two or more propositions to each other, but not as a consequence, but in the form of a logical opposition, the sphere of the one excluding the sphere of the other, and at the same time in the form of community, all the propositions together filling the whole sphere of the intended knowledge....There exists therefore in disjunctive judgments a certain community of the different divisions of knowledge, because if taken together, they constitute the whole contents of one given knowledge." In this sense, the exclusive disjunction represents certain properties of being we identified earlier. As a mutual exclusion representing the whole of a sphere of knowledge, Kant's disjunction is an expression of the oppositional co-constitutional nature of existence. He refers to the terms as "co-ordinate, not subordinate, determining each other, not in one direction only, as in a series, but reciprocally as in an aggregate.... A similar connection is conceived in the whole of things, in which one, as effect is not subordinated to another as the cause of its existence, but is coordinated with, simultaneously and reciprocally, as cause of the determination of the other." This condition also represents the prohibition against contradiction, i.e., one possibility is in opposition to or exclusive of the other. Because one alternative must be true, the simple propositions together represent the whole of possibility and also reflect the law of the excluded middle: One or the other must be true. It is either A, or any other proposition, which is –A.

The question of what is elemental, i.e., of what are the simple irreducible qualia of experience, is fundamental to the enterprise of returning to the source of consciousness itself. It could be argued that we have already gone far enough. Disjunctive normal form expresses the whole of logical statements with the three symbols of negation, conjunction and disjunction described above. Perhaps even this small set is larger than is needed, given that De Morgan's laws show we can express conjunctions and disjunctions in terms of each other and negation. The question is whether these separate terms reflect distinct qualia of thought, i.e., true elements of judgment, or if the proliferation of symbols is just a matter of the efficiency of shorthand. We can reduce our operators to the above, but they become rather unwieldy, just as the 1's and 0's of computer instructions are inefficient for human activity. The fact that a core set of logical symbols, consisting of the above plus the conditionals, has become an accepted standard suggests that there is something basic about in these terms with respect to the operation of the human mind. With regard to the conjunction and disjunction, it does not appear that the reduction of one to the other has some advantage in simplicity. This would suggest that they are existentially constitutive of each other, have equal primacy and should remain as basic terms. They are rather like figure and ground. We cannot get rid of one or the other. Likewise, as we will consider next, there seems to be something fundamental in our thinking with respect to notion of implication that goes beyond its representation through conjunction and disjunction.

The Material Conditional ($\rightarrow$), "if-then", pertains to affecting relationships such as causality and condition, although it does not specify the nature of these relations or have quite the same meaning of "if-then" in ordinary language. The meaning of the expression is defined by the truth value assigned to it for each combination of the truth values of for its component propositions:

A	B	A$\rightarrow$B
T	T	T
T	F	F
F	T	T
F	F	T

With the first condition, where both A and B are true, we have the start of its meaning in that it posits an association of A and B. We would not be talking about A and B at all if there were not some association between them. This however is insufficient to define the relation. Implication means more than two things existing together. It is really the second condition with A true and B false, the falsifying condition that is essential to the relation. In plain language, B must be true where A is true. B necessarily follows A. This does not say anything about why B comes, and must come with A. The implication is simply defined as being invalid where A exists without B. All we need do is recognize that the existing state differs from the condition of "B where A". However, in the real world we are not really satisfied with simply noting mere correlation, even if perfect. We want to know the reason for the connection. We posit ideas such as causality, with "forces" that compel things to occur. Here we have described the relation as an existential co-constitutive interaction. How this works is really the question of all questions because it is the question of how anything emerges out of being into existence in opposition to something else.

The third condition of the truth table, with A false and B true, also yields a value of truth to the implication. This outcome specifies the relation further since it tells us that, while B necessarily follows from A, A is not necessary for B. The requirement for necessity in both directions is expressed in the material equivalence ($\leftrightarrow$), "if and only if", operator. The final condition, where both A and B are false, also yields a truth value to the conditional. This violates the natural language understanding of "if-then". No one would think they were making a true statement in saying "if the moon is made of green cheese, then 2+2=6". Such a statement would be considered nonsensical or simply false, since there is no reason to believe such a relation would hold should the moon be found to consist of a coagulated dairy product. Yet in the meaning of the logical conditional, it is a true statement. However, this formulation does illuminate the meaning of logical analysis and valid inference. Logic is really only concerned with fundamental law of non-contradiction. A positive inference can only be made when all other possibilities are eliminated as contradictory. We will consider this in more detail below, but unless an argument results in both A and not A, it cannot be ruled out. If other possibilities cannot be ruled out, then we cannot assert a specific implication. The condition where two propositions are false yields no contradiction since with the falsity of proposition A, the defined contingent relation to B never comes into effect. The material conditional with two false propositions is perhaps not true as we would consider it the everyday sense of truth, but as it renders no contradiction, it does not invalidate an argument.

The purpose here has been to get to the elemental qualia of thought consciousness. We return to the question of whether we can justify affecting relation as an elemental parameter of consciousness. It goes to the fundamental issues raised by Hume. As noted above, the material conditional can be eliminated in disjunctive normal form. We can summarize its truth table outcomes with the formulation of "–A or B". All that is required to make a judgment is to compare the truth status of the individual propositions to that required by the truth condition.

However, we are concerned with fundamental conscious experience and the question is whether we actually think in such terms. Consider the statement "If you shoot yourself in the head you will die". Is this the really the same as the formulation of logic: "Don't shoot yourself in the head or you will die, or both"? This does not quite correspond to the way we think. We immediately think "shooting results in death." We do not think of it simply as identity to a set of truth conditions. We do not merely recognize correlations but immediately think in terms of consequential relations. A causality of "forces" that allow things to act upon one another may be problematic, but we do understand that objects and events are not isolated independent entities. They exist as relations and interactions with other things. They become or cease to become what they are through those relations. The material conditional remains in use, so it seems that logicians as find something fundamental about it.

We have not yet considered the modal operators; however, we will defer further discussion on these to the topic of the qualification of judgments to be addressed below. For now, it appears that the basic logical operations and symbols considered above confirm and form an adequate minimal set to represent the basic categories and relations of being as addressed earlier.

How logic works and why we need it

The above outlines the basic elements of thought, but how do we carry out a process of logical analysis and why is such a process necessary?

That which exists does so necessary in interdependent relation, yet we do not automatically recognize these connections, especially where they are at distant remove and many possibilities exist. The conclusion may perhaps already exist in the premises and be merely a restatement of it, but we do not immediately grasp that this is the case. An obvious example, and perhaps the most important in the real world, is in chains of cause and effect. We do not immediately sense how a change at A entails a change in Z through each intermediate link between them.

Logical argument proceeds by stringing together a series of propositions, each of which may be of a compound and contingent nature, which in sum lead to a conclusion. The question of interest here is what exactly this activity of "leading to" actually is. We will use the method of the truth tree as an example to examine what a logical proof is really doing. Again, we will step back and meditate on its absolute simplicity. In this method, each compound proposition is broken down into simple propositions or their negations. Implications are converted to branches representing lines of possibility, with one branch led by the negation of A and another by B, as demanded by the possible truth outcomes (that is, -A or B) as described above. Disjunctions themselves also split into branches for each possibility. For conjunctions, since each component proposition must be true, all must be included in every line of possibility. Once the premises are converted to simple propositions in lines of possibility, we simply check each line for the presence of the impossible, i.e., contradiction, a proposition and its negation occurring in the same line. To determine validity of the argument, we negate the conclusion. In other words, we are checking to see if possibilities other than conclusion of the proposed argument can be true. Consider the simple example below. The argument holds that if that A implies B, and A is false, then B must be also false. This is of course an invalid argument, as this is not the meaning of implication. When the argument is broken down per the rules of the method, we find that paths remain open where B is true:

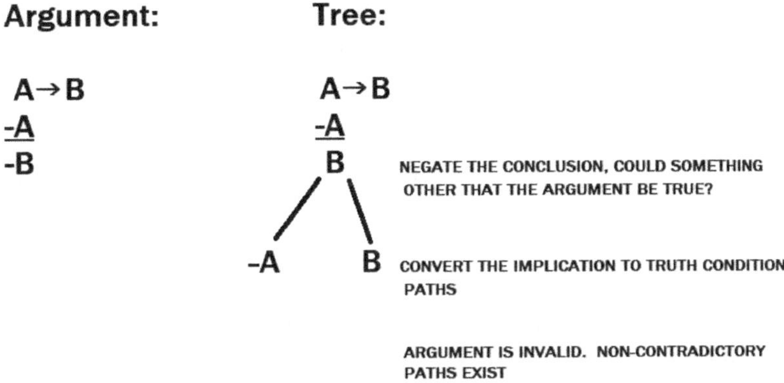

The paths remain open; hence the argument is invalid. Yet what did this procedure actually do? We converted the implication to its disjunctive equivalent, creating the paths of possibility. The negation of the conclusion in effect turns the question to "can something other than the asserted conclusion be true?" All we are really doing is breaking down the argument into its simplest components and looking for contradiction, i.e., paths with A and –A or B and –B.

We find there are no contradictions, as it should be, because implication does not demand the necessity of A for B. On the other hand, if we argue validly in accordance with the definition of implication, the negation of the conclusion yields no non-contradictory path:

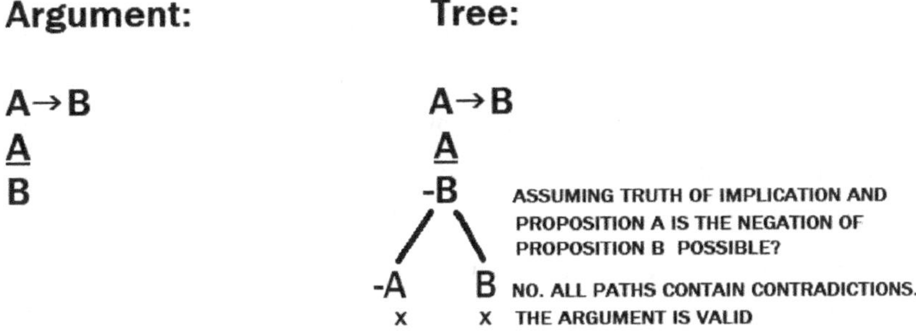

The point to note is that all we are really doing in evaluating such an argument is laying it out in a way such that we can apply the operation of judging identity with respect to the state of contradiction. We are only breaking down the propositions and conclusion into a form where we can detect violation of a basic law of being, i.e., that a thing cannot both be and not be.

Now let us consider a second logical form, that of the syllogism. We can look at the workings of the syllogism to see what we are actually doing when we progress through our premises to reach a conclusion. It embodies the process of inference. The word inference has its roots in the Latin *inferre,* meaning to carry or bring into, and that is precisely what the syllogism does. It allows us to carry the results of one judgment into the next. The questions here are what exactly are we doing, what is the judgment that tells us we can do it, and why do we need such a procedure? Consider a classic example:

All men are mortal.
Socrates is a man.
Therefore, Socrates is mortal.

We start from the assertions that men are mortal, and that Socrates is a man. From those statements we infer that Socrates is mortal. Why do we accept this inference? We have applied an unstated assumption regarding the nature of abstractions and class membership that goes something like: Anything that belongs to a particular class must have all the qualities necessary for membership in that class. Mortality is a property of men, hence, to call Socrates a man is to call him mortal. We can put it set terms: Subsets of sets that are subsets themselves are also subsets of the set to which their parent set belongs. We are still on track with the notions of implication and non-contradiction above. To be a particular thing is to have certain qualities. That which is necessary to be a particular thing must be there, or it is not that thing. This same principle applies across the various parameters of experience. The example above is about consistency in qualities of being, but we apply the same logic to other categories. For example, with space we arrive at similar inferences with respect to the properties of enclosure or orientation. An interior of an interior is also interior to that which the second is interior. On the axis of spatial dimension, if A is above B and B is above C, then A is above C. The basic continuum of quantity is that of greater and smaller magnitude, and we draw inferences with respect to position on this factor. In mathematics we call it the transitive property, where if A > B and B > C then A >C (and the same for equality as in if A=B and B=C then A=C). In affecting relations, we can infer chains of cause and effect: If A $\rightarrow$ B and B $\rightarrow$ C, then A $\rightarrow$ C.

In effect, the syllogism posits an identity or equivalency in some way between the first and second terms, where the second becomes a proxy for the first, allowing it to be carried forward in relation to the last. To say Socrates is a man is to say that "man" can function as a stand-in for Socrates. Whatever we say about men, we say about Socrates. The syllogism provides a means of expanding a web of connections. By confirming identity between two elements of immediate connection, the second may stand in for the first and connect it to its own immediate connections, creating a chain of association.

Why it is necessary to carry out such a process? Why logic? What is implied in the necessity of it? It might seem reasonable to expect that, when facts already exist in memory and we have a brain that unconsciously creates remote associations, that logical inference chains would form without deliberate conscious effort. Yet, such is not the case. Of course, this sometimes does occur. Some associations are so well established that we immediately make inferences without really thinking about it. In the example above, if we saw Socrates about to jump off the roof of the Parthenon, we would not need to consciously think through the relations of relevant sets and subsets before we began to fear for his life. However, where do not have well established relations at hand we do need to do carry out a procedure in consciousness. This suggests that we do not have the ability to automatically and unconsciously bring together new and/or remote associations and implications of a particular fact. We do not immediately recognize the possible consequences of an event or our possible responses and their likely outcomes until we specifically evoke them to mind and consciously think them through.

We do not do this unconsciously because we can't. As we have proposed above, the function of consciousness is to forge new relations. Our ability to make judgments with respect to identities and relations is limited. The ability to check conditions of identity and contradiction, i.e., what we are doing in logic, is local and binary. We can only make judgments on direct connections. This is consistent with the idea that attention is applied to one thing at a time. This is how consciousness works. Consciousness is the place where things come together. It is the place where they can both exist, but only in immediate connection. The outcome is the establishment of a relation. Inference, as in the syllogism, is in effect a leap of faith. We do not directly "sense" the connection of A to C, but once we have sensed an equivalency between A and B, we tag B as a proxy for A. When we directly link of B to C, we accept that we can link A to C. Socrates is a man, so what can be said of men can be said of Socrates. All the rest of mathematical and logical proof takes off from here.

In conclusion, thought consists of a couple basic judgments. This first is the determination of identity or difference. Something is a particular thing, or it is not, depending on its identity with the properties defining that thing. These properties are the specific values of the parameters through which it manifests its existence: A thing has or does not have a particular set of sensory qualities. It exists or does not in a particular place, time, quantity, relation, activity, etc. The second judgment is of the existence of contradiction: Does the truth of one asserted proposition nullify the existential conditions for the truth of another? Something cannot both be and not be a given thing. One cannot be in two places at the same time because locations exist precisely through their opposition to other locations.

Judgment and Qualification

After potential identities, possibilities, outcomes, and actions have been worked through, a verdict is rendered. The state of things is determined to be this or that. An opinion on the likely outcome of events is formed. Optimal actions are settled on. The result of the process is a determination of "facts" about the world: what is the case, what exists, what will happen, etc. These facts become the basis for action. Judgment is the process of assigning truth status.

We use the word "fact", but these determinations are not always accepted as certainties of what is. Our knowledge may be uncertain. We may have insufficient information to confirm the necessity of a particular conclusion. There may other possibilities that cannot be ruled out due to contradiction, or outcomes that may depend on unknown or uncertain variables. Thus, we qualify our judgments. A definitive assertion of fact or reality is just one possibility. Here we enter into judgments of modality and probability. What truth value do we assign to assertions? Is something necessary or possible? Is it fact or belief, likely or unlikely, etc.?

To judge something as fact or truth, is to accept it as being the case. Such a judgment is based on criteria such as identity of the concept to sense data, conformance to the condition of existential necessity, the absence of contradiction, or perhaps some social corroboration. This does not mean the assertion is really true. We "know" lots of things that are not confirmed. However, we accept that the evidence, whatever the source, is such that we can posit a particular statement as reality. We take it to be a basis for action. When we know the evidence for a proposition does not meet the standard of certainty, we call it belief, or a working hypothesis. We know there is uncertainty, but the assertion is our best bet. We take it "as if" true and use it as a default assumption for understanding and acting in the world.

The basic operators of modal logic, necessity and possibility, and the modal verbs of natural language (e.g., can, may, must, will, should, etc.) express this notion of the qualification of a statement. In the last chapter we described relations of being as existing on a spectrum, where on one end the existence of an entity depends on another and on the other is annihilated by it, with a range of accordance and opposition in the middle. A similar spectrum exists with respect to the judgment of truth. Necessity is the strongest form of truth assignment, while the impossible, which is the contradictory, is the absolute denial.

The basic categories of modal logic, necessity and possibility, are not adequate to capture the whole of qualification. They only cover the extremes of judgment. As with the contingencies of being, where the relations of existence are not limited to necessity or annihilation but exist over a range of opposition or support, so the qualification of propositions exists on a continuum from the impossible, to a slight chance of reality, to equal opposing possibilities, to preponderance of evidence in favor, to absolute necessity and assertion of certainty. Thus, qualification also involves a quantification that is the judgment of likelihood or probability. Here, the category of quantity enters into judgment.

There are several different meanings of probability. The simplest case perhaps is where there are a fixed number of possibilities and there no known factor favoring one or the other. This is the scenario of the casino game and is what mathematics formalizes as classical probability. As we noted earlier in considering the consciousness of the quantitative, we do not have an innate sense of the whole of countable numbers. What we do have is the general sense of proportion and we recognize broad degrees of dominance. It is only with formalization of a number system through mathematical inference that we acquire a theory of the meaning of probability and with it, probability assignments.

Similar to the conditions where classical probability applies are situations where there is not a finite set of possibilities, but data shows what has actually happened where particular conditions are present. When a doctor says there is a 30% chance of dying from a disease, he is not saying there is fixed number of possible random outcomes and three out of every ten involve death, but rather that a 30% death rate has been observed in known cases. It is an empirical probability. Regardless of whether they are mathematical or empirical probabilities, our understanding of their meaning is based on the same sense of proportion and dominance.

However, in real life the determination and qualification of facts is usually not reducible to the calculation of random event frequencies and does not have statistical data at its disposal. Most decision points are unique and complex, involving a number of factors that may vary in the degree to which we have information to evaluate them. In evaluating the likely behavior of another person, if we know nothing about them, we might use personal experience or analogy: This is what I would do or what others have done in similar situations. If we have some information, perhaps a particular group we can place them in, we can apply our knowledge of that group and perhaps gain confidence in our assessment. If we are well acquainted with someone, we might feel quite certain about our prediction of their response. Here judgment is based on a subjective assessment of probability.

Desire in Judgment

Judgment is not only a determination of the facts and their degree of certainty. Ultimately, knowledge is in the service of desire. We want to know what will best serve our interests. Our facts always have a valence of desire. Something is good or bad. It will have this effect on me. If I want Y, I must do X. The evaluation with respect to desire is not unlike the evaluation of facts. Things and events come with an association to desire just as they consist of associations to sense qualities and relations. As we evaluate scenarios, we also imagine how we will feel about them in terms of good or bad. We reject actions with bad results just as we would reject ones with contradictory outcomes. The evaluation of desire is not restricted to imagining and feeling desire outcomes, and in fact, that sort of process is not what usually occurs. As with our knowledge of the world, we hold "facts" of desire. We think, "I like this" or "I don't like that" and reject a choice of action without really feeling that desire in the present. As noted earlier, we can hold such "facts" even if they do not accord with bodily affect.

The calculus of decision making also includes the weighing of desire along with uncertainty. Mathematically this is the technique of the weighted average. A small probability of great gain or loss might have more influence on a decision than neutral impact of near certainties. This also depends on the specific psychology of the individual. Some people are willing to take large risks for large gain, regardless of the possibility of devastating losses. Others are extremely loss adverse and tolerate little or no loss even if it means forgoing a high probability opportunity for great gain. These alternatives are described in decision theory with terms such as "maximax" or "maximin".

EMOTION

Emotion is the mediator of thought and desire. It is an assessment of the relation between self and world with respect to desire. Thought provides the "what" of the world. It supplies the "facts" we posit about what is reality. These facts, however, are simply that which is (or what we accept as being) and are intrinsically neither good nor bad. It is their relation to desire that gives them their significance. Emotion is the interpretation of the facts in relation to desire and is what motivates action. Emotion not only motivates behavior but also includes a physiological response that assists the body in carrying it out. The emotions are therefore not elemental qualia but are a compound of sensation and thought.

To say that emotion is an assessment with a component of thought does not imply the presence of a conscious rational deliberative process. Emotion does sometimes follow from conscious deliberation, as when the outcome of rational analysis results in a particular realization, but emotional responses are more likely to arise immediately and unconsciously. Emotional response existed in some form long before the capacity for rational thought, so in what sense is it an assessment?

The essence of life processes is response and adaptation to changes in the environment. Species that acquire genetic variants making them more efficient in sensing and responding to change will likely have a better chance of surviving and reproducing than those without them, shaping evolutionary development in the direction of a more sensitive and differentiated response to the environment. Heightened reactivity to unfamiliar stimuli or increased pleasure/aversion to life enhancing/harmful elements provides the physiological roots for basic emotions such as excitement, fear, disgust, attraction, etc. Variance in reactions towards others such as approach/bonding vs caution/aggression provides the beginning of social emotions such as love and empathy, hate and anger, etc.

These precursors of human emotion are simple physiological reactions to the most general stimuli. True emotion becomes possible when a more specific response to the environment becomes possible. For most species, it would be more useful have heightened arousal in the presence of a snake or a tiger as opposed to a deer. This requires sensory and nervous systems that can respond to a specific set of qualities and the ability to extract essences from the pure sensory data. This set of abstract characteristics must then become associated with "danger" and link back to the primitive physiological emotional responses. At first, this might happen through chance variation and the shaping of hard-wired reflex circuits by natural selection or perhaps through learning via subconscious classical conditioning.

At this point, there is still only immediate response without any process of thought or reason, but it is already an assessment of a sort. The body and its instincts operate through a sort of logic whether we are explicitly aware of it or not. Instinctive response makes use of the same neural structures and activities (e.g., association and hierarchal contingency response) that we use in conscious thought. Here it just happens automatically and without the intervention of will and awareness. However, because conscious thought has the same form as these instinctive circuits there is a basis to link the early physiological responses associated with emotion to products of thought and to situations that could not possibly be a matter of instinct. For example, if in reviewing our financial statements we come to realize that our fortunes have been embezzled away, we have an emotional reaction of horror. This reaction could not have evolved by natural selection back on the savannah, yet we recognize the situation as a threat and link the event to primitive threat structures and reactions.

Still, most emotional responses seem to come upon us immediately without the conscious evaluation of alternatives that is characteristic of thought. However, we must remember that unconsciousness or semi-consciousness is the general characteristic of everyday thought. Once associations become well established, conscious decision-making is no longer required. Decision trees identifying different emotional structures and determining appropriate responses can become mechanically encoded even for complex situations, just as done in computer programs with a series of nested "IF" statements. Even unfamiliar situations might be assessed subconsciously though the operation of analogical processes.

This assessing aspect is so basic to emotion that we often detach the language of emotion from its physiological roots altogether and describe a state in emotional terms without any appreciable affective response. For example, if I say, "I fear it will rain tomorrow during the picnic", I am probably not feeling fear in the full emotional sense. I suffer little of the physical effect that would be present were I to suddenly notice a rattlesnake at my feet. It is as if we use emotional descriptions by analogy. The situation is structurally like that which evokes a primal fear response, i.e., there is some threat with respect to desire, but it does not elicit the same physical reaction. This can go so far to where seemingly non-emotional assessments are referred to as emotion. For example, "trust" is often included on lists of emotions, but is trust really an emotion? It seems that trust is better seen as the acceptance of the reality of a particular proposition: I choose to believe (take as if fact) that a person or thing can be relied upon to act in a particular way.

It seems that some of the disagreements between various approaches to the emotions arise because their theorists are often not talking about the same thing. Those who wish to cast psychology as a physical science look at things like which parts of the brain are active, or how neuro-modulator levels change during emotional experiences. This research is important, but it does not tell us the whole story. It is unlikely that we will find an exact one to one correspondence, at least on this level of large-scale structures, between the brain and emotional states. There are only a few basic physical reactions compared to the range of emotions, and further, the physiological effects are not specific to a single emotion. On the other hand, emotions are not mere constructions, cultural or otherwise. They do perhaps depend on the environment insofar as events take on their meaning in a particular setting or culture. The definitions and meaning attributed to particular terms may also differ in different languages and cultures. This, however, is a matter of talking about different things, not a relativity of emotion. Emotions are universal structures based on a small number of fundamental relations to being. Our experience of these structures is a function of the physical vehicle of consciousness, the human body, and as such do relate to physiological responses that evolved in the context of natural selection.

However, neither are physiological accounts adequate to understand emotion. For example, the amygdala in cited as having an important role in fear. We read of the effects of the fear response on the respiratory and circulatory systems, changes in hormones, etc., but nowhere do we find the subjective experience of fear. How do we live fear? How does it color conscious awareness and relationships to the objects of consciousness? How do we deal with fear or control it? What does emotion tell us about our perception of a situation? What does it mean in terms of the fundamental structures of being? We cannot adequately account for emotion with the idea that it is "really just" the brain doing certain things, or by relating it to hypothesized animal instincts. The external perspective has no priority over that the inner one. This is not to deny the connection between the two. From the start, we have asserted the unity of subject and object. However, we will be more likely to find this unity at most elemental level of consciousness and nervous system, i.e., in the connections and firing ontingencies of individual neural circuits, rather than through the knowledge of gross brain structures. Thus, an fMRI image showing what part of the brain is active during a particular emotional experience may tell us where to look, but it does not provide an understanding of the subjective meaning of an emotion.

The goal here is understand emotion from the perspective of subjective consciousness, i.e., how the meaning of emotion is lived in relation to the fundamental desire of being. Emotions can be understood as belonging to general families reflecting three basic aspects of experience with respect to desire: stimuli/objects entering into consciousness, intersubjective relations, and the status of the self. These three groups are not completely independent. For example, apart from the significance that the subjectivity of others may have for my own, I must also assess people with respect to non-subjective concerns: Do they want to harm me or take something from me, or do they want trade and alliance? Likewise, one's state of satisfaction is dependent on outcomes of the first two categories.

a. Assessment of the World

The assessment of and response to change in the environment, is the most fundamental emotional response. The essence of consciousness is difference. Perceptual systems are specifically oriented to detecting change in the environment. Emotional responses in this category are elicited when something unfamiliar, unexpected or highly charged with respect to desire comes into consciousness.

Emotions such as surprise and excitement indicate an initial neutral assessment: There is an unknown that requires attention, but its value is undetermined. The primary characteristics of these emotional responses are attention and arousal. Attention is drawn to the source of the stimulus. Consciousness zooms in with a laser focus and tends to evaluation of the situation at hand. Whatever thoughts or interests we had just before disappear. We are in bed at night and hear a noise in the house. All thought stops. Attention moves to the sense of hearing as we try to determine the cause. The second characteristic is arousal. We are energized and ready to move. The body goes into a state of heightened attention and readiness for action – the flight or fight response, or sometimes a freezing response so as not to draw a predator's attention. As we gain clues to what a stimulus might be, the emotion becomes more specific. If we realize there is nothing of consequence to the stimulus, e.g., the noise was just the cat; we quickly become disinterested or bored and pay no further attention to it. The rush of adrenaline subsides.

If the evidence begins to indicate a likely threat, we move into the fear family of emotions. The initial response to an unknown stimulus is vigilance and apprehension, but as the danger becomes more certain the feeling turns to fear. The greater the threat appears to be and the less we see a means to cope with it, the more the emotion moves to more extreme states such as terror, dread, horror or panic. Other emotions in this category are disgust, revulsion or aversion. These generally apply to threats of a physical, hygienic nature, as when we recoil from a putrid smell or maggot infested meat. Here the physical component is very strong and is an ejecting, repelling response. We might also feel disgust towards a person, which is analogical to physical disgust and means that like rotten food we find something literally or figuratively toxic about them and are driven to avoid them.

On the other side, if we recognize value or potential in the novel object we move to a positive emotional state. We start to feel interest, curiosity, and hope. We become eager and enthusiastic with a feeling of anticipation. We are attracted to and desirous of the object. We focus attention on it and are aroused for action, but this time so that we may do what is necessary to engage or acquire it. When the object reveals and approaches the absolute, the emotion becomes the sense of wonder, awe or astonishment.

b. Assessment of Being for Others

The emotions in this category arise not simply from the involvement of other human beings but relate specifically to the existence of others as subjects and their significance to the realization of our own subjectivity, i.e., how we see and are seen by them. As addressed earlier, other humans appear to be a potential means of fulfilling the desire to attain transcendence of self and consciousness of one's subjectivity as object. They exist for us as subjectivity in object. They can thus affirm and realize our own subjectivity in the world, or thwart it.

The emotional appraisal with respect to intersubjective affirmation or denial primarily exists on a continuum of love and hate. Love comes in variations that relate to the specific object of love and the expectations we place upon it. Included on the positive side of the love-hate spectrum is everything from casual "liking" to passionate romantic love. What they have in common is that in them we recognize (or imagine) the subjectivity of the other as affirming of our own, and we take on the other as our own self in object to some degree.

In romantic love, we want to take on the other as our self in the world. From its eternal persistence in books and love songs and drama, it seems to be the holy grail of interpersonal relations. It is the ultimate that everyone wants yet is hard to find. The aim of romantic love essentially is the project of fundamental desire: to transcend our subjectivity through the loved one in body and soul. Sexual passion is an intrinsic part of romantic love. Physically we merge with the other, aiming to overcome the difference and become subject and object at the same time. In romantic love, we speak of "soul mates", in other words, subjectivity mates. We take the loved one as ourselves in the world. We see them as seeing us as we see our see ourselves, and themselves seeing as we see. If they are an external extension of our selves, then their desire is our desire, i.e., our own self. We want to be wanted. In love, we wish to annihilate the separation between us. We expand the ego boundaries to include the other as part of our self, and accordingly we grant them the same care as we would give to ourselves. This is the ideal, but whether this project can be fulfilled is another matter. Most of romantic love is a projection and a mirage. We take on the other as being this thing and see what we want to see. Despite our desire, this fusion-like state of romantic love remains largely an illusion. In most cases, eventually the differences and divergences of desire cannot be denied.

Another zealous kind of love is the familial. In the love of family, especially that of a parent for child, the loved one literally is us in the aspect of the physical vehicle of consciousness, at least partly. Therefore, it does not have the physical passion. We do not sexually overcome the physical in this love. Like romantic love, familial love is characterized by the expansion of the ego boundaries to include the other. Physical being is the basis of consciousness, or more accurately of the objects of consciousness. We expect that the subjective will be similar in family members and take them to be at least a partial achievement of the fundamental desire for the transcendence of our subjectivity in the world. Of course, as with romantic love, these expectations are not necessarily realistic. Children are, after all, only partly of our own physical nature. With the shuffling of the genetic deck in sexual reproduction and the effect of environmental variables, there is no telling what the result will be. The subjectivity of the child is often discovered to be quite alien to that of the parent.

Positive intersubjective feelings less than the passion of love are categorized as affection or liking. Feeling affection in this way is, like love, is based on an affirmation of our subjectivity and characterized by at least a partial expansion of ego boundaries and bonding. Friendship does not demand the absolute status of love that comes with the connection of the physical and does not have the aspect of physical desire. We generally do not have the same investment in their welfare or the same expectations with those we call friends. On the other hand, in many ways friendship relations can be more satisfying. In terms of the actual sense of subjectivity, as noted above, the sense of unity with lovers is often more fantasy than reality, and children are often very different from their parents. However, we often become friends with someone precisely because of subjective affinity. We sense that they see the world as we do. They are interested in things we are interested in and do things we like to do. They have experiences similar to our own. We feel they understand us and can commiserate with us. Not being bound to us, we avoid the inevitable conflicts of the family relation. Friends can lend an objective eye on our problems. Out of our affinity, they may also become our allies and support our endeavors in the world. We may also have similar feelings towards people we do not directly know, as when we are drawn to an artist or writer or musician. Their creations capture and express our own experience and desire. They create concrete embodiments of our subjectivity.

We may also extend a certain regard towards others with whom we have no personal involvement, as in general humanitarian feeling. We may feel certain positive emotions and or extend a particular stance or behavior towards strangers. In empathy, sympathy and compassion we allow ourselves to feel the pain and distress of others and may feel driven to caring and altruistic behaviors to help alleviate their pain as if it was our own. In commiserating with others, we reflect their subjective state, objectifying it and in some sense putting it outside of them. In humility, we avoid displaying and/or demanding recognition of our own value, thus avoiding the objectification of others as inferior. This is opposed to the feeling of pride, in which we feel and display a sense of exceptional merit.

Extending this general good will to the heights of love we arrive at something like the universal selfless love referred by the term Agape and described in Christianity as the love of God for man and vice versa. It is the expansion of the boundaries of the self to include all. In other words, it is the complete unity of subject and object, or self-consciousness of being.

Love is the positive side of the intersubjective. The fundamental opposing emotion is hatred and its variations. If in love we take on the other as a transcendence of ourselves in the world, as the realization of our consciousness in the world as object, in hate we see the other as denying our subjectivity. Accordingly, hatred is desire for the annihilation of the other. Hate is not entirely a phenomenon of the intersubjective. We can hate things. We can hate our jobs, hate the traffic, hate a disease, etc. The underlying meaning is the same. These things bring pain and we would will them out of existence. However, despite this detestation of the object, true hatred is directed at other people. We may not like it, but we can resign ourselves to the hard realities of the physical world. It is not so easy to accept the sufferings imposed upon us by other human beings.

Closely related to hate is anger. Whereas hate reflects more of an enduring assessment of someone or something as a threat, with no redeeming qualities and with a desire for their annihilation, anger usually stems from a specific perception of an intersubjective slight. It occurs in the presence of an occasion for hate but need not continue to a wish for the non-existence of the other if the immediate situation is rectified. Thus, we can become angry with a loved one but also quickly get over it once the transgression is owned up to and an apology made. We place hate and anger mostly in the intersubjective because what really rouses our anger is not so much random frustrations in life or chance material loss, but a perceived attitude of the other that denies our sense of our worth or our fundamental ways of relating to the world. We are angry when we perceive others as devaluing us in some way. It may be a sense of a lack of regard with respect to our basic status as a human being and our basic rights, or as one knowledgeable or entitled in a particular role or context. If someone bumps into us on the street we likely are not physically hurt, but if they do not acknowledge the infraction (which immediately resolves the situation) we perceive the meaning as "you do not matter, you ar not worthy of basic consideration". Likewise, if someone commits a crime against us, even where the material loss or injury is small, what angers us is the criminal's seeming disregard for us as a subject. We do not get particularly angry at a bear that trashes our camp or even mauls us, even though the physical loss might be worse than that resulting from a criminal attack. We understand that bears do not have the capacity to think about us one way or the other and are acting on instinct. The subjectivity of the bear does not enter into the equation. However, when a human being seems to be not giving us our due as we see it, it is saying that our subjective existence is invalid or unworthy. This is also the case when someone opposes or demeans our core values and beliefs such as those of politics and religion. This calls into question our fundamental relation to the world.

Our reaction to this assessment of the situation is to fight to restore what we believe is rightfully ours, and this is what the anger response prepares us to do. Anger arouses and excites us, readying us for combat. In fact, it seems to put us in a state where that is all we can do. Anger is destructive desire and exhibits the characteristics of desire. It is as if all available resources are turned to combat and destructive capability. Reason drops away. As anger grows, there is no consideration of larger consequences or risks, which is why people get into trouble when they "see red" and are dominated by anger. Rational resolutions become impossible. Likewise, any social considerations are lost. There is no concern for the integrity of the other, no empathy, no compassion.

The desired outcome at the end of anger is restitution. The expression of anger is often a display and meant for communicative purposes. Anger evolved out of animal conflict response where the resolution might very well be physical combat and where displaying cues of the presence of anger and the readiness to fight might be enough to get the other to desist. Perhaps we do not come to physical combat so much anymore, but still exhibit the same signs of anger, signaling our feelings about the situation and communicating that there will be some kind of consequences. Supporting the idea that anger is primary an issue of our status in the eyes of others, restitution often is possible through a simple apology or clarification. We grant our wrongdoing to the other or confess our ignorance. We agree to make certain changes. If this is not enough, we fight in one form or another. If not physically, then legal or other remedies to achieve restitution may be employed, with the motivation and energy fueled by the anger response.

There are several additional negative social emotions we must briefly consider. In anger, we feel that we have been wrongly diminished by the other. We have not been accorded the status and consideration we believe we deserve. In other cases, the diminishment comes not as a perceived transgression of the other, but from behavior on our own part that exposes us objectively in a reduced status even by our own standards. The emotions related to this condition are embarrassment, shame, and guilt.

In embarrassment, the fault is not generally a wrong in a moral sense, but that we have not kept up certain social expectations for human beings in general or a particular social milieu. For example, there is a general social norm that we should rise above our animal nature. Thus, mishaps of the body are often a cause for embarrassment. To expose the body inappropriately, to publicly lose control of bodily functions, to seem overly dominated by needs of the body are typical examples. Embarrassment arises in situations where others witness our ignorance or ineptness in some way. Particular social groups have their own specific standards and manners to which a member must adhere. In a social group that imagines itself as being refined or of a higher social status, one would be embarrassed if seen as not knowing and acting in accord with its customs and manners, or if perceived as uncouth, ignorant or as having bad taste. In a group of teenagers, one might be embarrassed if exposed as not being "cool" or as too obedient to one's parents or still attached to things of youth. In a masculine or militaristic culture, it might be embarrassing to be seen as cowardly or weak.

To be seen as not living up to a claim one has made or being exposed as being less than the desired social image one tries to project are also embarrassments. It is not necessarily that we ought to be blamed or that we really have been lowered because of these behaviors, many of which everyone engages in to so some degree and would do the same under similar conditions, but it is that we have become an object to others in them. Where there is not compassion for one who has been caught in an embarrassing act, there is often a bit of schadenfreude. One person's lowering relatively raises our own status.

Shame is much like embarrassment only with a different type of transgression. If embarrassment is mostly about being seen as less evolved than one ought to be in some context, shame is more about moral transgressions: not acting in accordance with social mores with respect to what we owe are fellow members of society. That is, we are perceived as not acting in accordance with standards such as obeying the laws, respecting people's rights, showing politeness, consideration, honesty, generosity, etc. We may not necessarily agree with all these standards, but the perception that one is being perceived in a disapproving light is enough to bring about a negative emotional experience.

Guilt also pertains to these moral standards towards others, but unlike shame, in guilt others may not even be aware of our wrongdoing. The feeling of guilt is internal. We have done something wrong, and we know it is wrong. We feel that we are in bad faith in a social relation. If we cheat on our wife, lie to a friend, or swindle a client, we know that we have violated the assumed trust of the relation. If we feel guilt, we recognize that we made a bad move. We comprehend the value of these relations and know that we threaten them, whether through the possibility of getting caught or simply in knowing that we have not held to their conditions. In feeling guilt, we shame ourselves in an attempt to make it right or at least to avoid such behavior in the future. The public display of guilt is something different but has the same end of trying to repair the relation. When we publicly display guilt and admit our wrongdoing, we are trying to convince others we know we made a mistake, regret it, will not do it again, and hope they will take us back in their good graces as a reliable worthy partner in a relationship of some kind.

Two additional negative social emotions, envy and jealousy, are superficially related and often treated as synonymous, but they are distinct structures. In envy, we want what the other has. It is however more than that. If it was just a question of wanting, we might view the accomplished other with admiration. Their achievements might help us recognize what is possible and inspire us to pursue our own success. Envy though is not about desire for the particular success or possessions we lack. It is rather that the success of the other is felt to diminish ourselves. It exposes a feeling of inferiority. It is a reminder that we are not what we like to imagine ourselves to be or are not seen by others as we wish to be seen. It puts our subjectivity into question. As a result, we are more hostile than admiring of the other. Envy often has a component of wishing for the downfall of the successful, which we suppose will balance the scales and remove our own feelings of failure.

Jealousy is sometimes used as a synonym for envy. For example, one might say, "I am jealous of your success". However, this usage seems to be an imprecise use of language due to similarities of the two terms. Both involve a perceived threat to the self in response to what another has or may be acquiring. What distinguishes jealousy from envy though is that jealousy is about the desire of the other. We are jealous when we want to possess or perceive ourselves as possessing the desire of another and sense that there is some threat to our maintaining or acquiring that position. Jealousy appears mostly in romantic/sexual relationships, as we would expect, given that romantic love is about the transcending of our subjectivity in and possessing the desire of the other. Non-sexual situations where the use of the term jealousy seems appropriate are also those that involve the threat of losing the desire of the other. For example, we might appropriately speak of a child being jealous of a sibling. The child wants to feel he is the be all and end all of the parent's world. A girl might be jealous if she notices that a close friend seems to be forming an intimate bond with another friend. One might be jealous of a rival at school or work if their status (or desired status) as teacher's pet or the boss's favorite appears to be threatened. The concern in jealousy is that one is losing a privileged place in the desire of the other.

A final group of negative social emotions is that in which there is not so much an opposition or negating in our being for others, but rather a feeling that one is unable to engage at all. Here we have those emotional states referred to with terms like loneliness, alienation or isolation. One has limited ability to be with others. One finds no reflection of self in others and no connection with them. There is no interest in or from the other, or both. Others are not hostile and anger eliciting but simply do not seem to notice us or we cannot engage them at all.

c. Assessment of Self

The first two emotional categories were concerned with external relations to things and people around us. The third category is internally focused and consists of the sense of our own condition with respect to desire. Of course, external objects and the intersubjective affect our state of being. The quality of these relationships is the basis for it. The determination here is of our state with respect to fulfillment of the fundamental desire. That is, are we living in, or productively moving towards, overcoming separation and alienation from the world and transcending our subjectivity in it. Are we on a path towards the self-consciousness of being, or, on the contrary, are we alienated, blocked from the ends of desire, without connections or prospects for making progress towards them?

The basic emotional continuum in this regard is the axis of happiness and sadness. On the positive side are the degrees and nuances of happiness such as joy, ecstasy, contentment, fulfillment, hope, optimism, etc., and on the negative side unhappiness, sadness, depression, despair, meaninglessness, etc.

Whether a person is happy or not is affected by their status at each level of desire and the level of completeness to which they have developed. Being in a state of chronic physical suffering, where ones one's world is contracted into one's pain, makes happiness and even the will to live problematic. Being free of pain and having physical needs met is a first prerequisite for an openness to the world. Finding some transcendence of self in social relations, especially love and sex is adequate for many. Perhaps for the majority of people, achieving love and some degree of transcendence in the creation and continuation of the physical through children and a family life is the main purpose and source of contentment in life. Happiness is also found in mastering tasks and effectively acting upon the world, which is, in the end, to become more conscious on one's own nature as being and to overcome alienation from the object. A productive seeking of knowledge does the same. Self-expressive and artistic activities transcend the individual self, and as they become more universal in their objects move towards the self-consciousness and transcendence of being itself. Creative activities increase the differentiation of being and reveal more of its potentiality, which in turn can be integrated back into the source.

Research shows a connection between creativity and mood. We might almost say that being in a creative state is happiness. Earlier we noted that one of the attributes of fear was a narrowing of focus where our attentional resources are focused on the potential threat. Creativity on the other hand is characterized a broad expansive cognitive mode with loose and remote associations. This making of new connections is the integration that brings us to consciousness of being. There is elation in an insight or creative breakthrough. Suddenly we see how things are connected and how they work. We are a little more in harmony with the world. Seeing that there is a road ahead, a path to progress where we can act towards our goals is as important to happiness as our actual position. When we recognize that there are tasks we can engage in that will advance us towards our goals, there is hope and the feeling of meaning in our activities. We are positively energized. Activity in the service of desire is effortless. We are happy in activities that cut across the barriers between subject and object, for example in physical activities such as eating and sex, in creating, building, knowing, and relating with others, etc.

The opposing state, a contracted consciousness, where we feel cut off from connection to the world and see no possibilities for new ones, is experienced as sadness and depression in their variations. Depression is associated with loss. Loss is a cutting off from our connections to the world. When affirming relationships cease and when we fail in activities that seemed the path to progress, we are severed from the world, often without immediate possibilities for reconnection. We cannot easily give up connections of desire even when they are no longer viable. The physiological mechanisms that bond us to others in the obsession of love or motivate us to pursue particular activities cannot be turned off at will. Without taking Freud too literally, his casting of desire in terms of the investment of psychosexual energies in an object provides a good metaphor for the feelings we experience in emotional bonds and their termination. The withdrawal of these "cathexes" and the relinquishing of the object do not come immediately or without pain. We remain fixated on the lost object for a long time and have difficulty establishing new ones. We may find consolation in knowing that sometimes letting go is just a physical process that must work itself out at its own pace and in accepting that things will not always be this way. Sometimes it is only time that heals our wounds.

Because we have lost connections and see no possibilities for new ones, we have nothing inciting us to action, thus the low energy and lethargy of sadness. As with the other emotions where the body gives us something we need to cope with the perceived situation, what positive value is there in the low energy and fatigue of sadness and depression? It may be that being placed into a physical state that disinclines us to activity and interaction with others makes it possible for us to focus internally on coming to grips with the loss, understanding what went wrong and on finding new ways ahead.

This completes our survey of the emotions and subjective consciousness. Regarding the place of emotion in the understanding of consciousness, it seems that, however important, emotions are not fundamental elements of experience but are compounds composed of thought, desire and sensory qualia. However, this still leaves a problem for both the emotions and their component elements which are the qualia of sensations and thoughts. We have identified the simplest qualia of sense and thought but have not accounted for them. They seem to be ineffable, stand-alone building blocks with no connection to each other and offering no understanding of how they relate to their physical correlates or why they appear as they do. We can know everything about the physics of light, how the eyes discriminate frequency, and how the response of the eyes triggers a chain of neural activity in the brain when we see an apple, but we cannot explain why this flurry of neuron firings is experienced as "redness". This issue is what has come to be known as the "hard" problem of consciousness and is the subject of the next chapter.

CHAPTER 5

The Hard Problem

That there is a relation between mind and body is not in question. Yet the nature of the interaction between them is not clear. We may understand how the sense organs respond to physical stimuli and how such stimuli create electrical activity in neurons and transmit it to the brain. We are fairly knowledgeable about which areas in the brain are associated with particular kinds of experience and even which correlate with consciousness awareness itself. As neuroscience progresses, we will undoubtedly come to understand these relations even more precisely. Even so, knowledge of how the physical mechanisms work does not explain why that which appears from the outside as electrical activity in neural circuits comes to be subjectively experienced as colors, sounds and tastes, etc. It does not tell us why a particular frequency of light stimulating a response in the cone receptors of the eye is accompanied by consciousness of the color red for example. David Chalmers, who coined the term "hard problem" of consciousness, posed the question as follows: "Why is it that when our cognitive systems engage in visual and auditory information-processing, we have visual or auditory experience: the quality of deep blue, the sensation of middle C? How can we explain why there is something it is like to entertain a mental image, or to experience an emotion? It is widely agreed that experience arises from a physical basis, but we have no good explanation of why and how it so arises. Why should physical processing give rise to a rich inner life at all? It seems objectively unreasonable that it should, and yet it does. If any problem qualifies as *the* problem of consciousness, it is this one."

A couple of clarifications are necessary as to how we should understand this question. First, the notion that experience arises from the physical does not mean that the physical holds the status of a higher reality that creates consciousness as a byproduct or an illusion. Consciousness itself is not secondary to the physical. What we know as the physical we only know through conscious experience. Rather they are correlated perspectives. We can only say experience arises from the physical insofar as the specific kinds of objects and qualities available to consciousness are a function of particular physical structures and processes. The question of how consciousness exists at all was addressed in the first chapter. The remaining problem, then, is to account for the specific qualities of experience, i.e., colors, sounds, sensations, judgments, etc., in relation to their physical coordinates.

COGNITIVE EXPERIENCE AND ITS RELATION TO THE PHYSICAL

Considering experience as a whole, it is not difficult to understand much of it as a psychophysical parallelism with a direct correspondence between the qualities of subjective experience and those of its physiological counterpart. Earlier we distinguished between the senses as media, i.e., carriers of information, and the higher cognitive processing that extracts patterns contained in these media. The former, which are subjectively experienced as the elemental qualia of color, taste, sound, etc., are the more difficult problem and will be addressed in the following section. Here we will consider the experience derived from the cognitive processes operating on these media and show that this part of experience, which makes up a good portion of our overall consciousness of the world, consists of the same categories that constitute the scientist's third person comprehension of the physiological objects and processes correlated with it. The views from within and without reveal the same forms through different media. Beyond the specific mode of appearance, the inner and outer views are constructed with the same categories and have the same meaning.

Earlier we identified the basic properties of neural structures and activity, summarized briefly as follows: 1) Neurons either fire or they do not. It is all or nothing; 2) Intensity of stimulus is coded in the rate of firing; 3) The effects of neurons on other neurons across synaptic connections are either excitatory or inhibitory, making them either more or less likely to fire; 4) Specific patterns of neural activity are a function of the connection structures (e.g., direct, indirect, hierarchal, etc.) and firing contingencies.

How do the characteristics of the nervous system as described from an "objective" viewpoint correspond to subjective experience? Consider the experience of space. Earlier we identified the properties of spatial consciousness. We experience space as a whole or a field, but also grasp it as consisting of separate points within the field. Physically, a visual field has the same makeup. The retina is a field of individual receptors, but the cells are also connected such that we can perceive the field as a whole and recognize specific locations in that field. This field structure is passed on to a similar field like map on the visual cortex. Although there is in part, there need not be a precise physical duplication of the retinal image for there to be a correspondence between space as experienced and its physiological correlates. The structure of points and wholes only needs to be encoded such that it preserves the relational information carried in the sense data. That is to say, it needs to have a similar structure in terms of the basic elements of consciousness, i.e., the connection, continuity and contingency relationships of the parts. Despite the fact that the retinal field is two dimensional, we see, or think we see, objects as existing in three dimensions. This is due to simultaneous processing of additional information that in total represents and creates a subjective consciousness of a 3D space. As noted earlier, comprehension of the third dimension is rooted in movement and the somatosensory, but is also inferred through interpretation of various visual cues such as object size, interpositions, binocular disparity, parallax, etc.

Space has dimension, as does the visual field created in the retina and visual cortex. A cortical map derived from the retina is inherently two-dimensional and turns into three in relation to bodily movement and the higher visual processing as outlined above. The asymmetry of the body in three dimensions also provides a basis for the experience of dimension as does the vestibular system. The quantification of space is a function of the existence of individual points of space created by individual receptors and neurons that are also connected and grouped into new unities. The continuity or discontinuity of space is modeled by the continuous (or discontinuous) stimulation of contiguous receptors/neurons.

While the pure sense or media of time must be understood on its own, the tracking and management of time is spatialized and based on quantification of events. Thus, most of our experience of time parallels the same physical structures that we considered above to account for space. Clocks use counts of discrete events. Calendars and timelines represent time through ordered spatial pictures.

Thus, regarding the secondary processing that operates on differences in raw sense data to form the objects of the senses, the appearance of what the brain is doing from the perspective of scientist is not so different from what we experience subjectively from the perspective of that brain from the inside. As an analogy to the relation between the perspectives the scientist looking at a brain and that of first-person consciousness through it, consider the viewpoint of an experimenter watching a blind mouse running through a maze compared to that of the mouse. The experimenter sees the maze as a whole - the paths and their lengths, the turns and dead ends, etc. He sees the mouse negotiate the paths. This is not so different from looking at a neural net and path of electrical activity flowing through it. The experimenter can measure the paths and time the mouse's rate of movement. He can watch it follow the corridors of the maze, change direction when it runs into a wall, change the pace of movement, etc. The mouse, on the other hand, sees nothing. Yet as he moves through the maze, he comes to know it and his movement through it in terms of the same parameters of experience only carried in different media. He experiences the passages of the maze, their lengths and changes in direction, etc., through the body feeling of movement and contact. He knows he has moved faster or farther along a path from the quantity of movement and feeling of exertion. He knows the path has ended because the wall resists his movement and stopping his progress. He knows a left or right turn by their orientation with respect to the body and the different feeling associated with each. Eventually he learns the sequence of turns and solves the maze. In the end, both man and mouse end up with a model of the maze based on the same categories. The maze has passages, lengths, boundaries and changes in orientation. It has continuities and discontinuities. The rate of movement is a count expressed as change over time. The two have different experiences, but they are alike in existing through common categories and attributes of space, time and quantity. The two perspectives differ in that the values of these parameters are carried in different qualia. There is a similar parallelism between the view of the neuroscientist observing the connective structures of neurons and the flow of activity between them, and the experience of a subject perceiving a stimulus associated with that activity.

We can extend the same analysis to the activities of thought and judgment. While the precise mechanism by which thought processes work is a question for neuroscience, the basic elements of neural operation both account for and limit the kind of thought that is possible. We return to the elements of logic in the context of neural correlates. Propositions are statements in the general form of "X is Y". They are assertions of relations. Relations are a fact of neural connection. "Neurons that fire together wire together". To say an apple is X means that the visual/acoustic stimulus of the word "apple" (itself the culmination of the processing of a chain of spatial or sound elements) is connected to a set of other neurons representing various qualities (each of which is also at the end of a network of other neurons relating to sense and other properties). The word is a binder of these qualities and tethers the elements together to make a distinct entity. The truth of a proposition is the existence of a state of excitation (i.e., firing) in the collection of neurons needed to activate the neuron representing the set name. The identity of objects, "X is a Y" is sensed in the consciousness of identical states of firing. The recognition of identity or difference is the elemental judgment made in accepting the assertion.

If neural excitation correlates to being and truth, the lack of excitation corresponds to negation. If there are no neurons firing, there is no differentiation. If the associated activity that makes up an object is not there, then it is not that object. Another form of negation is existential opposition, where the existence of one thing precludes that of another, i.e., contradiction. A proposition may not assert both A and not A. This active negation correlates with inhibitory neural processes. The activity of one neuron makes another unable to fire. Their firing is mutually exclusive. These observable basic properties of neurons map to unique states experienced internally as the judgments of thought.

Continuing along these lines, in the experience of association or conjunction we are consciousness of two things existing together in some way. A state with two firing neurons (or sets of neurons) along with an additional physical distinction specific to this state would in effect show the same structure externally as the internal lived judgment of conjunction. The truth condition of conjunction is embodied in a simple neural circuit where neurons A and B feed into C, and where C requires the excitation of both A and B to reach action potential. The internal perspective of this state is the subjective judgment of conjunction. The internal and external are two appearances of the same condition.

The judgment of disjunction, the "or", can be created physically with a similar mechanism, the only difference being that the excitation of any one of a set of potential input neurons is sufficient to elicit response in the neuron marking condition of disjunction. The exclusive disjunction, A or B but not both, is a little more complicated but not difficult to construct. The alternative inputs might connect to two hierarchal condition circuits. The first is the standard disjunction cell C just described. The second target of the input cells could be an "AND" cell

D, which fires in the false "both" condition. From here, C and D feed into another "AND" cell E, where D has inhibitory effect. The result is a circuit that would yield a truth (firing) condition if either one of the inputs were true but would be blocked via inhibition if the conjunction is also true.

The same approach works for material implication, "if A then B". The beginning of the judgment of cause and condition is in the truth that B follows A, or B exists where A exists. This alone is just another case of association, i.e., we see A and B together. However, we do not infer a necessary connection simply because of joint appearance. In the conditional, there is evidence of a necessity relation: B appears every time A appears. The negation of implication is the appearance of A without B, i.e., the falsity condition of the truth table, where A is true and B is false. Again, multiple operations are required, but it is not difficult to model the experience physically. First, there must be recognition of an association; otherwise, there would be no reason to contemplate a relation of necessity. Therefore, we start with a conjunctive circuit, i.e., both neurons A and B must be excited to bring neuron C to action potential. Next, we need a mechanism that represents the negation of implication, i.e., the existence of A and −B. This can be accomplished by having A and B feed into a second circuit where the firing of A creates an excitatory response in neuron D, but the firing of B produces an offsetting inhibitory effect. When both A and B fire they will offset, and the output neuron remains inactive. The same is true in the events of B alone firing or where neither A nor B fire, since in both states there is no activity. However, if A alone is present, i.e., the condition of falsity, the result will be excitation of the output neuron D. This second circuit specifically flags the falsehood condition of the implication. It creates the truth table of the material conditional. We can extend this to material equivalence (if and only if) by running the same test in both directions. In sum, the subjective judgments of negations, conjunctions, disjunctions, conditional dependencies, etc., are literally embodied in neural structures. Beyond the level of pure sensory qualia, subjective experience consists of the same categories as those making up objective perception of the brain and its activity associated with that experience.

This is not to claim that these are the precise structures and operations by which these particular categories of judgment actually work but to show that these basic neural principles are sufficient to account for subjective thought experience and that the number of possible distinct states also limits the possible judgments of thought. In actuality, these operations might involve millions of neurons, but they all work through the same limited set of operations. In addition, conscious awareness itself requires more than the existence of these structures. As discussed earlier, consciousness requires a kind of repetitive feedback mechanism that integrates the flow of difference. Without that, the mechanisms we have described are not different from reflex circuits or logic gates in a computer, neither of which attains to conscious awareness.

Other phenomena are a mix of simple sensory qualia and these common parameters of consciousness. As an example, consider the experience of music. The creation of music in the body starts with the internalization of sound waves through their effect on the eardrum, a vibrating membrane that registers the physical wave characteristics of frequency and amplitude. Vibrations on the eardrum are transmitted to the cochlea, where coiled inside this snail like structure is the basilar membrane. This membrane responds differentially along its length according to frequency. In a typical compound sound consisting of different notes and overtones, the constituent frequencies stimulate movement at the appropriate positions across the membrane. In effect, the auditory system performs a Fourier transform that breaks down complex sounds into their simple components. The movement of the basilar membrane stimulates movement of hair cells at the organ of Corti. This movement results in the production of electrical signals that are transmitted to the brain for further processing.

In matching the phenomenological qualities of music with their physiological correlates, we find that for some properties of music there is no obvious connection between subjective qualia and their physical counterparts, while for others, the experience consists of the same categories constituting the "objective" comprehension of their correlates in the body. The only difference is the media through which the categories find expression. For example, the elementary sound quality of pitch has its physical counterpart in the position of the stimulus along the basilar membrane. Yet there is no obvious reason why this material structure and activity should be experienced as particular tones. Likewise, the experience of loudness is associated with the extent of movement of the hair cells, but we can see no direct relation between the two. These are the elemental sensory qualia, the problem of which will be addressed below. We only note here that there is a one-to-one correspondence between the conscious experience of these qualities and their physical counterparts.

On the other hand, the temporal/quantity-based elements such as tempo, duration and rhythm are the same in our auditory experience of them and in how they appear from the outside in observing the activity of the auditory system. We hear a fast or slow tempo and sense the longer or shorter duration of a note, or alternatively we see and measure differences in the rate of vibration on the basilar membrane. We subjectively experience rhythm as different recurring sequences of longer/shorter and accented/unaccented beats. As scientists, we can measure and comprehend the correlative vibration patterns in the auditory apparatus in terms of the same temporal/quantitative categories. The same categories are present in both perspectives only expressed in different media.

Other musical elements appear to be a mix of sensory and cognitive experience. For example, melody, considered strictly in the aspect of the succession of tones and their intervals, might belong to the problem of elementary sensory qualia. However, other characteristics of melody are experienced from both the subjective and objective perspectives. For example, we can both hear and measure intervals as greater or smaller. The succession of notes can be continuous or discontinuous in lesser or greater degrees, which can be both subjectively sensed and objectively measured as a magnitude of difference on the basilar membrane. Melodies can have narrower or wider ranges both to the ear and in the ear.

They may exhibit directional tendencies that are both heard and seen, etc. Harmony is similar to melody in having distinctive tone qualia, but it is also true that we consciously experience the presence of multiple simultaneous tones, the sense of which also belongs to objective quantitative measures. Timbre, the tone color that distinguishes the sound of a piano, violin or a flute, for example, might at first seem to be an ineffable purely sensory quality, but it is possible that we consciously recognize some of the objective elements that account for it. From the perspective of physics, timber relates to the complexity of the waveform and how it changes over time. It depends on differences in frequency, amplitude, harmonics, and their specific temporal patterns. Perhaps an astute listener can distinguish temporal and quantitative differences such as the specific change of volume in the attack of a piano note, or the quantity of audible harmonics, or the rates of change in vibrato and tremolo, etc.

The main point we have been trying to demonstrate here is that for large parts of conscious experience, namely that which is beyond elementary sense qualia, there is no mystery in understanding the connection between first person consciousness and how the scientist understands its physiological correlates. Both perspectives are constructed through the same categories and attributes of space, time, quantity, and being. The real problem, then, is the relation between the material and the simple sensory and cognitive qualia that carry the specific values of these parameters.

ELEMENTAL QUALIA

While the above sheds some light on the connection between complex subjective experience and its physiological coordinates, illustrating that the parameters of conscious through which we understand the latter are identical to many of those constituting the corresponding first-person consciousness, it does not address the more difficult problem of accounting for the relationship between the physical and the simple sensory qualia that carry these patterns of relation. While we may understand the correlation between subjective experiences and physiological structures, we cannot cut open a brain and see redness, or hear the sound of a violin in the temporal lobe or find sweetness in the dissection of taste receptor. Yet because of this correlation and because experience is altered or ceases when physical systems are disrupted, we know that there is some relation between them. How can we account for the appearance of these simple sensory and cognitive qualia and their relation to the body?

Consider again the basic relation between consciousness and object. The consciousness of objects comes about through a differentiation of the wholeness of being/consciousness followed by an integration of the parts. This differentiation, or limiting of being/consciousness, creates what we experience as the physical world. Each physical state as seen from the outside has a corresponding inner perspective of being. As a physical vehicle develops to create wider and more complex integration, it makes possible the consciousness of increasingly intricate objects and the relations between them. The specific appearance of the world to human consciousness follows from the particular development of human perceptual and nervous systems. How might qualia have unfolded into their current form in relation to the development of their physiological counterparts?

Imagine the start of conscious awareness as arising with a response to the differentiation of light. Whether or not the perception of light was actually the beginning of consciousness is not important here. Most likely it was not. Living organisms existed long before the development of anything like the eye. Yet we must start from the notion of some single differentiation through which consciousness first emerged, with each subsequent experience developing in relation to what preceded it. Because existence is relational and oppositional, it should not matter where we begin. The world starts from a first differentiation and each phenomenon becomes what it is in relation to what came before. In turn, what came before also changes since it now exists through a new set of relations to what came out if it. What follows is not a proposed account of the evolution in time of perceptual capabilities, but a hypothetical logical dialectic of the unfolding of qualia.

In the beginning, perhaps the perception of light was a simple binary response to a quantum of electromagnetic energy, a simple fire or not response at a particular quantity threshold. Consciously (assuming the capacity for integration is present) this would result in a simple distinction between two states. What qualities could this associated subjective experience have? All that really exists at this point is a consciousness of something and something else. We cannot really describe qualities such as light per se or color because these experiences are a function of relations with a million other discriminated experiences that have arisen since. There could be no consciousness of a specific category of color since at this point there is nothing in contrast to color. It is like the fish that does not know it is in the water until it is pulled out of it. There was nothingness, and then something, a simple experience of difference itself, without additional quality. This qualityless sense of something and nothing is precisely how we think of black and white: The blackness of nothingness in contrast to the equally qualityless wholeness of being. Even now that is how we understand light. White light is the undifferentiated. We only see colors when we separate out individual wavelengths, i.e., make a further differentiation. The experience of light and color as we know it now is what it is only in the contrast of all known colors, and for that matter in opposition to all other sense and non-sense experiences in their current differentiation and relations. In the beginning, we could not have known light as colors as we know them now and could not have had specifically visual experience until there was some sense other than vision.

One might ask why not silence and sound as our visual starting point. Perhaps this could have been, but at this point could we know the difference? As with visual experience, the sonic only takes on its appearance in relation to everything else that exists and at the beginning there is nothing else there to provide a specific sound quality. Another factor is that the appearance to consciousness of any sense medium is not independent of the nature of the source. In this context, we can reverse McLuhan's well-known phrase "the medium is the message" and say that it is also true that the message is the medium. That is, the phenomenal appearance of a sense medium is influenced by the characteristics of the stimulus it to which it responds.

For example, the phenomenon of color starts in the fact that different objects absorb or reflect different wavelengths. Visual objects are generally stable in the wavelengths they reflect or absorb. Their appearance may change with different conditions of illumination, but unless the object is a state of transition, color is not a medium that unfolds in time. Objects with color are extended in space. Differences in wavelength reflectance exist in stable discrete patches in a spatial field. These fields are modeled internally by spatial patterns of excitation on the retina and visual cortex. How visual consciousness appears is in some part due to the qualities of what it reveals: It appears as a temporally stable spatial field.

Sound on the other hand exists primarily in time rather than space, and we make sense of it through its temporal changes. Each unit of sound such as a phoneme or musical note is fleeting and gets its meaning in relation to what precedes or follows it in time. While we can often locate the source of a sound in the outer world, for the most part we do not experience sound as a projection in space. Music is spatially ambiguous. Were this reversed and tone was medium of light and color of mechanical waves, both media would take on a different feel. The appearance of the qualia themselves are thus to some extent determined by nature of what they reveal, in this example whether the phenomena reveal differences across space or time.

We will come back to this idea below but let us continue tracing the differentiation of visual experience. We have imagined the beginning the appearance of a world to consciousness as a simple binary response to light. Suppose the visual system evolves to a new level of development where it responds not only to the presence or absence of light, but to difference in the intensity of light. How would this new world appear to us? There are two aspects of light intensity to consider. First, there is the light source itself and the amount of light it makes available. The meaning of higher or lower light intensity is more or less light: More or less luminous energy and thus more or less ability to do work and have impact. We would expect a new subjective quality expressing difference in intensity to reflect this characteristic in some way. If lightness or whiteness is the initial experience of light, then the simplest additional differentiation would be to have more of the same. The subjective quality associated with perception of differences in light intensity is brightness. Phenomenologically, everything about a bright light is "more". We see more detail, we see further, we see with less strain. If we stare at a white light source as its intensity is increased, it remains the same white, but is somehow more. We feel more effect on the eyes. At some point, the power of the light overwhelms the sensory system, and it blinds us. In contrast, dim light places us closer to the black nothingness where there are no distinctions. The addition of a new quality such as color does not do the job here. Besides being a further evolutionary leap, adding a new kind of quality as opposed to only a change in degree, color presents only as a variation of light without conveying the sense and significance of increased energy.

A second aspect of light intensity has to do with the appearance of surfaces. We see objects because light reflects off their surfaces. The amount of light a surface reflects is a function of both the intensity of the ambient light and the reflective properties of the surface. This second aspect accounts for the property called lightness or value in color systems. In the original binary condition, where the sensory system responds identically to any amount of light beyond a particular threshold, the subjective experience is limited to black and white. However, now that the physical response varies with differences in light intensity, we need new subjective qualities to go along with them. What should we expect these qualities to be? Just as physical evolution proceeds in an incremental manner and building on what already exists, the subjective correlate of a new physical development will unfold out of and in opposition to the objects of consciousness that preceded it. The subjective experience must differentiate the quantity of light energy, but also preserve the original appearance of light. It would also emerge out of and in relation to the prior experience. It seems that the simplest way for this to appear in consciousness would be as a mix of black and white, or something like the perception of shades of gray. Prior to the development of true color perception, this is what we see. We have reached the world of the black and white photograph.

Continuing on, eventually the visual system becomes capable of differentiating not only the intensity of light, but also of distinguishing particular wavelengths, i.e., what we experience as color. Physically this comes about through the development of the cone cells whose particular chemistry makes them more or less responsive to specific wavelengths. Subjectively, a new kind of experience would emerge with the new physical state. It would not be entirely new, as it is only a finer discrimination of light. It would emerge out of and preserve the characteristics of light that already exist, i.e., reactivity to light in general and sensitivity to its intensity, but also add an additional quality associated with the wavelength. Here, a color-like experience is what we would logically expect. The new experience must emerge in contrast to what preceded it. The new experience must preserve the distinction of both the presence of light and differences in intensity while adding something to it. The ability to distinguish the presence and intensity of light is preserved within the perception of color. Color reveals light in general (every experience of the visible has color (treating white, black and gray as colors)) and can be assigned value (i.e., comes in lighter or darker tints and shades), yet also reveals a new quality, hue, which distinguishes wavelength. Perhaps this still does not account for the particular appearance of colorfulness in general or the qualia of particular colors. We might try to imagine some different appearance, but any radically new subjective presentation is neither consistent with the principle of differentiation in relation to current experience nor with the incremental change of physical evolution, since a large discontinuity in the quality of experience would likely require the same in the physical vehicle. This becomes clearer when we consider how the different sensory modes use very different sense organs.

The sense of hearing is a response to a different kind of physical differentiation. Rather than waves of electromagnetic radiation, the physical stimulus consists of mechanical, usually air pressure, waves. From an evolutionary perspective, it is a useful thing to be able to distinguish since it affords some knowledge of the environment when there is no light or line of sight. On the other hand, we can experience sound simultaneously with light. In fact, doing so increases its value because we can use the two senses together to get a better picture of our surroundings. However, to do so requires a different mode of perception. If we experienced sound waves in the same manner as those of light, we would need a clear way of telling them apart and distinguishing one kind of information from the other. As a distinctive physical state of the body, the sense of hearing has its own specific qualities.

As noted above, while to some degree the source of sound can be located in the external environment, it is primarily experienced as existing across time rather than space. We can make use of sonic cues to situate the orchestra, but music is not really of space. Sound unfolds temporally and is spatially ambiguous. Accordingly, the subjective experience of sound takes on very different qualities than those of light as appropriate to the structure of the underlying information conveyed in sound waves. At the start, there is a different kind of something and nothing consistent with a stimulus that comes and goes in time rather than lingers across space. The perception of sound, like light, also discriminates differences in stimulus intensity, experienced as a "more or less" quality that develops in reference to the initial sound experience and appears as loudness. A loud sound has more effect and is easier to hear. With sound, the addition of discrimination of wave frequency becomes the subjective quality of pitch rather than color. The addition of sound qualities and their contrast to those of light distinguishes and lends a distinct quality and appearance to both. It also creates new categories of existence in that we can now discriminate vision per se as a sense mode in opposition to hearing. The contrast provided by a new sensory mode responding to temporal change makes possible consciousness of the specific spatial quality of vision and vice versa.

Smell and taste respond to another distinct aspect of the physical world, in this case molecular composition. As a new kind of information different that provided by light and sound waves, they must be experienced as new sensory modes. We can watch and listen to television while we eat a meal and experience its tastes and smell sensations and recognize the distinctive qualities all at the same time. They exist in a kind of logic to one another. As with sound, to some degree taste and smell can be located in space. They can be associated with external objects but are mostly experienced internally. In contrast to sound, while they often have duration in time, they do not generally present their qualities in a relation across time as does sound. Presumably, taste and smell developed because of their usefulness in guiding organisms toward nutritive substances or other assets, and away from toxic ones. Accordingly, they come with a quality of valuation that motivates us towards or away from particular substances and organisms. They are pleasant or unpleasant. The chemical senses thus contrast and clarify the world of light and sound in that they reveal the distinction of inner vs. outer and good vs. bad.

The somatosensory system discriminates changes within or at the surface of the body, but what does it respond to from a scientific perspective? Largely it has to do with, and is the source of, the basic physical concepts of energy and mass. These are in fact aspects of the same thing, each formally defined in relation to the other. Mass is the resistance to change of movement, and energy is that which changes movement. Of course, this is the unity formalized in Einstein's equation, $E=mc^2$. The somatosensory system is the means through which we interact with the world. It is what allows us to move things, manipulate, and interact with them. Energy must be expended to do these things. Effort is required. Therefore, somatic sensation must appear to consciousness as opposition and force. The sense of touch is the quality of contact, which is a resistance or stoppage of movement of self or object. The proprioceptive sense of body movement and position depends on the sense of muscle tension and stretch provided by the Golgi tendon organs and muscle spindles and hence is also a phenomenon of effort and resistance. The interoceptive feelings providing a sense of the internal state of the body are to some extent related to these same categories (e.g., pressures and distensions), and others such as pleasure/pain, temperature, and arousal, etc., are also function of changes in certain energetic/chemical processes.

The somatosensory system must present its own distinct qualia, but it also exists and takes its meaning in relation to the other senses and vice versa. For example, it molds the sense of visual space, especially the third dimension, which only makes sense in the context of movement and effort. The cues imbedded in the two-dimensional image take on their meaning through their significance to interaction with their objects. It is the same for the cues of space and location in sound. Taste and smell become linked to interoceptive feeling.

In conclusion, the subjective qualia are first, largely a function of the characteristics of the stimulus with which they correlate. Secondly, as separate modes develop and differentiate from each other, they do so in relation to what precede them, both preserving the earlier differentiation and presentation of the stimulus but making further distinction. Further, each differentiation not only adds something new but also redefines the existence of its predecessors. Thus, in the example above, the experience of light begins with a nondescript binary differentiation. The emergence of sensitivity to intensity creates a variant of the same experienced as brightness. The further discrimination of wavelength must emerge out of and preserve this consciousness of light and luminance. Something like color seems the most efficient continuous means to provide this. As sense modes and qualities proliferate, each enhances the meaning of the other. What we end up with and how we experience the world today is the overall logic of differentiation and relation of all sense experiences. The outcome is the experience of the "real" world as we know it today. The development of the conscious experience arising from the senses works much like the procedure of Hegel's Logic, only applied to the logical unfolding of the development of sense experience rather than to categories of thought and being.

Above we asked the question of why the perception of light takes on what we know as visual qualities as opposed to appearing to consciousness in a sound-like manner. We pointed out that even if the raw medium of light perception were sound, then sound would likely appear very differently to us because of the specific relation of light to the objects it illuminates and how it exists in space and time. It might be useful to pursue this line of thought in more detail and try to imagine a world with a different sensory coding. Could it have been otherwise? Could sensory modes have been exchanged such that we would hear light, smell sounds or see odors? Note that that we are not concerned with physical issues such as the fact that the eyes are only sensitive to light and the tongue to chemical composition, or the relative sensitivity and discriminating ability of each sense organ. Here, we are assuming that at the level of the senses, there is no direct relation between the physical and specific subjective qualities. The seeming lack of connection between any particular physical structure or activity and lived experience is what prompted the question of this chapter. However, at the same time, because light has a particular relation to spatial extension and its perception also exists in relation to other forms of stimuli, it is not apparent that the world would necessarily take on an entirely new phenomenal appearance if such an exchange were possible. Because of the logical interrelations of the sense modes, we might end up back in the same place.

The idea that experience normally associated with one sensory mode might take on the qualities of another is not entirely in the realm of imagination, as people with the condition of synesthesia do just that. For example, some synesthetes experience colored music, where particular notes or keys or instruments may elicit particular color sensations. Dozens of kinds of synesthesia have been documented. Color mappings are common, for example, seeing letters or numbers as having colors, or to have colors associated with touch, taste, smell, pain and emotions, etc., but other cross sensory associations are also known, such as sound to smell or taste, or smell to touch and touch to taste. Now this is not quite the same as what we are getting at here. Synesthesia does not swap out sense modalities. The effects of synesthesia are generally supplemental to the "normal" sense and does not replace it. It is not that music becomes visual in all aspects and loses its sound qualia. However, synesthesia does lend support to the notion of cross-sensory experiences and help us imagine they might be like.

Suppose, for example, that we could switch the media of light and sound, with the former experienced through the subjective qualities of the auditory and the latter through the qualia associated with sight. Rather than the first differentiation of light taking the form of a quality-less black and white, it would have the corresponding sonic qualities of pure tone and silence, while the perception of sound waves takes on the analogous visual quantities. Discrimination of the intensity of the stimulus substitutes loudness for brightness and vice versa. Differentiation of frequency/wavelength trades the spectrum of colors for pitch, and so on.

How does this new world appear to us? As noted above, we cannot assume that these exchanged media would exhibit their current appearance. Each gains its full appearance through whatever else exists in relation to it. A second point made was that the nature of the stimulus affects appearance. In considering the transposition of the qualia of sight and sound, we must look at how light presents itself to the visual system. Light appears on the retina and in the visual cortex as a field. It is spatial in nature. Visual objects are generally stable. They do not come into and quickly pass from existence in the way of auditory objects such as speech and music. We know the visual field because our eyes move through it. It does not pass by in time. While perception may change with lighting conditions, visual objects consistently absorb and reflect the same wavelengths. Thus, visual experience presents as a stable spatial field usually consisting of distinct patches of color with distinct borders and taking up proportions of the visual field. In other words, color presents within the previously described properties of space.

If light is now imagined as presenting through the medium of sound, then sound must appear spatially. As we "look" across the room, perhaps what was the white ceiling is perhaps now experienced as a constant A note varying in loudness as our glance moves from areas in direct light to those in the shadows. Where the ceiling meets the blue wall, perhaps we now hear a distinct change to F#. We make out the gold frame of the picture on the wall by the change to Bb as our eyes follow along its border. As our eyes scan the picture itself, we experience a flurry of 1/16 or 1/32 notes of different tones reflecting the ever changing "color" and tiny details of the scene. We would know the size of objects by the duration of a particular note as we scanned the scene and its by its dominance of the total field of "view". Some of this might seem difficult to imagine because we are not used to hearing in this manner, but this is what we actually do now with sight. Our eyes constantly saccade across the field of view and our brains perform exactly this sort of processing. The point here is the any medium of experience would quickly take on qualities appropriate to the characteristics of light.

Now consider how "visual" sound might be experienced. The primary medium would be color, but it would no longer present as a spatial projection. We would rather be ambiguously immersed in it as we are with sound. We would exist in a pulsating wash of colors, color being the equivalent of pitch. Because of the way the auditory system works, there would need to be some coherent relation between the color and the phenomena of intervals and octaves. Melody would exist as the patterns of change from color to color. Harmonies might be mixes of colors. Tempo, rhythm and note duration would be captured in how quickly the colors changed and in the sequences of change. Timbres might be experienced as the changing patterns of colors, their blends and changes of brightness across time. As with sonic vision, the visual qualia we know today would be very different. When the two modes differentiate and exist simultaneously in opposition to one another, they co-constitute each other in the same relations as before and will create much the same world.

We can continue this line of thought with the other senses. Taste or smell vision would work much the same as sound. If we can conceive of such sensory media exchanges at all, it is because everything exists within the elemental parameters of consciousness, such as space-time and quantity that carry patterns of difference. They have starts, stops, boundaries, continuities, magnitudes, contingent relations, etc. Again, they would also function very differently. We would need more than five tastes to adequately substitute for the differentiation of light provided by the perception of color. We also earlier mentioned the element of desire in taste and smell. A gustatory sense mode would not be as useful from an evolutionary perspective if it was not connected to desire and revulsion, so it would seem that color serving in this function would have to take on a motivating valance of desire. Color would have to become a very different thing.

With the somatosensory, it becomes harder to imagine the application of a different form of subjective experience. We naturally coordinate vision and touch. Can we imagine reversing them, feeling textures as we look around us, while the body "sees" the contact of touch in the continuity of colors? As we already considered, pain and other interoceptive feelings are intimately tied to desire and motivation with respect to the homeostasis of the body. Pain could become associated with color, as has been known to happen in some forms of synesthesia, but it does not work as color alone. Because movement has a cost in energy, color experience would have to include a sense of resistance and effort in some way. Can we even describe the feeling whereby we know the position and movement of the body in space? The body is spatially mapped on the cortex (albeit in a distorted way) and perhaps it would be known directly as a visual picture of the space of the body.

We might imagine the possibilities of these transformations, but in the end, when they all come together in their contingent relations, we must come to a world that works like, and which we understand, exactly like the one we have now. The world is the sum of logical connections and relation, and the sense qualities as we know them take on the subjective feel they have because they are co-constituted in contrast to one another via specific relations. The world is exactly what it has to be.

THE RELATION OF CONSCIOUSNESS AND OBJECT

Have we made the case that the qualia of the senses are the result of a logical and necessary development, and that they do have some inherent relation to the sensory and nervous systems as understood from the external perspective of science? We have perhaps illustrated how post-sensory cognitive experience embodies the same basic parameters of consciousness that we see in the observation of external objects. Whether we look at a form or the activity of the eye that sees the form, we understand both perceptions through the same categories of dimension, size, continuity, interiority, etc. We both hear a rhythm and "see" it in the ear in terms of sequences of distinct units existing for various quantities of time and appearing at different rates of time. We have seen that judgments of thought are literally embodied in neural circuits.

We have shown that the form of sense experience takes on much of its subjective feel from the nature of the stimulus with which it correlates. Following from the characteristic of light that it reflects off objects in space with generally stable reflective properties, the appearance of light to consciousness through any medium must present in that manner, just as any qualia of sound will express the temporal nature of sound stimuli. Smell, taste and interoception must refer to the body and its well-being. Touch and proprioception, pertaining to movement and interaction with matter, must reflect the properties and relations of mass and energy. As each sense mode develops to further differentiate its physical correlates, the qualities of that mode unfold in a logical relation to their predecessors, as do the sense modes to each other. The appearance of qualities and the world we know is the result of this overall logical structure of this development.

Yet it seems there is still some part of sense experience that has not been adequately accounted for. We can understand how the perception of light might develop from a simple consciousness of light/no light subjectively experienced as a qualityless black and white, to a sense of intensity grasped as a relative mix of the two, to a sensitivity to wavelength appearing through color-like variants of this experience which emerge out of and preserve the distinctions that preceded them. On the other hand, it seems that this does not really explain the specific raw sensation of color or a particular set of colors.

We will come back to the question of sense experience later in the book. However, perhaps we also ought to consider the question itself and ask if we really need to or even can completely explain the subjective. The very way the question of conscious experience is often posed takes for granted certain materialistic assumptions. For example, "why does physical processing give rise to experiences with a phenomenal character", or "why is there awareness of sensory information", etc. The formulation of these questions assumes that the material has some objective higher reality status, and that consciousness is an unreal by-product of the physical that requires special explanation. This ignores the fact that the material world only exists through the subjective. Any scientific observation we can make or any physical properties we can describe consists of subjective experience and only appears through the subjective elements of conscious experience that creates them. Qualia are no more or less of a mystery than the physical phenomena with which they correlate. We do not need to explain redness any more or less than we need to explain the existence and properties of brains and quarks and electrons.

The assumption of a relation between mind and body is not in question. There is obviously some connection between the two views, but we are not justified in taking one perspective (which actually consists of the second) for granted and in assuming that the second is wholly generated by and an effect of the first. The real question is why these two appearances, your experience of my brain looking at an apple and my consciousness of the apple, are correlated.

This brings us back to the fundamental question of the relation of subject and object, which is a relation of perspective. They are the same thing from two different views. The subjective and its qualia are the perspective from inside the brain/body, i.e., what it is to be or exist through this brain/body. When we take the brain as an object of consciousness, we are experiencing it as it appears from the outside.

In the end, we may not be able to explain why qualia are what they are. The redness of the apple is simply what it is to be this brain and this body in this environment in relation to this something. Perhaps we cannot ultimately explain why anything is what it is. It is simply the nature of its being. All qualities and objects are always a function of a particular relation and perspective. The apple is always the apple for me, i.e., it is what appears to this particular vehicle of consciousness in a particular state. There is no apple "in-itself". There are neither "secondary qualities" belonging only to the subject, nor "primary qualities" of the object constituting its real essence. There may be a "something" that the object brings to the relation, but it has no absolute existence outside of a relation to what knows it or co-constitutes it. It is the nature of existence for objects to exist in opposition to one another. Existence is precisely the fracturing and subsequent integration of being. If some qualities seem more of the subject and others of the object, it is only because in the case of the former the relation between them is more obvious. Atoms are "for me" just as much as redness. The perception of atoms is after all, built with the constructs the human mind has at its disposal.

While there are many similarities between different perspectives of being, ultimately, for some aspects of qualia, it may just be that being is what it is, and we cannot say anything further about the way it appears. A particular qualitative experience is simply what is to be a particular mind-body complex in a particular state. Whatever out in the world may have contributed to that state, it has no absolute nature in itself that is the true reality. It only exists in relation to consciousness. In the end, it seems that if anything can claim to be the ultimate reality, it is subjective qualia, since these are the perspective from inside a thing, or of its being. Even these are only the being of a particular relation, the existence of a particular body in a particular state. There is never an independent, absolute thing in itself.

CHAPTER 6

Knowledge

We have examined the basic elements constituting the objects of conscious and have considered the relation of subjective experience to the human body through which it comes into being. Yet this only brings us back to the world of natural consciousness and the sense of separation between subject and object. We may understand at some level that the world, as the being of the body, is really our own self, but we do not experience it as such.

The world resists us and opposes us. We are not born knowing how to act effectively upon it and cannot instinctively predict the effect of most interactions between its objects. We do not instinctively know what will be good or bad or even what we will like or dislike. We do not immediately understand the subjectivity of other people or know how to predict their behavior. We do not know if they understand us or see the world as we do. We do not know how to live with others. All this must be learned through experience and then only with partial success.

Yet the world is not entirely unintelligible. It comes to us with recognizable properties even if we cannot consciously articulate their meaning. We have a certain intuitive sense of the world, if not innate than at least learned at an early age. Our survival depends on it. We grasp basic sensory properties. We have an intuitive physics that allows us to effectively move our bodies about in the world and negotiate its forces.

We are capable of interacting with and manipulating objects. We can adapt to their masses and resistances. This world comes to us without reflective consciousness. It is an animal consciousness based on instinct, a knowledge encoded in the body, in chemical reactions and hardwired circuits. It is prior to the knowledge obtained through the mediation of consciousness and language. We only come to understand this world through experience and thought.

The world is a construction of our own sensory and cognitive processes but is also experienced as alien and unpredictable. The desire to overcome this alienation underlies our wants and activities. This is the fundamental impulse of being towards consciousness of itself. At its origin, as the source of all, being/consciousness initially has nothing outside of itself of which it could be aware. The first step towards self-awareness of being is the differentiation of the wholeness of being. This differentiation was the creation of what we know as the physical world. At first, the concrete entities in this world are only isolated fragments of being. It is only when they are integrated, i.e., joined such that there is movement and transition between them in the moment, that there can be awareness. The integration of the parts restores the whole, but now as an object of consciousness.

However, this new whole object of consciousness is not immediately the full self-consciousness of being. An object of consciousness reflects being only to the extent that its parts differentiate the full potentiality of being. Integration of even a single differentiation enables consciousness of a whole of a sort but is a whole of opaque objects that still hide their secrets and only begin to reveal the nature of being. Thus, for a simple undeveloped vehicle of consciousness with limited discriminatory ability and integrative capacity, consciousness is characterized by a sense of a separation and alienation from the world. The ideas we have of this world are not adequate to what it is and can do.

A full self-consciousness of being requires the spinning out of all the possibilities of being, followed by their integration back into a whole in relations of consciousness. The only relation that connects everything to everything is a relation that passes through being itself. The realization of this relation is to restore the wholeness of being in integrated form where it exists in consciousness. To fulfill this relationship is thus the self-consciousness of being. This process of integrating the facets of being through consciousness is the acquisition of knowledge.

WHAT IS KNOWLEDGE?

What does "knowledge" mean? Knowledge is that which one knows. A typical dictionary entry provides several different senses of what it means to know. One meaning of knowing is the simple notion of awareness of or acquaintance with something, i.e., we have heard of a thing or seen it before. A second sense of knowing goes beyond awareness of existence or passing acquaintance but is the idea of having some understanding or information with regard to the object of knowledge. This is closer to our concern here, although we need clarity regarding the meaning of understanding and its relation to being. A third usage of knowing goes to the assertion of a status of certainty or truth for some content of consciousness. This is the emphasis in standard philosophical definition of knowledge as "justified true belief". Rather than telling us anything about the content of knowledge, this definition specifies criteria for accepting something as knowledge. We shall return to this definition later, but first we need to take a step back and ask what in the most fundamental sense knowledge consists of and what it means in relation to being and consciousness.

In its essence, knowledge is relation. Knowing is grasping and setting a relation between objects. Everything we know is a positing of connection. The most general relation is in the form of "X is Y". This is the relation of being, i.e., what qualities a thing has or the state it exists in. Every other assertion of knowledge is a specification of this relation of being, i.e., what particular qualities things have or what relations they have with other entities. What are these qualities and relations? In their most elemental form, they are the parameters of consciousness addressed earlier. They are ways in which we can experience.

First are the qualia of the senses, the pure sensory elements such as color, tone, taste, smell and touch that seemingly cannot be broken down to anything simpler. In reality, the distinction of quality and relation is only a convenience. Even these qualia exist in relation and opposition to other things. One color only exists in contrast to another, for example. However, we typically make a distinction between qualities which to belong to a thing and relations between things. If something is red, we do not think of it as a relation to other colors. Alternatively, if something is rectangular, we see that as a quality of the object (its shape), even though form is a relation of spatial and quantitative qualities, defined by the boundaries of what it is not. An object's mass and solidity might seem to be its nature in itself, but even these only exist in relation to the balance of internal and external forces.

What are the relations of knowledge? These are the elemental parameters of consciousness identified in Chapter 3 and 4. First are the general relations of Being: 1) Existence –Being at all: Something is or it is not; 2) Inherence – Determinate being, i.e., to be a particular thing or to have a specific quality; 3) Identity/difference – To be the same as or similar to another thing or not; 4) Conjunction/Association – To be with another thing in any parameter; 5) Affecting – To have an effect on the state of existence of something; 6) Accord/Opposition – The specific direction of affecting. Does something create or strengthen the existence of another entity or oppose or annihilate it?

Next is the dimension of Space and its sub-parameters such as relative position, dimension, contiguity and boundary. Time has similar sub-parameters, with entities and events existing on a dimension of past, present and future, and inside or outside of intervals. Quantity is relation of magnitude, the dimension of greater or smaller, more or less, and proportion. Opposing the static category of being is that of Becoming. Becoming pertains to relations of change in all other parameters. Change in relation to being is transformation, and in change in space is motion. A thing or relation changes with respect to other things or its current state. Motion is relative to other objects. Lastly, there is the category of Desire. Desire assigns objects and events a place on a dimension of value. They are good or bad. We like them or dislike them.

To gain knowledge is to assign to entities specific values on the parameters through which through they exist and to connect them through their relative positions on the continua of these parameters. Thus, we describe a physical object in terms of particular qualities of inherence. It has a particular color and shape. It has a specific size, number and relation of parts. It exists in a particular place or in relation to some other object. It used to exist, exists now, or will exist. It has effect on other objects. It is moving in space or changing its qualities. It makes us feel good or bad, etc.

How is relation possible and what has it to do with the self-consciousness of Being? In order for relation to exist, there must be some ground of relation. There must already be some form of identity between the terms of the relation. The elements or parameters of consciousness, the fundamental characteristics of things through which they exist, and which constitute their existence, are this common ground. They are its dimensions or spectra on which we assign things a place and value in relation to one another. As the ground out of which the existents emerge and gain their identities, these spectra are in effect the earliest differentiation out of the wholeness of being. When we relate objects on this ground, we become conscious not of just fragments but of the source that makes them possible. That is, integration through relation is the move towards move towards the consciousness of being itself.

As an example, consider knowledge regarding "where" something is. Anything we can say about an object in this regard will always be the assertion of relation to something else. Further, this relation is only possible because the two terms of the relation both exist in and through some common ground, in this case space and its qualities. If the apples are in the kitchen, we can only say this because we grasp that a kitchen exists as a separation and bounding of space, and further, that those apples also exist in space in a particular relation to that boundary, i.e., on the side of the boundary cut off from space at large. If the apple is near the bottom or top of a tree, or on the left or right side, we can make such statements only because we understand space as dimensional. Location in dimension is relative and requires some frame of reference. In this case, the apple exists in a spatial dimensional relation to the tree. Dimensional terms also have a larger frame of reference that allows us to describe these relations. Categories such as left/right, forward/back, and up/down largely refer back to the asymmetries of the body and to natural phenomena. For example, "up" is towards the head, but is also the body's relation to the force of gravity, or the direction of sun and sky versus the earth. The statement that "the apple is next to the refrigerator" depends on the spatial attributes of divisibility, continuity and perhaps magnitude. "Next to" means there is either no space or a small amount of space separating the objects. Knowledge is the assignment of specific values and relations on the parameters of existence.

It might seem that some properties such as form, for example, "belong" to the object, but this is also a matter of spatial and quantitative relation. Form is grasped in relation to what it is not, that is, where it stops. A shape is defined by how a boundary changes in space. Is the boundary continuous in a particular dimension (a straight line), or does it change in two dimensions at a particular ratio (perhaps a curve). Are the sides equal in magnitude? How many discontinuous changes in dimension are there (i.e., the number of sides), etc.? Likewise, location is never absolute. It only has meaning in relation to other objects in space. A map or globe is a larger more encompassing frame of reference, but the positions of towns and countries and their coordinates are relative both to each other and to the earth and its shape and movements.

What is true for spatial information is also true for the other parameters of experience. We understand time with similar qualities and in terms of relation to standard units. The same is true of quantity. Number is a system of relative proportions. Movement and change are relative to other objects and prior states in time. Properties of being are defined through contrast to other entities. This is the fundamental oppositional co-constitutional nature of all that exists.

The content of knowledge is relation. Relation is unity under a general parameter of being. By integrating individual fragments of being in relation, we become conscious of an earlier less differentiated level of manifested existence closer to being. In establishing knowledge, we track the tributary upstream and become conscious of something closer to the source, the increasingly earlier differentiation out of the whole. Integration is what allows consciousness of this whole, as opposed to the original state of immersion within it without awareness. Of course, we do not return to Being as a whole all at once. Each fragment of knowledge is only partial and limited integration, i.e., a relation of partial differentiated being. Each connection is a small step back to the whole. Integration is only as revealing as the completeness of the differentiation that precedes it. For example, if we separate the red wavelengths out of a white light, we will have red light and its complement of cyan in the residual light. The two together preserve the whole of the white light in visible differentiated form. However, this tells us little about the possibilities of color that exist within the nature of light. We must break out the white light as with a prism into all the colors of the spectrum to know its potential. Thus, the need for generative activity that spins out all the possibilities of being, with integration of the whole to follow. The self-consciousness of being itself only exists in the common relation of all potential manifestation, i.e., where everything enters into relation with everything else via passage through being.

The sense of separation and alienation from the world exists because we do not have consciousness through the full separation and reintegration of being. Sensory and mental objects, and our knowledge of them, only reflect the truth of being to the extent that our sensory systems can differentiate the possibilities in being and our cognitive systems can have adequate ideas to grasp the ground of their relations. Without that, the world remains opaque and unpredictable. What would it mean to have knowledge of these relations? Here we reach the question of the validity and criteria for knowledge. When do we have knowledge? How do we know we have it? What are its limits and what exactly is being related in knowledge?

THE LIMITS OF KNOWLEDGE AND ITS RELATION TO THE REAL

What is this knowledge of relationships about? Is it the comprehension of a "real" objective world that exists independently of us? From the position set out so far, it should be obvious that it is not. The phenomenal world for humans is the being of their bodies. Whatever is "out there", we know only insofar as the as the body can respond to and differentiate it. We must say with Kant that any world existing outside of us is ultimately unknowable in itself and that appearances to consciousness are a function of body structure and response. What we can know is ultimately ourselves.

As an example, let us return to the consciousness of light. If we had no sensors that responded to light, such as with certain species adapted to living in cave environments, as far as we knew there would be no such thing as light. Alternatively, if we only had a simple on/off response to a particular energy threshold, we could know no more than the presence or absence of "something". Experiences of brightness and color would not exist.

We can also look at the visual world as we know it now and consider what it might be missing. We experience color and brightness, but through the development of instruments have come to understand that visual experience is associated with wave phenomena of which we have no direct perception. Further, we know that these waves exist on a spectrum that continues far beyond the frequency range associated with the visible, and that these waves correlate with non-visual phenomena such as radio waves, microwaves and x-rays. They are also connected to the transverse waves of the associated magnetic field. All these phenomena thus have a common ground on the electromagnetic spectrum, but we would not have known that this unifying aspect of the world existed if we had not invented this instrumental extension of the senses. As it is, we still do not have direct experience of this aspect of the physical in terms of its own qualities. We still only perceive different colors and intensities. We know of it only by interpreting its effects on instruments as grasped through the parameters of consciousness we do have, i.e., space, time and quantity.

What else might be out there? Are we doomed to alienation from the world because at present we lack the sensory and cognitive equipment to perceive and process its finer details? Perhaps a complete consciousness of being is impossible given the current state of human evolution. The paradoxes and incompleteness of logical systems, the intractable problems of physics, the unanswered questions of philosophy, etc., may be an inevitable consequence of man coming up against his limits. Perhaps mankind has not yet evolved to a state where it is capable of truly returning to being in consciousness. Man, as he exists now, may only be a stage in the process. The universe is nearly 14 billion years old. It took over 9 billion years to arrive at the formation of the earth and virtually all of its existence to reach the consciousness of mankind. Time means nothing to the universe. If it takes another 14 billion years, or even if mankind turns out to be a dead end and the universe needs to start anew, it would be nothing in the scheme of things. It may be that at the current level of human physical development we are incapable of fully comprehending the universe and thus will remain in some degree of alienation from it.

Whether or not this is the case, and whether or not our knowing is limited to ourselves, this does not necessarily mean that the whole project of knowledge is entirely hopeless and that what we know has no significance to the ultimate nature of things. Perhaps the most amazing thing is that we are here to contemplate these issues. Living organisms are fragile, seemingly impossible things, and if not in violation are certainly struggling against the second law of thermodynamics. The world is hostile, and organisms must hold up against the forces of physics and competition with other organisms for resources. What survives is what can survive. What can survive is what is in some sense in accordance with the world. Organisms must be equipped to operate in the world as it is, to withstand its forces, to find resources, to fight off competitors, etc. This struggle has been going on for billions of years. The fact that we are here suggests that what is encoded in our bodies, and what we perceive and think, does in no small degree model the reality of the universe. At least it does so well enough to allow our continued existence in the world. We would not be here if it did not. In fact, when we consider the accomplishments of science in predicting the behavior of and transforming the physical world, we recognize that our knowledge goes far beyond pragmatic and crude tools for survival.

The physicist Eugene Wigner wrote a paper in which he referred to "the unreasonable effectiveness of mathematics". Whatever the ultimate metaphysical status of mathematics is, not only does it work extremely well but seems to work far better than we would expect if it was only a product of natural selection pertaining to immediate survival issues. For example, if our everyday sense of a quantified space is at all in accordance with reality, it would certainly be of survival value to have some means to measure and operate on those quantities in some manner. It would be valuable to know how far away resources or enemies are. We need the ability to sense the precise relations between body movements and distance in order to grasp and manipulate objects. We also benefit by knowing how the effort applied in moving the body would change when carrying heavy objects. A quantified sense of distance and mass undoubtedly enhances fitness. Yet it is not clear how these senses would develop such that we can determine a precise relation between the two as codified in Newton's law of gravity. In the course of evolution, we had no reason or opportunity to experience forces of attraction changing in relation to distance or mass.

This is one simple example, but there are many more instances where we have been able to describe the behavior of nature with exact quantitative formulae, yet without there being any apparent experience in the past struggle for survival that would have shaped bodily knowledge of these relations to such precision. The fact that these mathematical notions have such widespread application, and the fact that they work so well, and we can do so much with them, leads to the conclusion that they must in some degree encode the underlying nature of existence, or at least that which is relevant to survival. Yet, the elementary quantitative mechanisms that have evolved seem to include within them the seeds of something far greater than what is needed for immediate fitness purposes. The fact that we have survived and have consistently extended our ability to understand and act upon the world with quantitative thought suggests that this sense is at least some partial window into the ultimate nature of things.

THE CRITERIA FOR KNOWLEDGE

What does it mean to assert a claim of knowledge? What are the conditions or criteria that lead us to believe we have knowledge? To have knowledge is to be cognizant of a particular relation and hold it to have some "truth" value, but what does this mean? The content of knowledge is relation. Yet the question is complicated because there are different senses in which we use the term. One kind of knowledge is what we might call "knowing of", or what is sometimes referred to as "knowledge by acquaintance". This is the sort of knowledge we are getting at when we ask questions such as "Do you know John Doe?" Here the knowledge is simply of being aware of something in some vague way without explicitly calling out facts and relations pertaining to it. If I say I know someone in this sense, it means something to the effect that I am aware such a person exists. Perhaps I have a visual image and maybe some vague sense of what this person is about, but the specific qualities and relations attributed to them are not the issue. It is more that I am aware of the existence of a particular entity. Nevertheless, it is a kind of relation in that I make a connection between the name and an image or other unarticulated qualities.

Perhaps we could go on to describe this person and would then be demonstrating a second sense of knowledge that is the associational or propositional. This is what we are most concerned with in questions of knowledge. Here it is not a matter of simply recognizing the existence of something, but of holding a set of facts and relations about it. We can define its qualities and its effects and significance to other things. I might know who John Doe is in the sense of being vaguely aware of him in the first kind of knowledge, but here I posit a specific set of facts. Perhaps I know his background and history, things he has done and accomplished. I might know the traits of his personality. I know what he likes and dislikes. I can predict how he will react in a given situation. Academic knowledge also falls in this category. We hold in memory a set of relations pertaining to some topic.

A third sense of knowledge is of how to do something. This "how" is not just acquaintance with a set of procedural concepts, but also includes the ability to execute them, as when we know how to play a musical instrument or perform a dance. To know in this sense is to be able to carry out actions that will bring forth a result, for example making music or executing a set of defined movements of the body. In performance knowledge, in addition to a conceptualization of actions, a relation is formed with the body, between the idea of the desired outcome and the inner will and bodily feeling of the movement that brings it about.

We understand knowledge as relation, but acquaintance or assertion of some relation is not enough. We require that these relations have some reality or truth value. This leads to the question of what is meant by "truth". Most simply, truth means that the asserted relations are the way the world is. The propositions we hold are what we will experience in concrete existence. In the previous chapter, we noted that the categories through which objects appear to us from a first-person perspective are not different from the categories through which we think about the objects of science. Our concepts are essentially hypotheses we believe will be in conformance with observations of actual objects and events. We take these hypotheses to be true when there is identity between the thing seen and what we expect to see, between the idea and the reality. They look as we expect them to look; they act as we expect them to act. The recognition of identity and difference is at the heart of knowledge. In knowledge, there is identity of inner and outer or of perception and apperception.

That said, given that our knowledge of the world is knowledge of ourselves, i.e., it is a state of the body in response to something, and given the fact that manifested existence is always limited and fragmented, we also must say that knowledge and truth are always provisional and contextual. We cannot claim truth outside of the specific context in which we have experienced the confirmation of identity. We cannot claim a relationship of more than what we have actually seen. As we know, correlation is not causation. Until we reach an absolute relation to the whole of being there is always another factor that could render our knowledge void or limited. For example, Newton's law of gravity accurately predicts the motion of bodies in most circumstances. It is only under certain extreme conditions that it must be replaced with Einstein's relativity. It is not so much wrong but contextually limited. There may always be another set of conditions that will falsify an assertion.

The assertion of knowledge is not as simple as confirming the existence of a truth-identity condition. What we mean for something to be true is different from why we accept it as true. The idea of truth itself is separate from its justification. To accept that a proposition is true is to believe there will be a state of identity between it and any concrete instance of existence to which it applies. Justification is the reason for accepting that such a state exists. Is there a definitive standard for acceptance of an assertion as true and hence as representing valid knowledge? What constitutes adequate justification?

Just as truth itself is conditional and contextualized, there is no definitive criterion applied in awarding the status of truth, and hence valid knowledge, to a proposition. The standard of science is high. The fact of having observed a correlation is only the beginning. We must statistically demonstrate the improbability of our results have come about by chance. We must run experiments to tease out conditions that eliminate out alternative hypotheses.

In practical life however, the standards for what we take as knowledge tend to be much lower. We do not run experiments or statistical analyses in everyday life. A casual observation or two may be enough for accept a proposition as true, or at least enough to treat it "as if" true and as constituting a reasonable basis for action. Perhaps the greater part of what we "know" does not come by direct experience of a truth condition. Much of what we believe we know is socially derived. We accept as true that which trusted others tell us is true.

This lowered standard has both its advantages and disadvantages. While perhaps we do not "know" what we have not seen with our own eyes (and even then, it is questionable) and taking things on faith has its own drawbacks, we also cannot do without accepting a lesser standard of justification. Knowledge serves as a practical guide for action in the world. It provides the basis for response to the environment: X will have effect Y. I should respond with action Z. It is a guide for survival. We do not have the luxury of running scientific experiments on everything that enters into our lives. We do not have the time to figure out everything by ourselves, so we accept the word of authorities and those who came before. We may accept the outcome of single or few experiences as what is likely to happen in the future, although these judgments generally are not absolute, and we will abandon them when they are shown to be discordant with reality.

Part of the problem in defining knowledge is that we use the term in reference to very different things and different standards of evidence. What constitutes "justification"? For example, in one of Gettier's famous cases, the justification hinges the fact of someone having been told something by a seemingly credible source. In another, the justification consists of known prior associations and current observations consistent with them. These are not necessarily bad assumptions to make. They are valid reasons to be drawn to a particular conclusion. On the other hand, they would not hold up in a logical or scientific context or in a court of law. One might argue that the entire critique of knowledge as "justified true belief" (JTB) is not much of a challenge if stricter standards are applied. Yet in everyday life, we often make decisions and presume to know things based on much less. We cannot define knowledge as if the term means just one thing. We must specify the standard of knowledge. The only thing in common to all forms of knowledge is the positing of a relationship.

As part of the common philosophical definition, we must also consider the meaning of "belief" in relation to knowledge. The first question regarding belief is what is it about? In belief, we are concerned with truth. Is the subject of the belief actually the case? Does it exist? Does the world actually work in the way the belief says it will, etc.? The next question is what are we actually doing in judgment of belief? When we believe, we are treating a statement as if true, even though we know that perhaps it has not met an empirical test of truth. In a more practical sense, we are admitting it into our book of facts that we use to interpret and act upon the world.

We will get into the meaning and variations of belief in more detail in a moment, but first there is the question of what belief has to do with knowledge. Why must it be justified true *belief*? Suppose I am a student of physics learning about quantum mechanics. I might be well versed in the various concepts of quantum theory and may be familiar with the experimental evidence supporting the theory and be capable of doing the calculations, yet perhaps some of the theory just sounds too crazy to really believe it is correct as formulated. Can it be said that I do not "know" quantum mechanics? I certainly know *of* it. I know what the theory says. I can explain it and make predictions with it. However, the JTB definition says I must believe it to be true. It implies that this acceptance of the truth of something is crucial to the meaning of knowledge. Perhaps if we do not recognize something as true, it just is not there as knowledge. It has no practical significance and no bearing on our existence. We do not know it because we do not know it as reality. Possibly, we can think of it in terms of the truth condition for knowledge. Suppose quantum theory is absolutely true as formulated. If I am unable to believe in the truth of something that is in fact true, does that mean there must be something lacking in my understanding of it and hence I do not really know it?

However, truth is always provisional and so is belief. Belief is a kind of acceptance of the truth of a thing, but it also has degrees. The term "believe" as opposed to "know" is often used precisely to express that we do not really have certainty of knowledge. When we say we believe, are we not communicating that we take something "as if" true or as a best guess at truth, but also acknowledging that we are lacking a certain standard of evidence that would provide the certainty of knowing? We speak of religious *belief* because we have no empirical justification for faith. Yet in this case, the belief is often treated as the most absolute unquestioned reality and standard by which we live. In other cases, belief means no more than accepting something as if true. The evidence is sketchy, and we know it, yet we are willing to take it is an assumption for action because it is the best we have. That is the practical significance of anything we call knowledge: It gives us the facts by which we interpret and act on the world. Arguably, there are propositions that function as knowledge that are neither justified, believed in, nor true.

So where does all this leave us in coming to a definition of knowledge? The problem with definitions is that the natural usage of language is typically not very precise, and words can be used in many different senses. The sense of a word drifts by similarities as described by Wittgenstein's notion of "family resemblance". When philosophers start from vague usage of a term and try to develop a precise definition, they inevitably run into problems because different things are referred to with the same word. Yet there is no Platonic form for knowledge that we can look to for its absolute meaning. If precision of language is the goal, it is just a question of choosing a meaning for formal use. Does knowledge require a scientific standard of proof? Does it just need *some* evidence of existence or have minimal justification? Must we be fully committed to it? Pick one. Earlier, in considering logical operators we noted cases where the formal logical meaning is not that same as that of everyday language. For example, as considered earlier, a material conditional proposition with two false statements may seem nonsensical to everyday thinking even though it is true in formal logic. We have simply chosen a particular truth table as the definition of "if-then" to be used in the context of logical analysis, whether this meaning aligns with everyday usage or not.

Even if knowledge is always provisional and contextual, and if there is no absolute standard for defining when we have crossed the threshold of knowledge, we can summarize its general characteristics. Knowledge is about truth, where truth is the state in which the ideas and relations we bring to bear upon objects are identical to the properties they manifest in their actual existence. The qualities and activity they display are identical to those we expect them to display. By "actual existence", we do not necessarily assert a particular ontological status regarding this existence but refer to that which appears as a "real" physical world around us. This is the pre-reflective world created by the early levels of sensory and cognitive processing, the world that appears to the senses with qualities such as form and solidity and an appearance of stability across changing perspectives. Also included are inner objects such as ideas and feelings as perceived in their immediacy as objects as opposed to the meanings we give them and the relations we construct around them. For example, how we feel when we are in love and how we try to conceptualize it may be two different things. In short, truth is the identity of perception and apperception that holds in actuality and will hold over the domain of possible existence. Knowledge is the consciousness of relations that meet this condition.

This is the ideal. On the other hand, what we generally hold as knowledge is not so absolute. In reality, knowledge is provisional and contextual. Observations are always made in concrete situations consisting of specific conditions. There is always another event or a different environment in which a relationship may not hold. Some other factor may overturn a supposed truth or show that its validity only applies in a specific context. What we take to be knowledge in the real world often falls considerably short of the standard of absolute truth. Knowledge often means little more than that accepting some proposition as the best we have to go with, even if the evidence is limited.

Knowledge thus always comes with an asterisk, but there must be some justification before we are willing to take something as true or recognize another's claim of possessing knowledge. We do not accept a product of pure imagination as truth. Neither is one thought to possess knowledge where a truth comes to be held through sheer chance or coincidence. If there is no absolute standard for the acceptance of knowledge, there are at least certain general criteria that support its feasibility.

First, the relation posited in any statement ought to have been experienced in concrete reality. As the number of events supporting a proposition increases, the justification for its truth grows with it. Greater numbers of observers with the same experience also strengthen the assertion. It also gets stronger as it becomes less likely to have occurred by chance. Confidence in knowledge is increased to the extent that an asserted relationship of knowledge has been observed under varied conditions, reducing the possibility of confounding factors. On the other hand, a claim of knowledge is weakened to the extent that it exceeds the actual conditions of observation, and it must be rejected when reality contradicts it. There may be something that can be salvaged from it or it may be recast in some way, but the proposition as it stands must fall. These criteria are in essence what makes up the scientific method (more on which in the next chapter), and it is the rigor to which they are applied there that gives science its status as the gold standard of knowledge.

The experience of the senses is generally considered to provide the strongest evidence and justification of truth. Personal sensory experience also lends certainty. We believe what we see. However, even in this case there no certainty. The senses can fool us, as in mirages and optical illusions, or perhaps, as Descartes suggests, due to the trickery of malignant demons. However, direct experience is not the only means by which we arrive at the acceptance of a statement. We may feel confident in extending the domain of knowledge beyond direct experience by the use of proper analogy or logical inference. In addition, we highly rely on the social transmission of knowledge. We accept what others tell us is true. We may take the word of others believed to have direct experience, especially where they are trusted or when it is in their interest to tell us the truth. We also accept various forms of authority and expertise, such as when someone is in an advantaged position to know something because of special training or experience with the proposition in question. The existence of an open forum of ideas, where a proposition of knowledge has been subjected to scrutiny by and gained acceptance from a community of such experts, strengthens the justification for acceptance. Once again, belief is conditional. The first time experience conflicts with what someone has told us, e.g., a teacher has provided incorrect information, a media outlet is proven to biased or inaccurate, etc., they become suspect as a trusted source of knowledge.

Having said this, we should also note what knowledge is not. Firstly, the fact that knowledge is provisional does not imply a complete relativism or skepticism. We must dismiss the idea that knowledge is ever complete or final. However, as long as a statement holds up in reality, i.e., we see what it says we will see, then it is reasonable to assume that there is some truth in it. As long as it works and helps us to navigate the world, it has value. Likewise, the fact that knowledge is contextual or perspectival does not support an absolute relativism. One idea is not as good as another. Some are supported by evidence and others are not. Some work in the real world and others do not. Some perspectives are wider and take more into account than others do. Finally, the social aspect of the development, determination and transmission of knowledge does not mean that it is merely a social construction. The truth of knowledge depends on more than the fact of consensus or authority. Regardless of its derivation, knowledge ultimately depends on the test of reality and the judgment of the individual. If a false narrative carries the day, whether because of a lack of understanding or deliberate propaganda, that is the risk in knowledge by social transmission. We simply cannot have direct experience of everything we need to know to survive in the world. We just need to maintain critical judgment and a certain degree of skepticism about everything we think we know.

In the end, we are not so much concerned with defining knowledge as understanding its place in the project of being. It is the aspect of truth that we need consider more closely. When conscious/being imposes its categories equal to its object, it is effectively a self-consciousness. In the state of identity between perception and apperception, the sense of difference and opposition to the world is overcome. We feel at one with the world. Yet this sense of oneness in any given relation is only partial. An object is known in one aspect but is still opaque in a million others. What we need to understand is the process whereby we come to a more complete consciousness of unity: the development of knowledge.

THE ENTRY INTO KNOWLEDGE

How do we come to know anything at all? Knowledge is relation. A thing takes on its meaning in terms of other things. X is Y. One term always refers to another. Yet how do we know the meaning of this other? It too refers on to something else, as does that something to another, and so on. We look a word up in the dictionary and find a set of relations to other words. Each of these words in turn has its own set of words needing definition. We look up one topic but find ourselves led on ad infinitum. We never come to an end or sometimes return to where we started. However, if everything is forever held in suspension, how do we ever understand anything? How is it grounded?

Everything exists in a web of relations. As described earlier, each entity exists in opposition and relation to other things, existentially interdependent with that which it is not, as in a relation of figure and ground. An entity is not a thing unto itself, but rather is a center point or perspective around which a set of relations exist. We can define this center as narrowly or widely as we wish, from a single point and its immediate connections, to broad sets of relations creating complex concepts and systems, to the whole of being. An entity ultimately gets its meaning from its specific place in the whole of manifested being, which preserves the whole of being in the sum of its parts. The referring on and suspension of definition is not an endless infinity that never gives finality. Rather everything is co-constituted and finds its meaning in the whole.

However, we do not start off grasping relations of the whole and understanding the existential relations between the parts. That is the end to be attained. If everything is always relation to something else, which is in relation to another something, and that to another, and so on, how do we find meaning? In seems that there must be some anchor point from which to start. This problem of knowledge is essentially the same as the developmental problem of how human beings enter into language. We start outside of language but somehow come to grasp the meaning of words and relational constructions of grammar. By examining how this development works, we can understand how knowledge follows from it.

It begins with experience of the senses. Concrete sensory qualities simply exist. We cannot initially describe these objects of experience through words, but rather we point at them. If we want to communicate blueness, we can only point to some existing blue object like the sea or sky. We can then associate this referent with a specific acoustic stimulus. Later definitions of these qualities make use of these concrete examples. Green is the color of foliage or yellow is the color of a lemon. Sometimes the word for the color remains the same as that of the referent itself. Oranges are orange and violets are violet.

Yet even at this level, it is not so simple. Already we must distinguish different aspects of experience. If one points to a lemon and says, "this is yellow", the specific referent is not clear. Is yellow the entity itself, is it the color, is it the shape, the fact that it is edible, etc.? If next a banana is introduced as yellow, we can start to close in on the meaning, since this eliminates the element of shape, but could still think that yellow referred to fruit. Better as a tool to learn would be a box of crayons which are the same in every way except color. We seem to have an instinctive ability to conduct a sort of "triangulation", based on the fundamental judgment of identity/difference, where we grasp the common element in a set of objects and thus zero in on the specific meaning of the signifier.

This initial anchoring process goes well beyond simple sensory qualities. Early on, we are capable of recognizing complex objects. A child quickly grasps "mommy" and "daddy", and "dog" and "cat" as referring to specific people and animals. He must early in development have solved the problem of recognizing a stable object within a changing series of views and must be able to extract a range of basic qualities and essences that make up a particular object. However, this sense of essence is a largely an unarticulated one. Children, and for that matter adults, are hard pressed to name exactly what distinguishes one person or animal from another. Perhaps they can name a few basic qualities, but even (perhaps especially) philosophers have difficulties in settling on basic definitions. Language is unconsciously grounded in the concrete before we use it to construct knowledge.

What are the essences that make things recognizable but are also intangible? They are the body states associated with the early sensory processing that make up perception. As we noted earlier, color categories, shapes and forms, proportions, etc., correlate with distinct physical and feeling states and thus distinct objects of consciousness. These elements are imposed on experience long before we can consciously define them, i.e., before we can place them in explicit relations to other things. We automatically and unconsciously make associations between sets of these elemental properties and specific signifiers. The instinctive recognition of the specific properties is the legacy of our evolutionary history as organisms surviving in the natural world. The hard-wired circuits that created such experiences were the means through which life came to know and interact with the world, long before the flexibility of language came along and enabled the conscious forging of knowledge relations.

The elemental parameters of conscious experience are what make up the appearance of the natural world. The sense of alienation and opposition from this world is a function of the instinctive, unarticulated relation through which it appears. This experience derived from the natural world provides a secure anchor point from which we can enter into knowledge and higher relation. Emerson spoke of this in his essay, *Nature*, in which he referred to nature as "the vehicle of thought" and "words as signs of natural facts". The elementary experience of nature provides the first line of analogy that grounds higher thought. In turn, we can identify this nature as composed of the elemental parameters of experience described in chapter 3.

Complex ideas start from here. As we considered earlier, the basic characteristic of thought is that it is built up with analogy and metaphor. We start from these simple notions anchored in the senses and elemental cognitive categories, and through them create analogies by which we construct more complex and abstract ideas. Our understanding of abstract concepts is shaped by analogy, where they are compared to and contrasted with known examples to distinguish what they are and are not. Earlier we made an analogy to the operation of a computer, rooted in the wiring of the physical circuits and controlled through successive layers of processing from machine language to assembly language to high-level languages, to subroutines within them, to the natural language instructions provided for the end user of the application. A programmer at any level may do his job without having any idea of what goes on at lower programming levels or in the hardware itself. Likewise, a user can play a computer game or work a spreadsheet without understanding anything about how or why it works. Knowledge works this same way, where we almost unconsciously grasp complex concepts without realizing how complex they really are, based on layers of analogy eventually grounded on elemental cognitive qualia.

THE DEVELOPMENT AND LEVELS OF KNOWLEGE

In addition to an increasing complexity of ideas, the development of knowledge can be viewed with respect to consciousness and the overcoming of the separation of subject and object. There is a qualitative and quantitative development with respect to the degree that we are aware of relation and the extent to which it exhausts the otherness of its object.

The earliest form of knowledge is the knowledge of the body. Here we do not mean consciousness and knowledge about the body as an object, but rather the knowledge held by and encoded in the body. Here we refer to the unconscious knowledge carried in instinct, perception and movement. It is the knowledge of the animal, although it is equally present in human beings. It is the body's adaptation to the world. Because it is unconscious, it might seem questionable to call it knowledge. The neural circuits of the body are, however, the objective vehicle through which the experience of thought becomes possible. They parallel the structure of thought and function like thought regardless of whether we have conscious awareness of them or not. Although body knowledge is the first knowledge, it is hardly the least and is likely the greatest. The ability to survive in the world, to move and adapt, to develop and judge perceptions without conscious mediation is an incredible feat. While computers can calculate in a manner and speed far beyond what humans are capable of, perhaps the greatest challenge for artificial intelligence research has been figuring out how to model these basic everyday abilities. As Nietzsche said, "There is more wisdom in your body than in your deepest philosophy." In fact, if we return to the conclusion reached above that consciousness is not of an independent objective world but is the inner perspective of the body as it interacts with whatever it is that it responds to, we come full circle. The whole development of knowledge is the process whereby this unconscious knowledge of the body is made conscious.

The next step is knowledge that is still unconscious and reactive, but not merely hardwired in genetically coded circuits. It is acquired through the development of flexible circuits based on learning. Here we refer to mechanisms such as classic conditioning. There is adaptation, although it does not yet come about through the mediation of consciousness. When neutral stimuli of one perception become associated with other stimuli that evoke some instinctive response, the previously neutral stimulus may become capable of evoking the same reaction. Thus, as in Pavlov's classical conditioning, when food is presented to a dog along with the ringing of a bell, it comes to salivate at the sound of the bell alone. A light touch to the siphon of a slug results in a reflexive withdrawal of its gill. When that touch is paired with a shock, the touch alone now results in the much more powerful withdrawal reaction. These changes come about through chemical modulation of neurotransmitters that strengthens existing neural connections or in the longer run through the growth of new synapses. These new responses may be temporary or may become hard to extinguish. Yet it is all automatic and unconscious. A dog does not think to itself "food comes when there is a bell, prepare yourself for it". The reaction simply happens.

Classical conditioning is dependent on physiological reactions. Generally, it depends on relations to stimuli that evoke desire responses of the body such as pleasure or pain. It depends on animal nature, on feeling. Conditioned learning does not stray far from the immediate reactions of the body. It is the beginning of learning and plasticity on which the acquisition of knowledge depends, but what really opens the door to complex knowledge is the intervention of consciousness. Consciousness, as we have proposed, is present in and serves the function of forging relations. Once the capacity for consciousness learning and language has developed, the physical restraints on learning (i.e., the fact of evolutionary timeframes to develop new structures, fixed chemical processes, etc.) are greatly reduced, accounting for the explosive development of knowledge in man.

Conscious knowledge begins in awareness of association. The essential fact is that we consciously make the association. It does not happen automatically as with classic conditioning, where the body instinctively pairs some stimulus with pleasure or pain without conscious recognition of it. We bring awareness to consciousness that A comes with B. I consciously make the connection between the shape of a track in the mud and the presence of a specific animal. I grasp the association between eating a mushroom with particular qualities and becoming ill. There is not yet any knowledge of underlying connections that account for associations, only correlation. There is only the fact of their existence. Yet from a pragmatic perspective, correlation alone has great value. Civilization reached its heights without much understanding of what was behind the association of events in the natural world. Man knew of connections between the movement of the stars and the seasons, between methods of agriculture and the size of the harvest, between metallurgical processes and the transformation of ores into metals, between building techniques and the erection of great structures that do not collapse, etc., long before he had any understanding of why these things worked.

Some empiricists might have us stop here and leave knowledge as a description of correspondences in observed interactions. Yet we have always sought-after reasons for these associations and have been good at making up explanations, whether gods or magic or postulated natural entities. This is the next stage of knowledge, where we come to grasp the "why" of associations.

What exactly would it mean to explain something? What is why? To ask why is to ask the question of affecting relationships, which is to say that there is some existential dependency between the terms of the association. Let us consider the meaning of this more closely through an example mentioned above, i.e., the correlation of the positions of the stars and the seasons. The ancient Egyptians were able to make use of this information to predict the annual deluge of the Nile and the change of the seasons, but they did not understand the connection between events as we do today. Yet why is there a connection between the stars and the warming temperatures and longer days?

We start with the movement of the stars, or rather why they appear to move. Of course, the answer we now give to this question is that the earth moves, more specifically it rotates on its axis every 24 hours, and it moves through the heavens in its orbit around the sun. The stars become visible at different times because of the change of perspective. To fully answer the question, we would have to answer additional questions such as why the earth moves as it does, why it circles the sun, etc., and would get into ideas like, mass, gravity, the laws of motion, perhaps the curvature of space, etc. We can also ask why what we see changes in parallel with motion and would have to get into topics like perspective and optics. We can always continue to press back with another "why?", and shortly we will consider where it all ends up. However, for now we will leave it with a partial explanation and say that what we see and when we see it is inherently dependent on perspective. There is no visual object in itself. It is vision from a place.

So far, so good. We have a sort of explanation of why the objects in the sky seem to change position at different times of the year. Yet what does this have to do with the weather? In order to understand the connection between the earth's movement (and hence how we see the stars) and the seasons, we have to get into things like the axial tilt of the earth. We must know that the earth's axis maintains the same relative orientation to the background stars but changes with respect to the sun, so that at different times of the year, the northern or southern hemispheres will be pointing towards or away from the sun. Then we need to understand that the angle of sun to different areas of earth (i.e., whether it is more or less head on) affects the amount of energy (heat) received at a given location. This angle also determines the length of time a particular area is has exposure to the sun. Thus, we find a dependency between spatial relations (angle and position of earth in orbit) and the primary characteristics that determine the seasons. The transmission of radiation is not absolute but depends on a web of relations. Again, we can push the explanation back further. In order to understand the fixity of axis orientation we must understand things like the conservation of angular momentum. We also need to understand how angle affects the density of energy over a region of space, etc.

However, we have reached at least a partial explanation: The changing view of the stars depends on the movement and position of the earth, and this movement also relates to the earth's axial orientation to and energy distribution from the sun. The relation is possible because both elements exist in space, and the existence of particular states depends on the specific positions and movements of objects in space.

All explanation depends on the terms of the association being relatable. That is, they must exist on some common ground or parameter of existence. Typically, we do not push relations back as far as they can go. For a basic understanding of the world, we do not ask the secondary questions raised above, even though the whole explanation really depends on them. One would know more than most people, and probably feel he had adequate knowledge seasonal phenomena, by the simple understanding that the seasons depend on the revolution of the earth and the angle of the earth's axis with respect to the sun. Even most science as practiced does not question certain basic terms but takes for granted a reigning paradigm.

This is only a partial explanation, since there is much more behind it. In order to comprehend fully the existential relations between phenomena we really need to answer the deeper questions about space, time, mass, energy, thermodynamics, etc. To understand fully the relation and meaning of phenomena, we must understand their existential dependencies all the way to down to the most general ground of relation, i.e., being itself. The original emergence out of being is the question of all questions and is where we will find the unity of consciousness and object. Thus, we must press down to the most basic elements of conscious experience that are earliest appearance of the fragmented manifested world out of the wholeness of being and which are the general ground on which we can integrate this world back into a whole.

The development of explanatory knowledge is an advance towards a greater unity of knowledge, towards relating (and thus unifying) more distinct phenomena at a more general level. We can think of the web of knowledge as existing on two dimensions of the horizontal and vertical. On the one hand, connections can be narrower or wider in their relations and effects: A directly touches and affects B, but only indirectly affects Z through the intermediary chain of B through Y. This is the horizontal dimension. It increases by expanding association over greater distance and degree of separation. On the other hand, the vertical dimension is the continuum of ontological difference, climbed not by knowledge of correlation, but by the unification of entities through discovery of deeper properties held in common. It is ascended through greater abstraction and the reduction of difference. Its altitude is a measure of progress on the question of "why". For example, to establish that there is a chemical reaction between two elements is an advance on the horizontal. This is correlation, or the knowledge of "what". To understand "why" it occurs, through knowledge of a common atomic substrate in which they both exist, is to move higher on the vertical. It is movement towards being itself.

What is the end of the progression? The end of the process is where everything is unified and related to everything else. This is the point where all relation passes through being, the ultimate common ground of everything. There are two prerequisites to reach this state. First is the full realization of the potentiality of being, the state of maximum differentiation. This is the task of creative activity that draws out the possibilities of being into manifestation. Differentiation is followed by integration. This is realized in the relational activity of consciousness. The result is the self-consciousness of being. Conscious integration of the potentialities of being is the return to being in self-aware form. It is the end of the alienation of consciousness and object because there is no remaining separation of perception and apperception, no unexpected effects, no opaque otherness. Everything has its meaning it relation to the whole as a center or perspective within the whole. Each entity is a node within the entire web of relation.

This unity is the goal of all approaches to the pursuit of knowledge. In the objective approach of the sciences, it appears as the goal of physics to develop a "Theory of Everything" that connects all aspects of the physical universe. Subjectively, it appears in philosophy as the pursuit of being or "the one", or in religion as knowing God, the source of everything. The significance attributed to the unification of knowledge in being is exemplified in Herman Hesse's novel "The Glass Bead Game", where the highest activity of his Order of intellectuals is playing the title game, which consists of making deep connections between seemingly unrelated themes from all areas of knowledge.

We also have a sense of its meaning in our everyday lives, in the feeling we sometimes have in response to an idea, a book, or events in our lives, when a new idea suddenly clicks and all the pieces seem to come together, giving us a new way of looking at the world. Things become more holistic and meaningful. Ultimately, we aim to have this realization with respect to the whole of existence, where every relation is a relation that passes through being.

At the deepest level, what makes possible the relation and integration of experience are the basic parameters of consciousness, the elements from which all experience is constructed. These elements are the base upon which all complex objects, all higher analogies and metaphors making up our knowledge are built. They are earliest emergence of a world for consciousness out of the wholeness of being, thus the importance of identifying and understanding them. Having provided a preliminary accounting of what appear to be the basic parameters of consciousness and being, we now need to examine these elements more closely to see if further a unification is possible that leads us back into the nature of being itself.

Before doing that though, we will make one more digression. We return to the question of the meaning and objects of science in more detail. This goes back to the original question of the relation of mind and body and the notion that consciousness is an illusionary byproduct of the physical. We will look at the motivations for and methods of the natural sciences and consider whether these methods are adequate to all spheres of inquiry. We will also look at the objects of the natural sciences from the perspective of consciousness to consider whether they add anything to the parameters of consciousness addressed above.

CHAPTER 7

Science and the Physical

What is science? There is no definitive consensus as to its meaning among philosophers of science, but it is typically described as something like a systematic pursuit of knowledge about the world, perhaps with reference to particular methodological characteristics such reliance on observation, evidence, experiment, measurement, etc. We all "know" what science is in an everyday sense. We have a general notion of what is referred to by the term. Yet from a more philosophical perspective, these definitions are not really adequate. There are many ways of pursuing knowledge, and what makes something science is still an open question. Distinctions are made between science and pseudo-science, hard and soft sciences, etc. Many would equate science with the specific methods of the natural sciences.

However, if science is defined by a specific method, then its scope of inquiry will be restricted to what is amenable to study by that method. This becomes problematic when considering the subject matter of the social sciences and especially psychology as the study of consciousness. We will look at potential alternate methodologies for psychological research below. However, before focusing on a particular method, we should consider the purpose of science and what is essential to its goals. The first question is of the need for a particular disciplined approach to knowledge: Why science?

THE MOTIVATIONS AND AIMS OF SCIENCE

A rigorous method of arriving at knowledge is necessary because the instincts and inclinations that lead us to draw conclusions about truths of the world are not reliable. The price we pay for the infinite flexibility and capability for learning is precisely that the world does not come to us readymade with prescribed repertoires for action such as provided by the hard-wired circuits of instinct. Human beings must discover how the world works and how to act upon it. We must consciously forge relations between objects and events to create our facts about the world. Yet unless the ability to use this flexible learning capability of human beings is developed properly, we are perhaps worse off than the animals, given that our instinctive adaptation to any specific environment is relatively weak. The long human postnatal dependency on parents compared to animals means that a long process of biological development and education is required for man to attain even a passing ability to cope with the world. Even then, our naïve, everyday approach to knowledge is fallible. Thus, the need for a rigorous methodology as provided by science to validate what we think we know.

What is the character of natural thought and why is it problematic? The world as it shows itself in its sensory immediacy offers little precision and certainty regarding relations between its objects. As per David Hume, all we really perceive is association. B always appears with A or follows A in time. We do not "see" cause, which we understand here as a relation of existential co-constitution. Our understanding of the world is a projection. We impose categories of thought upon it. A causes B, A depends on B, A inheres in B, A supports or opposes B, etc. Things exist in particular spatial or quantitative relations, etc. It is the nature of the human brain to seek out patterns and generalities in what we see. We search for regularity and predictable outcomes that we can use to manage our actions. The immediate material of association is what the world presents to our eyes. As noted earlier, we are wired to attend to change and what is unusual in the environment. We interpret the meaning of the new by comparing and integrating it with knowledge we already have.

We register associations between phenomena and assume those associations signify the existence of underlying relations. We do so relatively quickly. A single occurrence of a particular association may be enough for us to assume that the world always works that way. We latch on to the obvious visible factor when the "cause" could be one of many or some underlying unseen variable. The natural inclination is to take correlation for causation. As we considered earlier, the human quantitative sense is not one of precise numbers. Beyond a quantity of three or four, there is only a sense of general trends and preponderances. The natural mind does not know exactitude and does not instinctively grasp the laws of probability. This is why the development of a formal statistics was necessary. If we flip a coin and it comes up heads eight times out of ten, we might be inclined to think it is a crooked coin. Yet statistics tells us that in any given ten flips of a coin, the result will be eight heads or more over 5% of the time. Applying the same standards he uses in his work, a gambling physicist would not accept this result as proof of cheating. Likewise, consider the claims made by a personal injury attorney of a link between some product and cancer. A jury might see the testimony of a large number of sick users as evidence of the claim. However, the rate of disease in product users may statistically be no higher than the rate in the general population. The link seems to be true because our impressions are dominated by immediate experience. The jury does not see the healthy users of the product that did not testify, or the afflicted people that did not use the product. We cannot "sense" the truth of the matter. We can only tell if there is a real risk associated with product usage through statistical analysis.

Another difficulty with naïve knowledge is its social nature, as discussed in the previous chapter. While the social transmission of knowledge is necessary and useful, allowing us to take advantage of the experience of the past, it also means that a lot of what we "know", we know without direct understanding or evidence. Errors and inadequacies potentially become the part of the canon until they are indisputably refuted. There is also an inclination towards a herd mentality. For whatever reason, we are disposed to accept authority and social consensus.

In sum, the relations of knowledge are imposed by the mind. Yet natural thought processes are often unreliable in producing valid relations. What we "know" is based on what we have actually experienced, which is the result of the particular manifestations and interactions before us. We do not take into account what we cannot see and cannot always distinguish which aspects of a complex entity or event are causative of an effect. Natural experience is vague, especially where the quantitative nature of the world is concerned. The reliance on social transmission of knowledge and adherence to group consensus makes us subject to mistakes of the past.

The aim of science is to get around these inadequacies. Consciousness projects certain relations beyond what is immediately given by the world. Science is fundamentally a means get outside of the impositions of the mind and put them to the test. We can understand the meaning of this more clearly by considering the methods of natural science.

THE NATURAL SCIENCE METHOD

Natural science begins with the hypothesis, which is in essence the relation that we would like to impose upon the world, and which originates in interior consciousness. A hypothesis might be informed by experience and data, but that data has always been generated in a particular context of concrete events. What seems like a strong connection between events might really be a result of some hidden factor or might reasonably have been a matter of chance. Ultimately, the objective is to comprehend the world in terms of reasons and underlying factors and not merely to generate a catalog of sensory observations. Scientific theories do not have any special qualities or metaphysical status about them. They are not independent of their creators. They do not do away with consciousness. They confirm it. However, they are informed and shaped by techniques that aim to get around the limitations of natural thought.

How do the natural sciences attempt to cope with the biases and inadequacies of natural theoretical constructions? First is removal of the relational categories of consciousness from the equation altogether. Whatever underlying factors he may hypothesize, the natural scientist only considers their observable manifestations. The results of an experiment must conform to what the theory predicts. Evidence must be based only on objective observation and not include what thought adds to it. Inquiry is stripped down to the data of the senses. The senses as we mean them here include not only the raw sense qualia, but also the early processing that constructs the basic properties making for the appearance of a "real" physical world. This includes qualities such as existence in space and time, magnitude, the sense of solidity and weightiness, i.e., that which is subject to measurement.

It is precisely the capability for measurement that makes reduction to the senses useful. Quantity is a general property of objects perceived to exist in space and time. Here we mean not just the inner intuitive sense of number, i.e., equality, more, less, dominance etc., but the possibility of numerical exactitude. As we noted earlier, exact quantification is based on the development of a technique. The basis of precise measurement is the notion of the unit, some specific (also sensory) object chosen as a reference point for counting. All numbers revolve around the chosen unit. A meter or a kilogram or a second has no significance in itself, except perhaps for the fact that these are good "human sized" quantities we can relate to in immediate and practical experience. The unit is simply a frame of reference. We will consider units of measure and their relation to consciousness in more detail later in the chapter. Their importance is that they give us a fixed way to tell us what happened beyond our vague feeling of it.

A second aspect of the stripping down to the senses is that it brings what we believe to be "objectivity". The assumption here is that all observers will see sensory objects and their measures in the same way.

I might interpret the meaning or cause of some phenomena differently than you, but if we both measure some object with a ruler we will generally concur as to its length. This allows replication of experiments and confirmation or disavowal of results because we have confidence that we are looking at the same thing. Beyond the senses, there is no assurance we constitute the object in the same way.

While not unique to scientific activity, the process of observation and gathering data is central to science. The value of generating new data is increased differentiation and broadening of context. Initially, perhaps the only difference between the casual observer and the scientist is that the latter applies a more rigorous and systematic approach. What science really adds is quantification of the data. Counting and statistically analyzing events serves to help avoid the cognitive biases of what we "feel" and "know" is happening.

Also characteristic of science is active intervention and the creation of new situations. Both in everyday life and in the lab, a lot of activity is just trying things to see what happens. Trial and error is a valuable technique that creates data and further unpacks the possibilities of being. What sets the natural sciences apart is the use of the controlled experiment. The function of the controlled experiment is to bracket off the higher constructions (i.e., theories) of consciousness and put them to the test. The controlled experiment isolates a term of a hypothesized relation such that we can say it must be this factor and no other that is responsible for the result. The experiment is an increase in differentiation, the teasing out of a particular element: It is this and not that. Even if the experiment fails, it still provides new data, new differentiation with which to work. Science also increases differentiation through the techniques and instruments it develops. Thus, microscopes and telescopes make things visible that we could not see before. Spectral analyzers, radio telescopes, particle accelerators, etc., opened up new methods of studying the universe. They expanded our experience beyond the senses. They provided new measurable correlates to subjective experience. We became able to see things from a different perspective with more information.

The social process of the natural sciences, while not unique to them, serves these same ends. Pre- and post-publication peer review provides the opportunity to look for holes in the research, point out flaws, consider alternate hypotheses, raise unanswered questions, etc. This process generates more data and leads to a further teasing out of possibilities. Experiments can be replicated and confirmed or discredited; counter experiments can consider other possibilities. The existence of this social process illustrates the need for a scientific method in the first place. It shows the extent to which theorists may differ in their interpretations of phenomena, and how much any one individual may miss the full picture and make incorrect assumptions when working from a single perspective.

In conclusion, the defining characteristic of the natural sciences is this stepping outside of the conceptual creations of the subjective mind, and their assessment by how well their predicted effects on measurable objects conform to the reality of these objects. A theory gains credibility when potential variables are isolated and controlled such that alternative possibilities can be excluded. In addition, it is not sufficient to have an appearance of association. Statistical analysis ensures that an experimental variable really did make a difference. It provides confirmation beyond the subjective feeling that B often occurs with A. The numbers tell us independently that it does with little possibility of it having been a chance event.

ISSUES IN THE SOCIAL SCIENCES

The primary purpose of the natural science method is to overcome the unreliability of pure theoretic activity by creating an external validation. Natural science makes its judgments based on whether or not the predictions of a theory correspond to observed reality in concrete instances of a given interaction. It relies on precise measurement of objects of the senses. The mere intuition that there is a connection between events is not enough. There must be demonstrated statistical significance. It uses controlled experiments that specifically isolate and control variables to discriminate between possible causative factors. It operates through a community of experts who have the opportunity to review and challenge each other's work.

However, the question arises as to whether this approach is suitable for all areas of inquiry. While the need for a rigorous approach, i.e., a means to manage cognitive imprecision and bias, limited data, the inability to specify operative variables, etc., is the same for all areas of inquiry, the specific method of the natural sciences, i.e., reduction to the sense object, measurement, controlled experiment, etc., is not necessarily universally applicable.

The true social sciences such as political science, economics and sociology are not particularly suited to controlled experiment. We cannot separate people into controlled economic or political categories. We can study examples of particular economic systems, socioeconomic classes, political systems or specific public policies, and generate comparative statistics, but social systems are so complex there is always the possibility of confounding factors such as unique histories, demographics, geography, political realities, nuances of policy, etc., that might influence the outcome of a particular policy or system. Research in the social sciences seems particularly at risk to the temptation of bias since its products are used as evidence in public policy debates affecting the material well-being of both politicians and their constituents. A natural scientific researcher who has invested a career in a theory might develop biases towards it, but theories in physics and chemistry usually do not have the same political implications.

The social sciences generally have quantifiable external effects, so they do largely have the statistical rigor of the natural sciences at their disposal. The number and variety of political economies in the world offers at least some opportunity to compare and contrast policies and systems. What these disciplines lack is the true testing and isolation of variables. There is a complexity in social systems and behavior beyond that of the natural sciences. Social variables are ever changing and must be interpreted by the participants. Unlike the natural world, the social world cannot be reduced to a few basic laws. Masses and molecules do what they must according to according to what seem to be a universal physical laws. It is not clear how these social sciences could do better. In any event, even if they do not perhaps reach the rigor and standards of evidence of the natural sciences, they still have value in revealing facts and new ideas.

However, as the subject here is consciousness, our main interest is in psychology, which essentially is or should be the science of conscious experience and its effects on behavior. The problem with psychology taken as a natural science is that its primary subject matter is precisely what these sciences strip away from inquiry. Natural science psychology reduces its subject to the external effects of mind. The result is approaches such as behaviorism, which limits psychological inquiry to the measurement of observable behaviors, or biological schools of thought that focus on physical correlates of behavior. These are useful lines of inquiry, but they are also incomplete.

If we are interested in understanding these external correlates it because they refer back to the perspective of the interior. The subject matter of psychology is the subject: The sensations, desires, thoughts, and emotions and how we live them. Our ultimate interest is largely in what is known as "theory of mind", the ability to understand the mental states of self and others as subjects. In other words, the motivation is precisely to understand the inner lived experience of self and others that is foreclosed by methods limited to measurement of sense data. We want to understand how personality and experience creates a person's perspective on the world and their motivations. What is the world of the "extrovert" or "introvert"? How do men or women see the world in contrast to the opposite sex such that they behave as they do? How do we understand the meaning of our emotions as we live them? As addressed earlier, emotion is not just a physical response, but also a reflection of how we interpret a particular situation. For example, anger is not merely physiological arousal, but an interpretation of how another sees us. Love is not merely a burst of chemicals or an ineffable feeling of attraction, but reflects a particular certain meaning, whether explicitly understood or not, granted to the loved one. The behavior of a person in love depends on how he/she experiences the emotion and perceives the object of love. In clinical psychology, if we want to understand pathological behavior and engage patients in a clinical relationship, we need to understand how they experience their situation. How do schizophrenics, depressives, the autistic, the traumatized, addicts, etc., live the world? Knowing that there is a problem in the functioning of neural circuits only gets us so far.

The interior perspective is not merely a curiosity. Consciousness is what drives motivation. The way we see the world, however realistic or unrealistic our assessment of it, is the source of the will to act. As we have proposed earlier, consciousness is where we forge new relations. If we are to change behavior, we need to become aware of and consciously change our interpretation of the world. Whatever the value of psychoactive medications in alleviating or managing certain symptoms, they generally do not cure anything and may have serious side effects. Changing our lived world takes the effort of consciousness. We should not expect that this kind of change could come from medications and more than we might hope we could learn calculus by taking a "math pill" or learn by passively listening to recordings while we sleep. This kind of learning requires the active engagement of attention to integrate the new material. In other words, it needs exactly what consciousness provides.

Any approach that has man take thought and affect as external object to himself loses the possibility of integrating the experience into consciousness and will. For example, Freud couched psychoanalysis in such terms with his energetic metaphors and hypothetical entities such as Ids and Egos, psychosexual stages and Oedipus complexes, etc. However, whatever insights may underlie these constructs, any value in psychoanalytic therapy comes not from relating our current lives to a theoretical construct, but from providing awareness of the tacit warped assumptions and beliefs that make up our lived world and contribute to the frustration of desire in the present. Likewise, knowing what brain mechanisms are involved with a behavioral pathology does not in and of itself help a patient or those around him. That requires the development of conscious coping mechanisms.

Yet these lived experiences are exactly what the natural sciences strip out. Behaviorism is perhaps the most consistent with natural science positivism in restricting its field of inquiry to sensory measurable behavior, but it is also the most impoverished with respect to the world of conscious experience. Biological approaches likewise meet the test of empiricism, where the correlates to neurophysiologic findings are observable events, but they are also lacking to the extent that they reduce psychology to the brain.

The problem is how to preserve and test the subject matter of consciousness in a way that satisfies scientific standards. This problem goes back to earliest attempts to develop a scientific psychology, such as Fechner's "psychophysics". Among other things, Fechner is known for the development of a law establishing a quantitative relationship between the subjectively experienced and actual physical intensity of a stimulus. The problem with this is, as we have examined earlier, that we do not have the precise quantitative sense needed to measure inner sensations accurately. Such methods might reveal general tendencies but do not provide the basis for a precise mathematical formula. Much of modern academic psychology has the same problem when it uses self-reports and surveys as a source of data. Anyone who has ever filled out a survey or evaluation form knows how questionable the data collected from these instruments is. Social psychology in particular has been a target of criticism for a low reproducibility of results. Among other problems, many social science experiments assume that the subject's interpretation and attitude towards the test situation accurately reflects what the experimenter wants to test. These experiments do not address the intentionality of the subject. The data derived from these methods is then subjected to statistical analysis, but this is putting a lipstick on a pig. The natural sciences do not have this problem. Quarks do not need to interpret anything. They simply change their state as the laws of the universe dictate they must.

As an alternative, qualitative approaches to psychology such as phenomenological description have been developed. These make it possible to preserve the experience of consciousness as subject matter but do really meet the key criterion of science, which is to get outside of and put internally constructed meanings to the test? These approaches collect descriptions of experiences as data and try to investigate them in a rigorous way, but no matter how many descriptions we compile, they still come from, and are interpreted through, the unreliable subjective perspective from which we needed to escape in the first place. No matter what kind of reduction we claim to perform, as soon as we interpret and impose a structure on the data, we are in essence creating a theory.

If we could rely on ideas derived only from careful observation, we would have no need for experimental science. The natural sciences force us to get outside of cognitively imposed structures and confirm their validity by comparing their predicted effects to concrete, "objectively" measured, sensory "reality". The activity of describing experiences and extracting essences is of the same order as theoretical activity. It never shifts perspective. Nor is there the possibility of isolating and teasing out essential and non-essential elements by creating a controlled finer differentiation of the data. Acquiring descriptions of experience from many subjects is perhaps a way of bringing forth more possibilities and perspectives, but most subjects comprehend their experience in vague terms, and it depends on the researcher to construct general essences from them. As noted earlier, we are all naïve theorists in our everyday lives. Our naïve ideas mostly consist of common social tropes, multi-layered analogies and metaphors, the origins of which are vague semi-conscious feeling, and folk psychology. This is obviously a useful thing. We have survived quite well with it, but we cannot necessarily claim it as truth.

However, while we need not accept the entire line of argument of eliminative materialism, we must acknowledge that naïve folk psychologies are not particularly clear, and how we naively conceptualize subjective life is not necessarily an accurate picture of what experience presents in its immediacy at the elemental level of conscious. Any attempt to find meaning and give structure to such naïve descriptions will require much to be imposed by the understanding of the researcher. This is not to say descriptive activity of this type is not worthwhile, and what it aspires to can be seen as a major aim of psychology, but it is only part of the process.

Is it possible to have a psychology that preserves and elucidates the inner world of conscious experience but also connects it to external objects of the natural sciences and allows for rigorous testing of what we imagine this experience to be? In order for consciousness to have objects, it must exist in a differentiated form, or in other words, it exists through a "physical" vehicle, however subtle. The nature of the vehicle creates the kind of objects available to consciousness. There is always an external "physical" correlate to conscious experience, and therefore neuroscience should ultimately be able to provide an external perspective from which phenomenological experience can be examined and tested in the way of the natural sciences.

The question is how to connect the inner and outer perspectives and to explore both without a reductionism to one side or the other. From the perspective of consciousness, we cannot say that experience is simply what we naively describe it as and think it to be. Making sense of experience to give meaning to it is a constructive theoretical activity. On the other hand, neuroscience cannot simply reduce conscious experience to physiological structures and chemical activities, as if love was "really just" a set of hormones and neurotransmitters activating particular centers in the brain. The point of knowing about love is to negotiate it as we live it. A person dealing with a lost love is not helped by being told they have too much oxytocin on the brain.

How do we connect the two perspectives? In chapter 5, we considered how inner and outer experiences often have the same structures consisting of the basic parameters or elements of consciousness, differing only in medium. It is at this level that we might connect consciousness to neurophysiology such that we can give meaning to lived experience and also describe its external coordinates.

On the side of consciousness, we must get beneath the higher constructions and analogies of our folk psychologies and understand experiences in terms of the elemental qualia categories that underlie them. All experiences can be broken down to raw sense qualia and the cognitive elements that find patterns in them and create higher objects. That is, we define them in terms of space, time, number, movement, etc., and their variations in the respective sub-parameters of each. We grasp them in terms of the basic relations of being, their inherences, identities and differences, their associations and conjunctions, their contingencies and effects, oppositions and accordance with other objects. This subjective perspective we can get at through introspection and phenomenological description, as well as by making use of empirical data of the type generated currently by academic psychology. However, as we covered earlier, these relational structures are also embodied in rudimentary neural structures and operations. Neurons are, in different media, spatial fields and quantities, assertion, negations, associations, contingencies, etc. Therefore, we should in principle be able to validate subjective experience by mapping to its neurophysiologic complements.

Exactly what such a psychology would look like is beyond the scope of this book, but we can provide some examples. On the subjective side, we would develop structures of experience in terms of variances on the elemental parameters of consciousness. Earlier in the discussion of self-actualization, we considered differences in the type of object that becomes one's preferred vehicle of desire. Variances between individuals in the presence and dominance of such objects and how they color one's conscious experience of the world provides a starting point for the study of personality: Is one oriented towards the immediate experience of the senses, the affect, the interpersonal, the somatic, or abstract objects of consciousness? Is there persistence or domination of particular objects, or a cutting off of others? We can also consider personality in terms of how we live in time and space. Is there a focus on the past or is the past cut off? How does one live the present and future? Is one dominated by the immediate emotions and sensations of the moment without any sense of the future consequences (also related to causality) as in manic states and impulse or emotional control problems? Does one ignore the present in pursuit of the future? Many phenomena can be viewed in terms of interiors/exteriors and boundaries such as when we disown or project our feelings to the world outside us. Earlier we described emotions as being a cognitive assessment of a situation along with an adaptive body response. We considered love as the inclusion of another within the boundaries of self. In happiness, we have a wide beam expansive openness towards the world and future. In fear, attention contracts to a laser beam focus. Psychopathologies can be understood, as alterations in the categories through which construct inner experience as noted above in manic states. Depression, for example, is a contraction and separation from the world the of future possibilities. The forces of resistance weigh us down, and we feel the lack of arousal and energy needed to act. We construct narratives limiting our possibilities based on flawed causality, etc.

Development of a framework for comprehending subjective experience and meaning is one side of the equation, but how do we attain testability and connect the phenomenological to the physical? Fairly recent technologies such as functional magnetic resonance imaging (fMRI) have opened up a new world for cognitive science. They are good at locating specific areas of the brain that are active during particular experiences and at least pointing us in the right direction, but the information gained is generally too gross to tie to specific structures of experience. As proposed earlier, the physiological parallel to the experience of perceptual forms and cognitive judgments resides in the wiring and synapse chemistry of individual neurons. It is found in the in the specific connections and firing contingencies. Thus, we would need methods than can discriminate microstructures of the brain, the detailed connectomes. We need to look at the brain at the level of detail of a circuit board.

Perhaps the science is not there yet, but the use of single-unit recording is a start. Perhaps improvements in research methods will bring us to a point where we can grasp the nuances of experience as lived in terms of the same categories through which we understand their correlate individual neural circuits. As an example, the discovery of grid cells has given us insights into the physical correlates of the ability to track location, but the workings of these cells might also clarify our conscious construction of space itself. Natural science and philosophy/psychology would be attacking the same problem from two directions, and each would provide insight to the other. How we live particular experiences will tell us where and what to look for in the brain, and what we see in the brain will help clarify subjective experience. The ultimate end would be to see the physiological as consciousness and consciousness in the physiological.

THE MATERIAL OBJECT

Our final topic in this consideration of science is the idea of materialism, the notion that physical matter is the true reality and that everything else can be explained in terms of matter and physical phenomena. Consciousness and thought are held to be epiphenomena of matter, side effects or illusions of a true physical reality. Again, in questioning this position we do not advocate a dualism or argue that there is no direct relation between the objects of consciousness and the structures and operations of the brain. The issue is not whether that which appears to consciousness has a relation to or even a partial dependency on the "physical". The problem is the primacy given to this specific type of object to consciousness. It is the idea that what appears in the guise of the material has some exceptional reality status. It's what "really" exists. It is effectively the acceptance of a metaphysical status where these material objects are an absolute "in-itself". A version of this idea is expressed in statements to the effect that we are really just atoms, the ultimate reality, knocking about by chance. What we are is just whatever happens to stick due to physical laws and with no additional meaning

Why is there support for materialist philosophy? Likely it is in part due to the success of the natural sciences. However, we can accept the value of the method without the metaphysics. We can acknowledge the usefulness of the natural science method and grant that it provides a rigorous standard of truth without claiming that the only valid way to look at things is as sense data and as external material objects. There is no primacy of one perspective over the other in their reality or value. It is just that we have not yet discovered as effective a method to test and verify inner subjective experience.

It does not make sense to deny or demote the consciousness that gives us the objects claimed to be its source. The observations of science exist through consciousness and are not independent of it. Objects of the senses have no special status in this regard, but only have a particular way of appearing to consciousness that lends this sense of their having an independent reality. Phenomenology tells us that this experience arises in how these objects present themselves as a predictable flow of views. There is an anticipated continuity with change of perspective. The awareness of perspective is perhaps what leads to the feeling of independence. The object changes its appearance as we move, unlike, for example, an afterimage of a bright light that remains the same no matter how we move our heads or what we look at, and so appears to belong to ourselves. This experience deriving from the change of perspective begins to provide a general framework for the sense of the transcendent, but if we want to understand the consciousness of the physical objects of the natural sciences, it seems we should consider the specific qualities of which they are composed and their relations.

The science of the physical relies on quantified data of the senses. If we want to understand what its objects really are, then we ought to look at what is actually being measured. There are many different units of measurement used in the sciences, but most of them are derived from simpler units. Just as the appearance of the everyday world is constructed from complex combinations of elemental experiences, most scientific measures are composed from simpler units. The International System of Units (SI) defines seven base units that are the building blocks from which all others are derived. As the basic properties measured in physical objects, a study of the meaning and origins of these base units should tell us something about what constitutes consciousness of the material world. We will see if there is anything new or special in the objects of science beyond the parameters of conscious experience we have already identified and if they provide and additional insights into the nature of the physical world. The seven base units are the second, meter, kilogram, ampere, kelvin, mole and candela.

The second is the unit of time, one of the previously identified elementary dimensions of conscious experience. In the SI system, the second is defined "by taking the fixed numerical value of the caesium frequency $\Delta\nu_{Cs}$, the unperturbed ground-state hyperfine transition frequency of the caesium 133 atom, to be 9,192,631,770 when expressed in the unit Hz, which is equal to s^{-1}." Earlier we questioned the extent to which there was an actual sense of the passage of time and saw that for the most part we mark time through recurring events assumed to occur over consistent time durations or through the quality and quantity of memories. Scientific thought does the same, measuring time through a count of atomic level cycles. We must accept that these events are of consistent duration. The intuition of time arises in the sense of the passing moment. In this case, we "scale down" from this basic sense by analogy and dissect time below the level of possible experience based on cyclical events only our instruments can record and count.

The meter is the unit of length, or unit used for the measurement of space, again one of the elemental parameters of everyday conscious experience. The formal definition of the meter is based on how far light travels in a specific fraction of a second (as defined above) based on the accepted physical constant of the speed of light. The specific SI definition is not important for our purposes. It and numerous previous formal definitions are really just approaches to standardizing an approximate unit in use since ancient times and chosen presumably for its human scale and practical usefulness. The formal definition of length does not provide any additional insight into the nature of space as experienced in everyday consciousness. The important point is just that measurable space is a basic parameter of science.

The kilogram is the measure of mass. Mass, along with its complement energy, is one of the most fundamental concepts of physics. We have not clearly identified it as an elemental parameter of experience and so need to closely look at its meaning and its origins in consciousness. There are a number of ways mass can be operationally defined, one of which is to see it as the quantity of inertia, or resistance to acceleration, possessed by an object. We see that mass and energy are inseparable and are reciprocally defined. The SI derived unit of energy, the joule, is defined as the work expended by a force of one newton through a displacement of one meter. The newton in turn is defined as the force needed to accelerate one kilogram of mass at the rate of one meter per second squared in the direction of the applied force. In other words, the quantity of mass of an object is defined as what it takes to move it, and the quantity of energy is how much it can move.

The sense of mass in consciousness arises in the everyday experience of heaviness and resistance in objects when we try to move them. The experience of weightiness is part of what leads to the sense of real material objects of substance. This sense originates in the somatosensory system, in the Golgi tendon organs that sense changes in muscle tension. We experience a difference in the tension associated with lifting, carrying, pushing and manipulating a range of objects. As with its complement, we sense energy in the amount of movement in relation to the tension and resistance of the object. We apply lots of energy when we strain at movement. We feel "energized" when we can effortlessly do many things. When we are moved without an accompanying consciousness of our own effort, we sense the presence of external forces acting upon us. We sense energy in nature when we are buffeted by the wind or feel the force of ocean waves and their ability to overpower our resistance. We know the force of gravity when we fall from a height or see seemingly strong objects shatter when they hit the ground. From the cradle, we develop an intuitive physics where we grasp correlations between object appearance and the phenomenal accompaniments of mass and energy. We develop expectations for how objects will change and move in interactions. "Real" physical objects act in certain predictable ways.

The measurement of mass begins on the human scale, based on quantities we can actually sense and on practical needs. The kilogram was originally based on the mass of a liter of water, a quantity that can we actually lift and feel the quantum of tension and effort associated with the act of lifting or pushing it. The direct sense of mass exists over a range, from the smallest discrimination of muscle tension to point where we can no longer move objects. Beyond that range, we cannot feel quantity, and only infer its meaning via analogy and the general principles of addition and proportional magnitude. As with number in general, the human ability to identify precise quantities of mass only exists over is narrow range.

Regarding the formal scientific measurement of mass, until recently (2019) the kilogram was defined by a standard physical artifact, itself based the original definition of a specific quantity of water. In its latest formalization, the kilogram is defined via the Planck constant, which relates the energy carried by a photon to its frequency. How this all works is rather complicated, but for our purposes it can be thought of as the force needed to balance the weight of the standard kilogram, i.e., an energy equivalent. The main point here is that mass and energy are elementary categories of experience and that they originate in particular subjective somatosensory experiences.

The ampere is the unit of electric current. In everyday life, we have limited sensory faculties and little experience of what we think of as distinctly electromagnetic phenomena. From the beginning, we would have observed lightening and experienced other static effects like shocks or attraction between objects. We would have experienced the attractive and repulsive forces between magnetic stones, although we would not have realized their connection to electrical phenomena. Our ideas and measures of electric current come out of the lab rather than from everyday experience. The need for a specific unit of electrical flow arises out of the importance and usefulness of harnessing electromagnetism for science and industry. Nevertheless, descriptions of laboratory phenomenon are still rooted in the categories that consciousness has at its disposal, and electromagnetism must be understood in those terms. The only difference from the previous measures is that here the focus is the laboratory observations themselves, rather on the experience of everyday life.

The concept of current has a natural analogy in the flow of river. In elementary terms, this reduces to movement through a bounded space. In an electrical current, the bounded channel is usually a wire of some length through which something moves at a measurable rate. What is it that moves? Electrical current is the flow of electrical charge past a point or region. The SI unit of current, the ampere, is based on the fixed value of the "elementary charge", which is the magnitude of charge carried by a single proton (or negative charge carried by a single electron). Now what is "charge"? Electric charge is a defined as a physical property that causes matter to experience a force within an electromagnetic field. Charges are either positive or negative, with like charges repelling and unlike charges attracting one another.

So here is the root of our science. Force, as noted above is an interaction that changes the movement of an object. In this case, the interactions are these attractions and repulsions. We can consider this strictly empirically is spatial terms, i.e., the objects move to have more or less distance between them. However, idea is also rooted in the experience in everyday experience when we feel pushed away or pulled towards something or someone, as in the feeling when we place two magnets in close proximity and effort is required to prevent them from pulling together or repelling each other. In other words, charge, and so electrical current, is another energy phenomena rooted in the sense of tension and movement of the body. The amount of charge is simply the multiple of the movement resulting from the interaction with a single proton.

The kelvin is the unit of thermodynamic temperature. We have an immediate sensory experience of temperature in the experience of heat and coolness through the thermoreceptors of the somatosensory system. Like other perceptions, our quantitative sense of temperature is imprecise, detecting general orders of magnitude rather than suited to determining exact temperature readings. We might be reasonably adept at estimating air temperature within specific intervals, whether it is in the 30s, 70s, 90s (Fahrenheit), etc., but not with precision. The real shortcoming of the body is that we can only detect and differentiate temperature within a limited range. When it gets too cold or hot, the sensors of the body freeze or fry. Old style glass thermometers that spatialized the effects of change in heat and made them measurable were adequate for everyday life. Man also learned to recognize signs of important heat thresholds such as boiling water or the color of the iron in forging processes for example. However, it seems that as with electricity, the need for precise measurement over a wide range of temperature came from its importance in science and industry. This became possible when scientists discovered the correlation of changes in temperature with physical effects observed at the atomic level. The current definition of the kelvin, the base unit of thermodynamic temperature, is based on the Boltzmann constant, which relates the average relative kinetic energy of particles in a gas with the temperature of the gas. In other words, it is another energy phenomenon based on the perception of movement over space and time, expressed in joules per kelvin (J/K = $m^2 \cdot kg/(s^2 \cdot K)$ in SI base units).

We need not spend much time on the mole, which is a measure of amount of substance. It gets its significance from atomic theory and its use in scientific contexts. The mole provides a reference point to equate the number of elementary entities in substances, these entities being atoms, molecules, ions, electrons or any other particle or specified group of particles. This reference point is the Avogadro number, $6.02214076 \times 10^{23}$, which was originally related to the number of atoms in a specified mass of carbon-12. All we have here is a counting unit. There is nothing descriptive of the qualities of physical objects except perhaps of recognizing them as consisting of the same kinds of elementary entities.

The final SI base unit is the candela, the unit of luminous intensity in a given direction. The candela can be related to the perceptual quality of brightness and developed in reference to the light produced by an actual physical candle. The need for precision and extension beyond the human range led to the development of a better-defined objective unit. In the recent SI redefinition the candela is defined "by taking the fixed numerical value of the luminous efficacy of monochromatic radiation of frequency 540×10^{12} Hz, K_{cd}, to be 683 when expressed in the unit $lm\cdot W^{-1}$, which is equal to $cd\cdot sr\cdot W^{-1}$, or $cd\cdot sr\cdot kg^{-1}\cdot m^{-2}\cdot s^{3}$, where the kilogram, metre and second are defined in terms of h, c and $\Delta\nu_{Cs}$." Simply put, this comes down to an amount of radiant energy over a fixed area, and so can be seen as another energy phenomena understood in terms of time, space, mass and movement.

With that, we have considered all the base units in the standard international system of measurement. Other units in common usage can be derived from or converted to these units. Along with phenomenological notions described above, we can view these base units then as a minimal set of qualities through which the formal objects of science appear to consciousness and render the sense of the physicality and independence. We find nothing additional to what we have described as the elemental parameters and qualia of everyday conscious experience. How could there be? The objects of science are only what consciousness gives to us and can only be thought of in terms of the categories and qualities of experience belonging to consciousness. We create measurement units to the extent that conscious awareness differentiates experience. Even some of these base units are not truly "base" and exist more for the convenience of working in the sciences to which they apply. One thing that does stand out from our review is the importance in science of the sense of weight and its movement, i.e., mass and energy, which unlike other elementary parameters of consciousness have their origins in the immediate qualia of the senses, in the somatosensory sensations of bodily tension and effort. These are of course some of the most important concepts in physics and most of our other measures relate to or derive from them in some way. We will consider the significance of this in the following final chapter.

There are specific characteristics associated with the objects of the natural sciences such as perception through the senses as existing in space and time, and with that being subject to quantification. These characteristics contribute the sense of "objectivity" and allow for social verification in that with such objects we tend to agree on what we see and arrive at the same measures. While we can understand adherence to natural science empiricism on pragmatic grounds, there is no justification for the granting a special reality status to objects that appear as physical. Yet we find much adherence to the notion that the "physical" world reflects a kind of "in-itself" true reality and the belief that entities named by science are real things. Atoms are real, etc. That is what we actually are.

However, even if it holds to a limited methodology and acceptable data set, philosophically, science has also moved on in its metaphysics. Some materialists talk of a false "folk psychology", but there has been an equally false folk science, much of which has been discarded over time. There have been many substances and forces that were taken to be underlying realities but were really just names given to explain certain phenomena. For example, phlogiston was supposed to be an actual substance held in combustible objects, but it seems that this was really just a name masquerading as an explanation for the observation that things catch on fire. Élan vital is just a word pointing to observed phenomena unique to life. It just postulates that there must be some special force to explain it. Even gravity is merely a name for the sense of a "force" that makes things fall. Nowadays the correct language is to speak of fundamental interactions rather than fundamental forces.

Science has moved away from metaphysical jargon and entities that are taken to be real things, and closer to descriptions in terms of a few simple categories. In the Standard Model of particle physics, the main properties of particles are mass, charge and spin. The first two we have already considered. Spin, if not the literal spinning of particles on an axis, is based on the fact that particles behave in ways that can characterized in terms of the mathematics of angular momentum and so still reduces to our other concepts. Modern physics moves towards terms which, while perhaps incomprehensible to most people in their relations, are based on increasingly elemental experiences. For example, string theory, one of the leading candidates for the "theory of everything", reduces particles to one-dimensional string-like objects, where particles and their properties are explained as differences in the vibration states of the string. If we think about the conceptualization of vibrating strings, it is only a product of the properties in consciousness of space, time, and movement (energy), all subject to quantification. Science understands the universe through the same basic elements of consciousness that make up all experience.

CHAPTER 8

The Unity of Subject and Object

We began in Chapter 1 with the question of the relation between mind and body. While it is not difficult to find correlations between sensory/nervous system activity and conscious perception, it is not so easy to understand how or why these physiological activities are "experienced", or why these experiences, with no obvious relation to the physical, appear with the specific qualities that they do. We concluded that consciousness itself is neither a separate substance nor a by-product of a primary physical reality. Mind and matter are two aspects of the same thing. The pure awareness that is consciousness *is* being, and the "physical" is a differentiation of that being into specific limited entities. Consciousness becomes "consciousness of" through these entities in the connection and transition between them in the timeless moment. However, the physical does not create consciousness, but rather provides the occasion for awareness and determines the kind of objects available to it.

However, this general relation still does not explain *how* mind and matter are one. It does not help us understand how relation between them is possible. In order to do this, we need to find their common ground and show how matter exists within and emerges out of the nature of consciousness in a continuous manner. In Chapters 3 and 4, we examined the specific qualities constituting conscious experience and considered their relation to the body in more detail. We arrived at a set of elemental qualia, or parameters of consciousness, that are the building blocks of all experience. As the most general qualities of conscious objects, these parameters make possible the relation and unity of experience. They reflect the early emergence and differentiation of the world out of being and thus are the path back to it. Chapter 5 continued this line of inquiry and attempted to clarify further the relation of the body to experience and the emergence and development of the qualia themselves.

However, while these parameters reduce the perceived separation and difference in manifested being, they are still outside of pure being. They still leave us with a separation of consciousness and object. The task, then, is to show that these elements of conscious awareness are not actually separate but are parts of a deeper whole. In this chapter, we revisit the parameters of consciousness to see if we can unify them further and trace them back to their ultimate source of being itself. The general categories derived in Chapters 3 and 4 are summarized as follows:

1. Sense
2. Space
3. Time
4. Quantity
5. Relations of being
6. Relation of becoming
7. Desire
8. Subjectivity

The sense category consists of the simple qualia of the sense organs as outlined in chapter 3. These are the immediate inputs of the senses prior to any additional processing of the patterns of difference carried by them. The elementary qualia of vision are color and brightness following the following the ability of the eyes to distinguish wavelength and luminance. The component elements of sound are pitch and loudness. The elemental taste qualia are the five basic tastes associated with different receptors that respond to distinct chemical compounds. The somatosensory system has a number of different types of receptors including mechanoreceptors, thermoreceptors, and nociceptors, which account for the separate qualia of contact, temperature and pain. Others such as the Golgi tendon organs and muscle spindles yield the sense of muscle tension and stretch.

The remaining categories we referred to as "cognitive" qualia, which are the experiences derived not directly from the input of the senses but from the higher neural processing of it. Space, time and quantity refer to the basic experiences of where, when and number. These appear in Aristotle's metaphysics as the categories of Place, Time, and Quantity and in Kant's system of a priori intuitions and categories. They include the general categories and the sub-parameters and relations that constitute the experience of them. For example, space and time are grasped through relations such as dimension, continuity and limit, etc. Quantity exists in relations of greater, smaller, equality and proportion, etc.

The category "Relations of being" refers to the general set of determinants regarding what exists or can exist and the conditions of its existence. Its content is what we have addressed under the topic of "thought", which in essence is the process of determining the facts about the world, i.e., what is and is not and what is possible. Another way to understand it is as the operations and determinations of logic through which the thought process operates. This includes the judgments of existence/non-existence, of inherence (i.e., having qualities), of identity/difference (i.e., comparative relations), of association, and of the conditions and dependencies of existence. This category largely addresses the same ground as that of Kant's system.

The category "Relations of becoming" refers to the consciousness of activity and change. It equates to Aristotle's categories of Action and Affection. It is the recognition of change in the other parameters and has a counterpart to each. Thus, change is space is motion and of quality is transformation. Change in relation to underlying conditions or dependencies is "causality". The remaining categories of desire and subjectivity are relatively simple. We covered desire extensively in chapter

2. The unique experiential form provided by desire is the dimension of valuation. We like or dislike things. It is the consciousness of psychological attraction and repulsion. Subjectivity is the sense of opposition between seer and seen, of a center through which things exist and which have value for it. Its projection onto the outer is the intersubjective, i.e., recognition of the other as subject.

These are the basic parameters through which we constitute and know objects of consciousness. We understand them as the most general forms and earliest differentiation out of the unity of being. This is, however, only a preliminary accounting derived from natural experience and language. Is it possible to find a deeper unity that underlies even these highly general differentiations of everyday experience? Ultimately, the end is to understand being itself and not merely its manifestations, however abstract and simplified. Having identified these elementary parameters of the objects of consciousness, the next step is to see if they can be traced back further to the common source out of which they arise.

We have already noted instances where these elementary categories are not as separate as they appear to be at first glance. One example was the category of time. We saw that the actual sense of time is in fact very narrow, if existing at all. We noted that our ability to judge the passage of time quickly becomes rather poor without external cues or time keeping devices. We are hard pressed to accurately estimate the passage of time much beyond even a few seconds without keeping an internal count. Rather than being a true sense where we truly experience a flow of time, time is largely a concept that we construct in order to be able to think about and make use of experience. The construction of time has its origins at the heart of consciousness in that it starts in change. We become aware via movement through difference, in the transition from one thing to another. The moment of transition is the passage from existence to non-existence and vice versa. We only sense time at the resolution to which we can register existence and change. We grasp existence on something like the duration of tick of a clock. Whatever the precise length of this sense of transition and time, the actual feeling of time has a short duration. Beyond this range, time is an analogical construct to track what we cannot sense. As with quantity, and its subitizable amounts being the limit of the true number sense, beyond the moment we have little or no direct sense of time. However, we can conceive of longer durations consisting of the addition of moments through the general idea of a number system such that we can grasp the idea of sixty moments as a minute, or sixty times sixty as an hour.

We conceptualize time as flowing like a river. We noted that time has essentially the same parameters as space. Perhaps this as not just coincidence but reflects the fact that the concept of time is actually one with that of space and its properties. We depict time spatially on time-lines and calendars. We sequence events in time as in a spatial order. We noted how the tracking of time, even its formal scientific usage, is based on a counting of events, ranging from sub-atomic cycles to large scale astronomic events (e.g., the rising and setting of the sun, the change of the seasons, the revolution of the earth, etc.) Our internal sense of the past and present is related to non-temporal quantities and qualities. We know something was long ago because of the number of events we place after it. Alternatively, we judge the place of events in time by the quality of our memories as they lose sensory and emotional impact and become more abstract. At some point, there may be no imagery to recall at all, and memories become nothing but assertions that something once occurred. They exist at a place in a sequence.

We conclude that there is no separate category of time consciousness beyond resolution of the ability to recognize difference. Time is the consciousness of being and becoming, understood and made pragmatic use of through the faculties of space and quantity. Objects and events in time and memory are much like objects in space. What is in the past is not "here". A memory is like an object in another room which must be brought into to our present location in order for us to see it, i.e., to give it existence in consciousness. It is understood as having a location in an ordered sequence. Time looks like just another coordinate of space necessary to locate events. This is how physics now treats time, having unified it with space in a single four-dimensional manifold of spacetime.

As space is linked to number in being quantifiable, we can continue along this same line and consider if there is a more essential connection between the two. Like that of time, the sense of quantity has less to it than we might at first think. We noted earlier that the true immediate grasp of specific numbers was limited to the "subitizing" range of about one through four. There also appears to be an innate sense of addition and subtraction over this range, but from there we infer meaning by extending the basic concept of counting and grouping within a system of units. In addition to this, we have a simple sense of quantitative relation. We know greater, lesser, or equal. Beyond these simple ideas most of what we do in mathematics is a construction built on such basic concepts and the laws of logic, i.e., the connection of concepts through the flow of identity. As the mathematician Leopold Kronecker is to have said, "God made the integers, all else is the work of man".

Within mathematics, explorations into its foundations reflect similar concepts to the quantitative as described here. Set Theory, which is often used as a foundational system for mathematics, reflects the same basic concept of grouping objects into wholes and extension of the process via recursion. Much of the foundational work is the application of formal logic to mathematics, so if we are to tie quantity to space it seems we can also tie both to our basic category of being and logic. We will return to this shortly but first we will consider the relation of quantity to space.

The first descriptor of space was the dichotomy of point and field. Space is both part and whole. It is understood as being quantifiable. It has individual locations which can also been grouped as a unity. We can think of the space in terms of the visual field. Individual points are distinguishable through differences their content, color for example. Wholes are formed through the categories of connectivity and boundary. We intuitively recognize a whole when there is no differentiation of adjacent points or where a continuous line defines a boundary separating it from the space around it, forming an interior and exterior.

These spatial groups are similar if not identical to the way we grasp the idea of a set of numbers. We speak of items being in or out of sets. These are spatial terms. We often depict sets in terms of circle diagrams, with the interior representing what belongs to the set. Sets are also depicted spatially with diagrams in the style of graph theory with a collection of interconnected edges and nodes. This parallels the structure of neural connection. Both types of spatial representations also provide for counting and recursion as pluralities become unities, which then become parts of larger wholes, and so on. We depict this as circles inside of circles inside of circles, or as hierarchal networks, where the nodes connecting a number of particulars at one level become the particulars of the next level.

We are able to immediately grasp one whole as being larger or smaller the same as another. As noted above, we have limited ability to grasp specific quantities, only the subitizing range of one to four. Is it possible that this condition is related to spatial judgment? Consider the four-color map theorem, which states that no more than four colors are needed to color a map such that no two adjacent regions have the same color. The extent of precise quantitative discrimination (subitization) is identical to the requirement for spatial discrimination, suggesting that they are the same thing.

As also noted earlier, beyond the immediate grasp of one to four, the human number sense is one of proportion rather than exactitude. We know greater, lesser or equal. We are fairly good at estimating close to exact proportions within the subitizing range, i.e., 1:1, 2:1, 3:1, 4:1, but beyond that, our estimates get inaccurate and the sense of things more general. We grasp broad relations like few, many, most, etc., but we cannot precisely tell the difference between 90% vs. 93% for example. This also reflects how our spatial sense works. Consider again the visual field from which we derive a large part of our information about space. We have the same field of view whether we are in a room or looking at a distant horizon. It does not come with axes marking off absolute magnitudes of space taken up by objects. The absolute value of any sector of the field is relative to the total space we can see. We can make judgments regarding the absolute spatial footprint of objects we see because we understand size relations between objects, and we know how to interpret visual cues of distance and the relation of distance to object appearance. Visual/spatial and quantitative judgments are both based on proportions rather than fixed magnitudes.

We noted the use of spatial terms like "inner" and "outer" in defining membership in a set. However, the use of spatial terms in the context of number is far more extensive than that. When we have more money, our bank account balance is "higher". The record that sells the most is "on" the "top" of the charts. The stock market is "up" or "down". When we include all things, it is "across the board". We run "over" or under a budget. A sum is "between" two amounts. An estimate is "near" a particular number, etc. One of the primary fields of mathematics, i.e., geometry, *is* the study of space. Its branches such as topology use and inform other branches of mathematics such as algebra and analysis. Number seems largely conceptualized in terms of space.

The higher structures and relations developed by the field of mathematics are built from these rudiments of number via application of the laws and procedures of logic and proof. Logic, as we have noted, is about the most fundamental relations of being and provides the basis for judgments pertaining to the possible truth of propositions and arguments based on them. Is logic, which thus constitutes the rules or categories of being, truly a separate category or is it too part of a single space/time/quantity composite?

Russell and Whitehead aimed to reduce mathematics to logic in their *Principia Mathematica,* and above we attempted to demonstrate the unity of quantity and space. We do find evidence for a further connection to logic in the many graphical methods created to depict logical relations. Perhaps most commonly known are Venn diagrams, but there have been many other similar constructions for this purpose such as Euler's diagrams and Pierce's existential graphs. These diagrams use simple pictures, i.e., spatial objects, and are capable of representing all logical relations of interest. We can see the connection between space and logic more clearly if we take a step back and meditate on the simple elements that make up these diagrams.

The starting point is the background on which the diagram is drawn. It may be only implied by the page on which it is written, but the background is frequently drawn as an enclosure in which all the figures to come are located (figure 1). It is useful to do this since the space surrounding the figures is also part of the relationships represented in the diagram. The enclosed field of play represents the totality of the space on which we place figures. As an undifferentiated whole, it can stand in for being, the undifferentiated unity of existence out of which all things arise. It includes the entire range of possibilities of what can be. It can also represent the totality of a specific domain, for example, as the entire set or "space" of numbers.

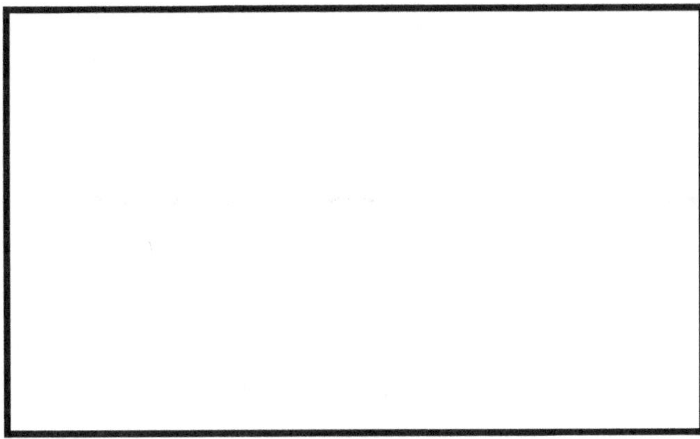

Figure 1

The next element is the differentiation of space, normally represented by a circle as in figure 2. It is an enclosure that separates a region of space from the whole. It establishes an irreconcilable opposition between what is inside and outside of the boundary. There is only an interior with respect to the division from an exterior. This is the basic principle of being: Things only exist in opposition to other things. They are existentially co-dependent. Entities are a separation and limitation from the whole of being. The circle creates a distinct entity consisting of whatever is within the bounded region, such as the properties of an entity, a collection of entities belonging to a class, or in logic the elements of a proposition. Mathematically it stands for a set.

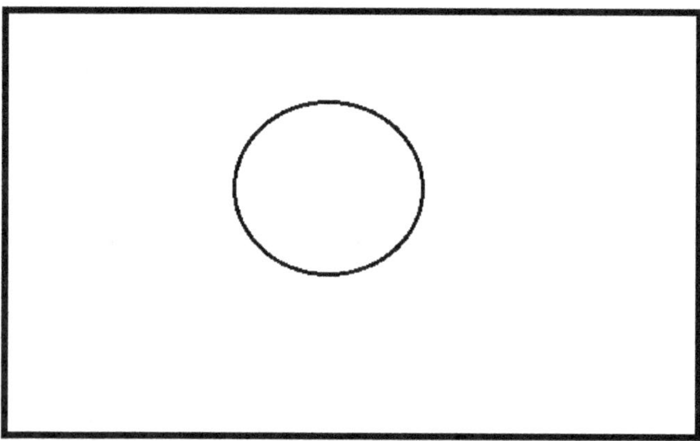

Figure 2

The addition of new bounded regions makes possible the representation of multiple entities and the relations between them (figure 3). Identity and difference are represented in the shared and unshared space of each entity. Figure 3a represents the idea of separate entities sharing no space in common, or from the perspective of being, having no common qualities on the domain of interest. Figure 3b shows intersecting spaces, where there are some elements in common. The shared area represents the intersection of set theory and the conjunction of logic. There could also be a complete overlap in which case we would have a completely shared space and identity within the domain. Figure 3c shows entities entirely within a larger entity, i.e., subsets. Figures 3b and 3C also represent the existential and universal qualifiers of logic. In 3b, there is some member of the left hand set that is also in the one on the right, whereas in 3c all of the smaller circles are entirely in the larger one. For all X, X is Y. Diagram 3c also depicts the beginning of basic quantitative counting function. Two unities can be grouped into a larger unity and this simple process can be applied ad infinitum to create a number system. All this is captured through basic spatial properties.

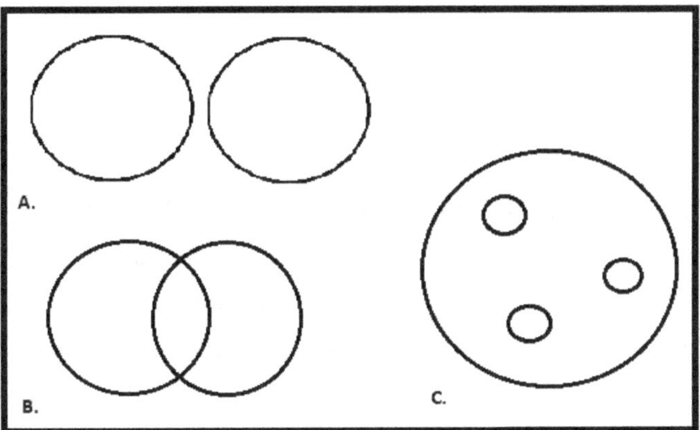

Figure 3

The final element needed to represent logical relations is a means to represent truth values, a designation of what must be and not be the case in order to have a truth condition for a particular relation. Customarily this is portrayed by coloring or shading the parts of the space that are true, and with falsity/non-being left as colorless as in figure 4:

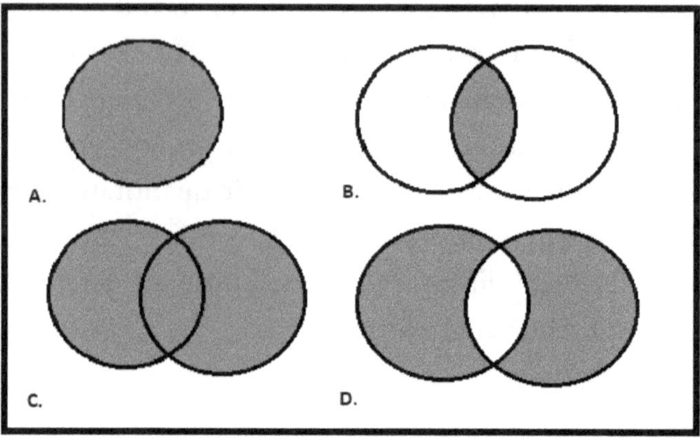

Figure 4

The first example (4a) represents an assertion of the truth of a proposition. The negation of the proposition is represented with a negative image: The circle would be blank, and the surrounding space is filled in, i.e., the truth of negation is what the proposition is not. Diagram 4b as noted above is the intersection or commonality of sets. The diagram defines the condition of conjunction. The conjunction is true only where both propositions are true. Example 4c represents the logical disjunction. Truth exists where either proposition or both are the case. Example 4d is the exclusive disjunction: One or the other propositions must be true but not both. It is of importance because it represents the notions of necessity, possibility and contradiction. For the condition to be true, one proposition or the other must be the case. On the other hand, both cannot be true. They are mutually exclusive or existential opponents. One makes the other impossible, i.e., they are contradictory, like being and not being.

The final example is the depiction of the material conditional: If A then B. We include this (diagram 5) because of its connection to the category of affective relation and issues of cause and condition.

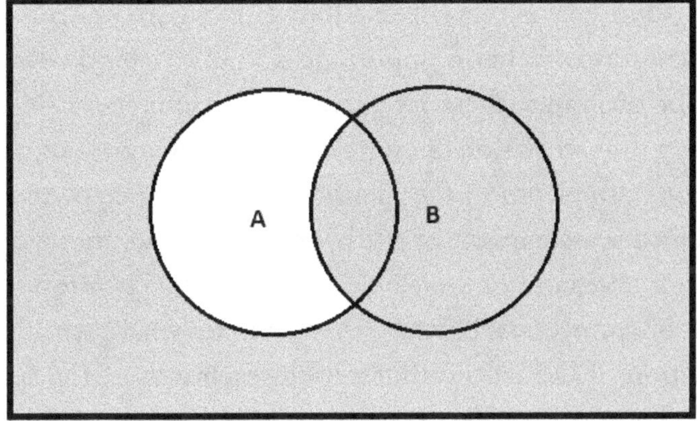

Figure 5

At first glance, this diagram does not immediately seem to grasp our intuitive meaning when we speak of a conditional relation. Intuitively we think of conditional relation as something like a latent necessity, where the truth of A must result in the truth of B. In action, through its introduction into a relation, A seems to act and exert forces upon some object, resulting in change. This is the notion of causality. However, we do not immediately grasp this sense from the picture. We noted this problem earlier when we considered the material conditional in terms of its truth table correlates and reduced its expression to conjunction/disjunction and negation. The diagram effectively does the same thing. It depicts in graphic form the truth table values for the formal logical meaning of implication. When we look at it more closely, we can see that it does tell us "B is always true where A is true", but it does not obviously communicate the sense of existential dependency. The diagram is also confusing to the natural sense of condition by depicting as true the vacuous case where both A and B are false. Above we considered why the operator is defined in this way. It only weeds out as false that which is contradictory. As the diagram shows, only the case of A without B contradicts the intended meaning of implication.

The main point here is that the relations of logic can be represented in simple spatial terms. What is important is to understand why this is the case. In the diagrams, there are three simple differentiations. First are the circles, a differentiation of being in the domain of space. Second are the relations of entities in the identity and difference of the space they share. Third is assignment of truth/existence value. In logic, there are propositions taken out of the whole of possibility. The propositions have relations or connectives between them, and they have truth values. The combination of the truth values within each part of the space of interaction defines the possible relations of being between the propositions. The graphic elements are spatial depictions of the same relations that make up thought. It appears that thought is carried out through spatial categories.

Logic and space can be unified because both the pictures and elements of thought depend on the same underlying laws of being. There is consciousness of a world only with difference. The recognition of identity and difference is the first awareness. Second is the concept that entities exist through separation and opposition to one another. Whatever exists is co-constitutive to its negation. A and −A must be separate to exist. This is the basic law of non-contradiction. Both A and −A cannot be true. What exists, and exactly in what state it exists, depends on the state of its relations. To say there is a condition or a cause between two things is to say that they exist is some existential dependence and the introduction or removal of one will change the other.

These properties are embodied in the principles of both space and thought. A circle is a distinct differentiation into an exterior and interior via the creation of boundary. Each only exists in opposition to the other. Likewise, a proposition exists in opposition to its negation. Separate enclosures can be related and share space, just as entities, sets, or propositions can have common properties or otherwise coexist in some parameter of existence. The existence or absence of color or shading in a diagram exemplifies the binary oppositional differentiation of truth and falsity.

It appears that there really is no separation between the basic properties of space and the categories of thought and logic (the relations of being). Is one primary and the other derivative, or are they equal different perspectives of the same thing? What is truly our experience at the simplest level of consciousness when we make a logical judgment? For example, when we think of a conjunction of some kind, are we really thinking spatially of a kind of "place" where one thing is juxtaposed to another, or is there some different quality that accounts for the experience? Space seems to be the common denominator, but in any event space, time, quantity, logic make up a unified whole.

Continuing along the same line, we now consider being in the aspect of change, or becoming. A large part of becoming easily ties into the foregoing because so much of change is understood as motion, i.e., change in space. From the perspective of physical science, all change is effectively understood in these terms. Energy, one of the most fundamental concepts of science is the capacity to do work, which is about moving something. All processes, as they are studied by the sciences, are understood as some form of physical movement, i.e., as change in space. Electricity is a flow of electrons. Chemical reactions involve the exchange and positions of electrons. Temperature is defined in terms of kinetic energy, or the movement of particles. Thoughts depend on the opening and closing of neural ion channels and the flow of neurotransmitters into the synapses. Everything that happens physically has a correlate of motion in space. When we speak, we move our bodies to move air that moves the membrane of the eardrum to set off the flow of electrical signals through the brain. Becoming is understood of change in space everywhere.

However, we are not just concerned with the perspective of the physical science but of becoming as a conscious experience. What makes up the consciousness of change? Becoming depends on time and the recognition of difference. An object existed and now it does not, and there is conscious awareness of the difference of states. This is the condition for any conscious awareness. There must be a juxtaposition of states and recognition of difference between them. Consciousness exists in the timeless moment of transition where difference briefly holds in existence. The consciousness of becoming is the same whether the change is in the "now" as with an object in motion before our eyes, or if it is consciousness of change from a more distant past. Memories exist latently out of awareness. We only have a remembrance when we evoke the contents of memory and place them in juxtaposition to other conscious contents in the present moment. To experience becoming is to put contents in the in the same "place" and experience the difference between them in whatever parameters in which they change and exist. There is no movement as such, but the particular experience of a sequence of differences over time. Think of how a film works or the illusion of a moving arrow on a neon sign. The sense of movement is created by a rapid sequence of small changes in individual frames. Consciousness of movement exists when difference is recognized in juxtaposed perceptions of an object in space. All consciousness of becoming is like that, even where the change is not physical motion with a transition in spatial coordinates. For example, if a light changes color, we know it has changed because the before and after events exist in effect in different space-time coordinates in our minds. To exist as change they must be brought together in consciousness. If a color, or an idea, or a relation in the parts of a machine changes, each gains a new set of local and remote links where it exists in relation to other things. The old and new states are set side by side such that there is consciousness of difference between them. The structure is the same as for the sense of spatial movement, only here the recognized difference is a change of quality in the same spatial region rather than a change in location of the same qualities.

Subjectivity is not really a separate experiential category that requires a specific reconciliation. In its primary meaning as the sense of "having" experience or of something that has experience, the subject is nothing other than the general subject of our inquiry, i.e., the possibility and nature of conscious itself. Therefore, it needs no specific accounting for, as it will derive its meaning in the whole. When considered in the sense of a "self" of which we are aware, the subject is effectively an object of consciousness. It is a unique object perhaps, in that it has sensations and defines a unifying center of conscious experience, but it is an object largely known through the same parameters of any other object of consciousness. It is described through qualities and a history in time and space. The intersubjective is a projection of this sense of having consciousness onto external objects, and while it has a special significance with respect to desire, its qualities are the same as those of consciousness of self.

We addressed desire in detail in Chapter 2 and described it in general as the attraction of being towards consciousness and knowledge of self, lived as an attraction toward the overcoming of alienation between consciousness and object. How does this sense relate to the other categories of experience? The initial relation between an aware subject and its objects is to draw a separation between inner self, i.e., the "I" within the body, and something separated from it "out" in the world. The immediate sense then is one of boundaries and discontinuities. The satisfaction of desire at all levels is in crossing the borders and/or the connectivity of spaces. To eat is to incorporate the material. To engage in sex is to merge with the physicality of the living subject/object and transcend one's being in the outer. To love is to expand the boundaries of the self to include the other. To know is to overcome the separation from object by connecting inner and outer. The world does what we expect it to do. The separation from it dissolves. We forge continuity between objects whereby one object flows seamlessly into the next. The self-consciousness of being, which is the integration of the whole, has its physical parallel in the completeness of and continuity of synaptic connectivity of the brain. Boundary and continuity are spatial categories. The differentiation of spaces reveals the potentialities within being and reveals its nature. Reuniting these spaces not by absorption back into the singularity but through the integration of parts in consciousness makes possible awareness of the nature of the One.

WHAT IS CONSCIOUSNESS (REVISITED)?

We have joined the parameters of experience but one into a single unified category. Not yet reconciled are the qualia of the senses, which we will consider below. The common element and one that seems to encompass all the others is the experience of space and its properties. Is space the primary source to which all the other elements can be reduced, or are they all equal but different expressions of the same thing? We can only describe space in terms of specific properties. To have anything at all there must be differentiation. In that sense, any description requires multiple perspectives. The sense of space, however, does seem to be the common denominator that accounts for everything else. Is it truly a unified source?

Let us return to the first question of what consciousness is. Here we ask the question not in terms of its ontological status or relation to the "physical" world, but from the standpoint of immediate experience: What is the experience when we say we are conscious or conscious of something? As noted earlier, we know what we mean by consciousness in that we can say when we are or are not conscious of something, but definitions are often circular or provide synonyms that are just different words for the thing we are trying to define. Consciousness is difficult to put into relation. In the end, when we say we are conscious of something, what we are saying is that "it is there", "it exists". If we are "conscious", we mean that a certain type of world exists for us. Consciousness is where stuff is. It is a place for stuff to be. This is also how we describe the experience of space. Space is where things are. In other words, conscious essentially is space.

One theory of consciousness is called the "Global Workspace Theory". Perhaps this should be understood not just as an analogy but as a literal description of the nature of consciousness. Consciousness is not just like a space but *is* the experience of space. Conscious is a "place" where things can be placed together in the timeless moment to make possible their existence (i.e., to have awareness of them). Here we also come back to the equation of consciousness and being. For what is being if not that which gives existence to, makes existence possible, that out of which existence arises. We also see intimations of this connection in the context of Eastern religions, where enlightenment states of consciousness are sometimes described as an emptiness", or as an open space or clearing out in which things arise. They too see only the present moment as real. These states presumably reflect an awareness of the ground of existence itself and are hence experienced and described, at least in part, in terms of this pure space-time/awareness.

Space is the ground of existence. That which arises out of being/consciousness/space to exist is a revelation of the properties and structure of space. What is and can be is a reflection of the possibilities inherent in this structure. That of which we are conscious is a differentiation of this structure into specific values. This differentiation is what we know as the object or content of consciousness. Exactly what this differentiation consists of and how it relates to conscious/space is obviously then the key issue the question in trying to understand the relation and unity of subject and object.

First let us give a little more consideration to the idea that everything, when stripped down to its most simple elements, is experienced as these basic spatial qualia (as revealed via the senses). Is this really all? Do we really grasp everything in these terms? This is what we tried show above. It seems fairly easy to comprehend with "physical" objects. Whatever we see or touch exists in space and is easily comprehended in terms of form and size, relations of continuity and interiority, etc., but when it comes to meanings, relations, thoughts and feelings, it is less obvious. However, as seen above, the processes of reason and logic, which create our understanding the world, depend on a few simple basic relations that are also spatial qualities.

If only a limited number of basic neural structures and activities are possible, then ultimately all experiences can be broken down to the elemental experiences arising out of these structures. For example, while emotions do have a pure sensory aspect (e.g., arousal, alertness, a particular orientation to objects, etc.), they also have a cognitive structure through which the meaning of a situation is interpreted (whether consciously or not). The details are beyond our scope here, but we have already noted some emotional structures that have a clear spatial component. For example, love and hate incorporate or eject others from self-boundaries. The world is contracted in depression and expanded in joy.

As an example of how the sense of space might constitute human experience even at the broadest levels of the whole of society and culture, consider the ideas set forth by Oswald Spengler in his major work, *The Decline of the West*. Spengler sees his great world cultures as coherent organisms with a unified world defined by a distinctive conception of space (its "prime symbol") that informs every aspect of the culture, from its art and architecture, its religion, its form of the state, its money, and even its mathematics. Thus, the Classical culture of the ancient Greeks is seen as having a "here and now", tangible space. This primary feeling of space is reflected in classical culture's exceptional accomplishments in sculpture, i.e., the art of the concrete body, and in its spaceless temples. We see it in ancient Greek religion, with its concrete, man-like gods, and in its social structure where the city-state is the political unit. It is there in the mathematics of solid Euclidean geometry, and in its histories that take the form of narratives of concrete events, etc.

In contrast, Western civilization (the "Faustian soul") is said to be characterized by infinite space, reflected in its soaring Gothic cathedrals, the development of music and perspective painting, its restless exploration and expansion. We cannot go into more detail here, but Spengler's ideas are worthy of further study if one wants to appreciate the primacy of space and how a particular feeling of space can permeate almost everything around us.

Consciousness and space then, can be understood as a "place" where entities can be, where juxtaposition and transition through differentiation becomes possible. The nature of what can be is a function of the properties of this structure. What can be arises out of this background and consists of the properties of this space. The differentiation of this space, the precondition for conscious of limited objects within it, is the revelation of its nature. The source is made manifest in what emerges out of it. Objects of consciousness are the limitation and differentiation of consciousness/space/being in its appearance as specific concrete values.

MAKING SENSE OF THE SENSES

There are still a couple of pieces missing. First is the question of how sense qualia fit into the picture. We still have not established a connection between the qualia of the senses and the other parameters of consciousness. Since sense qualia seem to be irreducible to anything else, it is not immediately apparent this how this will be possible. Second, if this unified space-time composite is the nature of consciousness, what is it that differentiates consciousness, and reveals its nature through a set of specific values on its parameters? In other words, what is it that is "in" consciousness? If there is a unity of consciousness and object, then the object must be a variation in consciousness itself rather than being some separate thing that interacts with it. The problem, then, is to understand how the objects of consciousness relate to its structure. What is it that differentiates the field of consciousness but is also of consciousness?

As it turns out, the questions of the senses and of the content of consciousness are one and the same. Sense qualia reflect the initial point of contact with the differentiated world. They are the "media" or carriers of difference and information that provide the basis for construction of the objective world. The senses are the revelation of the differentiation of space. They are that which is in space. This is actually the position of the natural sciences. Their object of study, which they take to constitute the "physical world", is the measurable experience of the senses. These qualia are what are "in" consciousness and make up its objects. Thus, the relation between sense experience and the structure of consciousness is where to look for the identity of consciousness and object.

However, the problem all along has been that the raw experience of the senses seems ineffable, incapable of being related to anything else.

Yet, while these subjective, first-person perspective experiences seem to stand apart, we do know there is more to them. Sensory qualia, when measured from the external "objective" perspective of the natural sciences, do correlate with additional differentiations and patterns of which we have no direct consciousness. If I look at an apple, I experience particular qualities. I see a color and shape. They reveal an existence and footprint in space. Variations in color and the changing appearance of the apple as I move with respect to it provide clues to its form in three dimensions. I verify this by wrapping my fingers around it. It is a sphere and not a flat circle. When I touch and move the apple, it yields a feeling of solidity and weightiness. Its surface limits the movement of my fingers. I feel a specific tension of the muscles when I lift and hold it.

On the other hand, instead of looking at the apple I can subject it to scientific instruments and instead read measures of the instruments. When I look at the apple, I see color and brightness, but the instruments reveal a cyclical phenomenon we understand as waves. We notice that objects of different color correlate with different specific wave measures. Not only that, but we also have discovered that these waves exist in measures that have no counterpart in visual experience at all, suggesting they are part of some larger phenomenon of which we have no direct awareness. We have learned that the visible is just a small part of what we call the electromagnetic spectrum, with unseen ultraviolet and x-rays and gamma rays on one side and the infrared and radio waves on the other. Our instruments also reveal characteristics of this spectrum with no visual counterpart at all, such as the transverse waves of the magnetic field. We do not experience any of these phenomena when we look at the apple itself.

The instruments of science provide a much finer differentiation of the world than the senses. As discussed in chapter 6, our knowledge of the world is really knowledge of our bodies. What we know is the response of the body to the world. Our picture of the world is only accurate to the extent that the senses and cognitive apparatus are adequate to the differentiation of the environment. Color and other sensory qualia are what appear given the specific response capability of the human sensory system. The senses are inadequate to fully discriminate all that existence must be. The problem of the ineffability of sensory qualia might be understood as a problem of inadequate resolution. The object is opaque and appears as an otherness because we cannot see it in its full existence. What appears through the senses is the limit of what can appear to the specific vehicle of the human body with its limited discriminatory abilities. For example, redness or blueness might be understood of as a sort of "blurry" perception of an electromagnetic wave.

From an evolutionary perspective, it makes sense that we have only acquired a limited, opaque experience of light. The human visual system in its current form has fitness value because it provides the ability to distinguish objects based on differences in the wavelengths they absorb and reflect. However, there seems to be no obvious fitness advantage gained from a finer grained perception of the electromagnetic spectrum relative to the costs of developing it. The visible spectrum happens to be the dominant spectral range of electromagnetic energy of the sun, so sensitivity to wavelengths outside that range would not yield much of a payoff in terms of increased knowledge of the environment. It is not clear how in early human development we would have benefitted from the ability to perceive electromagnetic wave properties in detail. Although we have learned to extract value out of such information, no additional physiological development was necessary to do so. The brain with the capability to make use of more detailed light information is the same brain that can develop instruments to acquire it without the need for nature to enhance the capability of the senses. The process of evolution only developed the senses to the extent of what was beneficial for survival. Yet we know that there is something more there.

However, perhaps there is a way ahead. Just as the development of the eye provided life with a new mode of experience, revealing a previously unknown differentiation of the world, so the development of instruments has made possible awareness of new phenomena. We can think of the instruments of science as being a kind of extension of the senses. This seems obvious in the case of a simple instrument such as a lens in a pair of eyeglasses. The enhanced experience provided by a man-made lens is just an enhancement of an existing sense. Glasses only give the near-sighted person the clarity of vision that others have without assistance. We do not think of this as going beyond the senses. The same goes for microscopes and telescopes, where we gain the acuity to see smaller objects or more distant objects than our nature given lenses afford.

Many instruments, though, such as the various non-optical telescopes or oscilloscopes, are not direct enhancements of the existing senses. These instruments detect invisible signals and convert them to a form we can perceive with our existing faculties. Can the data provided from these tools, which we interpret as wave forms and frequencies and energies, etc., be thought of as another increase in the resolution of the senses? What if the world as it appears to the senses is just a low-resolution version of the world as it can appear to our limited sensory apparatus? Imagine if our senses developed such that we could directly sense the world with the detail made possible through our instruments. With this finer grained sensory experience, the world would directly appear as wave-like phenomena that are characterized precisely in terms of the parameters of consciousness, allowing the possibility of a unification of consciousness and object. The problem of the senses would go away, and that which appears to consciousness would be of the same stuff as consciousness itself.

Using the data of science as a proxy for enhanced sensory experience, we can explore how this might work. Continuing with the example of the sense of sight, what is beneath the subjective experience of color and brightness? Science understands vision as the perception of light, a wave-like phenomenon (and per quantum mechanics also having a particle-like nature). Waves vary in the duration (frequency) of the wave cycle and the degree of change across it (amplitude). Different colors correlate with variations in frequency/wavelength, and brightness with the magnitude of variance. Physics interprets light waves as the propagation of electromagnetic energy. These fluctuations in waves reflect differences in electrical field strength, defined as force per unit charge. The energy of a photon is a function of its frequency, seen as color.

The energy carried by wave relates to its amplitude and experienced as brightness. Light is a phenomenon of energy.

Energy, as we noted earlier, is about moving something (or more precisely, changing its movement). The quantity of energy is a function of the three components of its measure: the distance moved (space), the rate of movement (space/time), and the quantity (mass) moved. We earlier described energy and mass as complements, the consciousness of which is rooted in the somatosensory system, in the sensations of bodily effort and tension felt when we move something or resist forces of movement. We have noted the elementary nature of this feeling as well as its significance to science, but in the speculations above on the unification of experience into space have not yet made accommodation for qualitative sense of energy. We have considered movement and change but have not addressed this sense of force and resistance. This may provide a clue as to the nature of the object

Let us imagine that sensory experience achieves the acuity of electronic instruments. Instead of seeing stable fields of color, we might see vibrations in the electromagnetic field, with different wavelengths represented by specific frequencies of change in a single medium rather than through different colors. Brightness, or amplitude, might be sensed as a change of magnitude of some quality in the movement from pole to pole in each cycle. Perhaps we might directly feel the force of photons.

The idea is that at a higher resolution the subjective experience of light no longer consists of ineffable color qualia but takes on the form of changes in the temporal-spatial-quantitative patterns that constitute the field of consciousness itself. Perhaps this does not totally solve the problem. There must still be something that carries and reveals the pulsations, some medium of difference. It would seem that if energy is to stand on its own ground, then the "quality" that varies with fluctuations in the electromagnetic field would have to be experienced as something like the force or impelling sense of energy. We will return to this issue of "primal" qualities below. The point for now is that if vision had the acuity of electronic instruments and the spectrum of colors were a single characteristic of quantified movement, we might experience objects of consciousness as being variations of space/consciousness itself.

As with light, science understands sound as a wave phenomenon and as being a propagation of energy. In this case, it originates in a mechanical wave, where the oscillations are alterations of compression and rarefaction of the medium, carrying potential and kinetic energy. It might be even easier to understand sound in terms of energy, since we can directly observe its effects as a force of movement acting on the tympanic membrane. The rate of vibration and the extent of displacement of the membrane is a function of the energy of the wave. As with light, we do not perceive energy as manifested in vibrational activity but with frequency and amplitude translated into the consciousness of pitch and loudness. However, if we imagine the development of a human auditory system that is discriminating enough to distinguish and allow consciousness of wave fluctuations, then "hearing" becomes consciousness of this vibratory activity. Again, a sensory mode reduces to the parameters of the field of consciousness.

Does this reduce sight and sound to a single medium? In chapter 5, we speculated that the need to distinguish different kinds of physical information led to the development of multiple sense modes with unique qualities. If the sights and sounds coming at us simultaneously were both apprehended as vibrational phenomena, it might seem that they would interfere with one another. Yet there are great differences between light and sound waves, with separate vibrational ranges. For example, the frequency bands of audible sound are much lower than those that visible light exists in (20Hz-20 kHz vs. 400-790 THz), so at this level of acuity they are quite distinguishable. It is also likely that waves moving through a physical medium would also have their own nuances and complexities. The auditory system as it already exists performs a kind of Fourier analysis on sound waves, breaking down compound tones into their component sound and allowing us to hear different voices and harmonies. Perhaps all existence is an extension of this principle. At this level of perceptual acuity, both light and sound might be directly experienced as wave/energy phenomena and be grasped as movement in space, time, and quantity, i.e., the parameters of conscious awareness. What about the other senses?

Science explains taste and smell in terms of chemistry. Matter consists of elemental substances. Tastes and smells distinguish the presence of different kinds of elemental substance or as classes of compound substances. Pressing deeper, science understands these elements as all being composed of the same set of elementary particles, differing in the quantities of the particles making them up, i.e., in terms of atomic theory. If we imagine a perceptual system that could discriminate objects at the level of atoms, we might feel that some progress towards a unity of experience had been achieved, with the diverse world of objects reduced to qualities and quantities of a few elementary particles. However, reducing the diversity of the world to a small number of common objects does not completely get us back to consciousness itself. Atoms and their component particles conceived in this way are just smaller objects, still alien external entities separate from that which has awareness of them. Therefore, we must press further to the latest understanding of physics.

Before doing this, though, we should also consider the somatosensory system and how its experience as well, enhanced to the acuity of scientific tools, might present its objects through the qualities of consciousness itself. Certain aspects of the somatosensory hold a special place in creating the experience of "physical" objects. The inputs of the other senses – colors, sounds, tastes, and smells - seem to be subjective, sensations produced in the observer rather than existing in the thing itself. They are what Locke called "secondary qualities. Of course, everything is really "subjective, but we can still recognize the distinction Locke is making. There is a difference between these surface qualities of an object that to a greater or lesser degree appear as sensations belonging to the sense organs, as opposed to those that seem to constitute the object itself. The latter are Locke's "primary qualities", which he identifies as solidity, extension, figure, motion/rest, and number. Even though these categories also exist though and for human consciousness, we must account for the appearance of certain objects of consciousness as being "real" or "physical". Most of these "primary qualities" derive from the same spatial/quantitative categories discussed above. However, we have not yet addressed anything like the quality of "solidity", to which we would also add the property of weight or mass, meaning resistance to movement. The sense of solidity and mass originates in aspects of the somatosensory. The word we use to indicate that something is real or physical, tangible, derives from the Latin *tangere*, to touch. Touch, as we described it earlier, is the sense of contact, which is a resistance to movement. The notion of mass or weight derives from the feeling of tension and effort in the body when we lift or move something. How do we get from these subjective sensory feelings to the categories of consciousness?

We return to the science of the atomic and its objective correlates to the consciousness of solidity and mass. A detailed explanation of the theories of modern physics on this subject is beyond our scope and knowledge. To explain solidity, we would have to get into the details of quantum mechanics and things like the Pauli Exclusion Principle. For our purposes, it is perhaps enough to say that is a property of matter that certain particles cannot be in the same quantum state simultaneously and therefore repulsive forces exist when one tries to push them together. The conscious quality of contact and solidity is the subjective perception of the restriction of movement due to these forces. The conscious perception of mass derives from the perception of muscle tension and effort felt when moving something. The scientific definition of mass as resistance to acceleration does not really help us understand it any better, since it really just seems to be a restatement of the subjective feeling. The amount of mass is also defined as the quantity of matter, which is the number of elementary particles. By analogy, we attribute the conscious notion of mass to these particles below the threshold of perception. Even if we could see and feel subatomic particles, it seems that they would still be in opposition to consciousness, and thus we have only pushed back the problem. Consciousness of smaller particles is just consciousness of smaller alien objects. We must then increase the magnification further and delve more deeply into the scientific understanding of energy and matter.

As we descend deeper into matter, we find that even protons and neutrons are not elementary but consist of smaller particles we call quarks. When we look at these component quarks more closely, we find that their mass is only a tiny fraction of the mass of the proton and neutron. 99.8% of their mass comes from gluons, the exchange particles for the strong nuclear force. This is the energy that binds the quarks together. Gluons however are massless particles. Their mass is primarily a measure of the energies of the quark motion, and so the protons and neutrons that make up almost all the mass of an atom really consist of energy. Pushing physics back as far as we can, we arrive at quantum field theory (QTF), where particles are understood as excitations in fields specific to each fundamental particle. Points in the field can be thought of as quantum harmonic oscillators. When the energy level at a particular location of a field is sufficient, it results in the propagation of a wave across the field. These waves are what we know as particles. Even QTF is not a "theory of everything" in that it is not reconciled with relativistic gravity. String theory, a current candidate for such a theory, sees what we have in the past conceived of as point-like particles as ultimately consisting of one-dimensional vibrating string like objects, with the properties of the particle such as mass, charge and spin being a reflection of the vibrational state of the string. Whether or not string theory is correct in its details, at the simplest most general level, our fundamental theories of matter and its variations come down to differences in vibratory activity that are ultimately a function of energy.

We conclude that what sensory variation represents and what makes the fundamental differentiation making up the varied objects of the world is what we know as quantities of energy. This actually is not anything new or controversial. As we know, $E=mc^2$. Matter is a form of energy. Now how does the idea of sense objects as energy help with the problem of their relation to consciousness? Once again, what is energy? Energy is ability to change the movement of something. More energy is the ability to move more mass or move a given mass faster or further. In other words, we mostly know energy in terms of space, time, quantity and change, i.e., the same stuff as consciousness itself.

There is still one element for which we have not yet accounted. If there is movement, there must be something that moves and through which movement is revealed. This is the phenomenon of energy in the form of mass, but what is it? Mass appears to consciousness through effort and resistance to movement. To the question of what is moving, we would propose that it is space-time itself, which contains an energetic potentiality. Space isn't nothing. According to QTF, the lowest possible energy state is not zero, and the quantum vacuum and quantum fields are not empty space. They are characterized everywhere by constant random fluctuations, with "virtual particles" popping in and out of existence even when there is not enough energy to create the propagating waves that are particles. If consciousness is space, then consciousness is also energy. This was in fact part of our definition of consciousness in that it exists through the movement or transition between limited entities.

Just as mass and energy are two aspects of the same thing, they also have an inherent relation to space. According to general relativity, the curvature of spacetime directly relates to the quantity of energy/matter. Every quantity of mass can also be defined in terms of a Schwarzschild radius, the size at which it creates a black hole. Relation is only possible where things exist on some common ground, so there must be some existential connection between energy, mass and space. Energy and mass are reciprocally defined in terms of the capability of and resistance to movement. Even with massless particles there is force exerted by movement. Where there is not yet mass, energetic potential must exist in the medium of movement itself, i.e., space. Movement and force/resistance exist in a necessary relation. Movement is always an opposition. Think of a car with its tires spinning out on ice. It needs something to push against and can only move with the resistance of friction. Movement is always movement against something. We would add the experience of this to conscious awareness as well. In addition to the parameters of consciousness described earlier and united in the experience of space, we would argue that the most elemental experience of consciousness includes to some degree a sense of opposition and effort in the transition from object to object.

If we had the ability to sense to vibrational fluctuations at the lowest level of massless particles, energy/mass might appear as pure movement, or really the same as conscious awareness itself. With the perceptual and nervous systems we have, we only know these effects in their accumulation as force, resistance and mass. Perhaps this experience is an effect of the interconnection of energy/matter and space. Not only does space vibrate, but curves on a larger scale. The sense of mass in every day experience might be understood as an effect of geometry in the same way that general relativity conceives of the force of gravity. Curvilinear motion is acceleration is energy is mass. There is a familiar quote from the physicist John Wheeler to the effect that spacetime tells matter how to move, and matter tells spacetime how to curve. It might be more accurate to say that matter is curved spacetime.

It seems that space-time and energy form a primal existential pair. There is no movement without a differentiable something to move in. Nor could there be any notion of space without movement through it. To the question of what we are aware of, or the medium of movement, at this initial differentiation it is consciousness itself, which includes energy within it. Above we equated consciousness with space. However, it is not enough to have a differentiated field. There must be connection and movement through it such that the parts become one. The impetus of energy is this movement and is a part of consciousness itself. With energy now connected to space, the characteristics of consciousness come together, and these same elements also make up the objects of consciousness.

Here we arrive at a unity of consciousness and object, mind and matter. In its baseline form, consciousness is the field of space, a massless but not empty grid in which things can exist and be juxtaposed by connective energetic processes to create awareness. To the question of the differentiation of space/consciousness of which objects consist, this can be thought of as a result of differences in the densities of this same energy. Objects are thus the same stuff as consciousness. As an analogy, we might imagine space/consciousness as being like a gelatin salad with fruit suspended within it. Like the gelatin, consciousness is a clear medium that holds things and gives them a place to be and be present to awareness. However, in the case of consciousness, the objects within are not like fruit, held in, but of a different stuff than the gelatin. Rather they are the same substance of the medium of suspension. They are more like areas of congealed, condensed bits of a gelatin mix that did not blend properly. Alternatively, we might think of consciousness as being like a spider web. It is a grid that can hold things, however in this case there are not flies trapped in it, but locations where the webbing has been disturbed and gobbed up into a mass. Matter is a gob of consciousness/space-time.

The consciousness described at this level is the pure sense of consciousness itself that gives awareness and existence. As we have emphasized, what we normally understand as consciousness and as the development of consciousness – from insect, to animal, to man, to sage, etc. – is really a development of the objects available to consciousness. Consciousness itself is always the same awareness and giving of existence. What consciousness is aware of is a function of what its specific vehicle differentiates. The baseline state that is the quantum vacuum - the field of consciousness/space which makes visible but is invisible, which is massless and empty yet not nothingness – is much like the light of physics. Massless photons exist as pure energy, moving unimpeded by the effects of mass at the speed limit of the universe, illuminating yet unseen themselves. Earlier, while considering consciousness as space, we referred to Eastern philosophies that describe enlightenment states in terms of "emptiness" or an open space. Yet the term "enlightenment" itself also reflects the energetic aspect of consciousness. Consciousness gives a "place" to exist, but it can also be understood as a bringing into existence by giving visibility. Buddhism speaks of the "luminous mind" or "clear light mind", which is the pure non-dual sense of "I AMness", the ground of being out of which all arises. This language of light is another way to look at consciousness along with space and emptiness. If not literally the light measured by physics, consciousness is functionally the same thing. Consciousness is like a light that shines on objects in the dark, making them visible. As we look out at the illuminated room, we see the objects made visible but forget about the source of illumination, the light itself. Yet if we turn our gaze away from the illuminated and hold our light to the mirror, we can recognize the nature of that which makes visibility possible. In the same way, we can turn our focus to the field of pure consciousness and recognize its nature as an illuminating, awareness giving field, which is also the source and stuff of the objects of which it is aware.

CONCLUSION

With this, we arrive at a unity of consciousness and object, mind and matter. Consciousness is the energized interconnected field of space, where awareness exists in the connection and transition between differentiated points in the timeless moment. The objects of consciousness (and that which we experience as the physical) are a higher density in the same field of the same energetic activity that is the structure of consciousness itself. In coming to this conclusion, what have we accomplished as regards the overall project of being coming to self-consciousness and the overcoming of the separation of subject and object?

On the one hand, we have identified the common ground of the two and the means of relation and transition between them. On the other hand, we do not live in this field of pure consciousness. Perhaps in certain mystic or "expanded" states of consciousness, in the condition of those beings we call "enlightened", there is an intuition of this pure awareness and how complex objects arise out of it, but this is rare and is seemingly incapable of articulation. For the most part, conscious awareness exists through a limited vehicle of consciousness, in a configuration that reveals being only to the extent that it can differentially respond to its possibilities in manifested form and can integrate them back into a whole. Having a notion of the general consciousness-object relation is not the same as experiencing consciousness of it through the objects of awareness. Knowing that in essence they are really just differences of vibrations in space does not help us live in the consciousness of being. It does not give us the ability to predict the behavior of others or to know how various objects will relate or interact. Consciousness and the self-consciousness of being can only come through the concrete relations and values of limited objects. It requires the full diversification of the potentiality of being and the subsequent integration of the pieces through the relation of being. We only know being through its appearances and their relation via consciousness.

Even this general unifying relation is still incomplete and vague. We only really know space and consciousness when we know the specific values and relations between space and energy and matter. On the one hand, this is the work of physics and mathematics. Only with a successful "Theory of Everything" can we have consciousness of being itself. However, a valid theory of everything also must pass through and have consciousness as a factor. Even if physics should have success in its endeavor, there is still the question of reconciling its objects with subjective consciousness. We need an equal understanding from a phenomenological perspective. For example, suppose that string theory proves to be correct and ten dimensions or more are required to give an accurate description of the universe. Can we ever really "live" that? Is a three-dimensional world all we can truly have lived experience of (at least without further evolution), in which case we could never truly know the "real" world directly, or is it possible that our 3D picture of the world is really just an inadequate construction of the mind which we can overcome and can learn to experience the world in a higher dimensional way? We can ask this question with regard to many ideas in modern physics, such as curved space, the relativity of space-time, the equivalence of mass and energy, the strange phenomena of the quantum world, etc. In the end, the perspectives of physics and lived experience must become one, not by reducing one to the other, for example by reducing of life and meaning to the language of the material, but by equally elevating the physical to include the subjective.

Perhaps we cheated a bit in substituting an external perspective for direct sensory experience in an attempt to get around the seeming inadequacy of sense perception. This allowed us to conceptualize a unified ground of consciousness and object, but at the same time, it is not how we experience the world. We still live through the senses as they are. If we cannot now realize a first-person sensory experience at the resolution at scientific instruments and mathematical thought, what can we hope for? What we can do is try to understand the relations and interactions in terms of the direct experience we do have. We can try to uncover the affecting relations of the sensory such that we maximize correlation between our experience of what occurs in the world and the internal ideas that we impose on it. The more we can comprehend and predict the results of interactions between the objects of consciousness, the less difference and opposition of the world.

This is the task and meaning of man and universe: To reveal and realize the nature of being. The first part of this project is the act of pure creation, the wringing out of all the potentialities of existence. Being must become all it can be. The second is the return of these fragments of being to the whole, however not by sinking back into the original undifferentiated totality, but as an integration of the parts through relations of consciousness. To connect the whole potential of being in consciousness is attain the self-consciousness of being itself.

As considered in chapter 2, this activity takes place on all levels of existence, from the "physical" to the most abstract, according to the inclinations and abilities of the vehicle through which consciousness exists. For many or perhaps most, the main task in life is reproduction, the continuation of consciousness and the creation and nurturing of new physical vehicles of consciousness. Every new life created, every new shuffling of the genetic deck, every mutation, every new life form, etc., brings forth new potentialities out of the source of existence and a new perspective of consciousness on the world. Many or even most realize their unique being and find their greatest meaning in interpersonal relations, in knowing and being known and in wanting and being wanted by others. While the daily tasks of work or home are necessary to support physical needs, they also require for success knowledge of the nature of physical existence, of the principles of organization, of human psychology, etc., and thus provide satisfaction in themselves as a form of mastering and knowledge from the world. We are motivated and content in activity that is creative, doing that which reveals the potentialities of being and reveals the source in their relation. Science aims at the theory of everything that unites all physical phenomena into a single framework. The arts aim at instantiating inner experience in its concrete sensory form. Religion and philosophy are in different ways the disciplines of the absolute itself from the perspective of the subjective.

The absolute is approached and made conscious to itself through the relation and unification, i.e., knowledge, of the limited objects made present to consciousness. We come to it first by revealing its potentialities, in spinning out all that is possible in the limited forms, and then by putting it back together in an ever deeper and more complete integration. We therefore must continue to play the glass bead game, bringing ever more diversified elements into a more complete relation. The process continues to where all relations are relations that pass through being, where the relation in consciousness is being become conscious of itself.